Sapphires, Monkey-Bread and a Coup d'Etat

Sapphires, Monkey-Bread and a Coup d'Etat

The Itinerant Ecologist Series

Malcolm Marks

Coeur de Rose Publishing

CONTENTS

I would like to thank my Great-Nephew, Zachary Rowe, for designing the front cover to this book. Your artist skills far outweigh my own and are certainly inherited from my lovely sister, your grandmother Sandra.

This book is dedicated to our two lovely grandchildren: Lilith and Nathan.

Your entry to the lives of Mamy Véro and Papy Malcolm has brought us both immeasurable joy. We hope that when you are a little older and can read and understand these books, you may see us as something more than simply two elderly and doting grand-parents!

By the same author in the Itinerant Ecologist Series:

'From Nigeria to Cracking Walnuts'
(Book 1)

Available in paperback (ISBN: 978-2-9590283-0-4)
and electronic version (ISBN: 978-2-9590283-1-1)

'There's a Crocodile in the House'
(Book 2)

Available in paperback (ISBN: 978-2-9590283-2-8)
and electronic version (ISBN: 978-2-9590283-3-5)

'Of Cows, Chars and Beautiful People'
(in preparation)
(Book 4)

Also produced by Cœur de Rose Publishing:

'A Bend in Time: Tales from la Savoie'
by Pierre-Antoine S. de Vrai (March 2024)

Available in paperback (ISBN: 978-2-9590283-8-0)
and electronic version (ISBN: 978-2-9590283-9-7)

1

Living the French Way

We have just arrived home to our little house in the tiny hamlet of Cordon that lies in the extreme south of the beautiful Bugey region of France. And this, after more than four years of work and life in Senegal. Our daughter, Mélanie, was a little girl of seven when we left UK for Dakar in early 1989; now it will not be long before she becomes a teenager. Our little boy, David, was an infant and now he is a cheeky, freckled-faced seven-year-old.

A new life beckons but we have to adapt fast.

The decision to leave my previous job in Senegal was bitter-sweet. What a glorious life we had *côté jardin* (the pleasurable side of life) with the beach, warm sea, domestic help and an interesting job with a great salary. But how stressful was the *côté cour* (the harsh side) with rife dishonesty to try to deal with and little support from those in the administration who were supposed to help. That is not to say that everything about my previous job was disappointing; not in the least. As a doctor of ecology from London University, helping to develop a centre for ecology in a lovely country like Senegal, and then starting to turn that project into a self-financing structure was both academically challenging and mentally stimulating; a real pleasure. I loved that side of my work and I would not have missed the experience for the world. But events overtook me or rather, if I am strictly honest, my capacity on my own to deal with them at that time was insufficient.

A well-financed second phase of the project began in 1991 and key among its requirements was that the expatriate staff should take an administrative and financial backseat while handing the steering wheel over to a government appointed coordinator. A great initiative, providing the person appointed was competent and had the project's best interests at heart. I doubt that person did, and he almost succeeded in driving the project into the ground to benefit his own political ambitions. My best efforts to warn the hierarchy both in Dakar and on the US east coast of the financial shenanigans were met with (let me say this politely) 'disbelief'. That is until a very senior person was finally convinced that an internal audit should occur. This rapidly discovered that I should have been believed a lot sooner! Too late, their disbelief led to my loss of faith in the system and worries for my health and safety (after the mysterious death of a close and dear colleague). Therefore, I requested that my contract not be renewed and we left the job and Senegal with very heavy hearts in July 1993.

One challenging but fascinating part of my job at the ecology centre was to determine how it could be helped to evolve into an autonomous and self-supporting structure. In general, development projects usually run all the time that donor money is pumped in but when that flow of cash stops, for whatever reason, the lights almost invariably go out.

The wish to move towards a self-financing status was both innovative and challenging for the team and me. This led us to look for clients for the centre's products and skills, both within Senegal and in the broader sub-region. One of our first potential clients was the government of The Gambia who, like Senegal, had been approached by the United Nations Environment Programme to be part of a pilot project determining National Inventories of Greenhouse Gases. Do note that this was in the early 1990s, way before the climate change bandwagon and the so-called "Greens" began to form in Europe. As part of the UNEP initiative, I had travelled to Banjul and worked with the relevant civil service departments as well as doing a little *pro bono* work for a friend at the local US mission. Several months later, that same friend invited me to join a private sector team bidding on an upcoming US-funded agriculture and natural resources project in The Gambia and, just prior to leaving Senegal, I heard that our bid had been successful and the contract signed. So, while we are sad to have had to leave Senegal, I do have a good job to go to, employment with an excellent private sector company and a great new country (The Gambia) to work in.

Of course, nothing comes easy. With this new job, there are a couple of major drawbacks. First, the initial contract is only for a period of twelve months and second, the full-time contract only begins in about six months time in the coming January. In the meantime, we have to make a big decision: what to do about the children's schooling? Do we enrol them in the French system for just the autumn term, then pull them out so that we can all go together to The Gambia in January, have them do a year in that country (in the English system) and then likely return to France and put them back in the French system? Or do we take the tough, tough decision and put them in the French system while I travel to The Gambia alone? Mélanie has already had her eleventh birthday and so it is a good time for her to integrate the first year of secondary education within the European system. To be honest, it is for her that we are the most concerned.

After long and hard discussions, we make the decision that neither Véronique, my lovely wife of sixteen years, nor I want: we will put the kids into the French system and I will go to The Gambia on my own. At first, this seems a very harsh choice since we are close as a family and have never been apart for more than a few weeks at a time. However, when we sit down to calculate how long each period of absence will be, we realise that I should be able to get back to France every half term while the family will be able to visit The Gambia every long school holiday. So, basically we will be together as a family every six weeks or so throughout that year.

The next decision we need to make is where to enrol the children for school. The first option is state/local. There is a primary school, for David, in our little village while Mélanie would have to go to *collège* in Belley, but that middle school has a poor reputation according to local friends. The second option is to put them into the private system at some distance from our home in Cordon, on the other side of the river in Isère. The negative here is the distance that we would be obliged to drive the children each day to and from school. The third and nuclear option is to try to enrol them in the International School of Lyon. This school has quickly obtained a fantastic reputation, being one of the top achieving schools in the city. It would enable the children to integrate the French system while still continuing to do some subjects in the English language. But the big negative is that we, or rather Véronique and the children, will have to move to Lyon.

First things first. We need to apply for entry to the school; a refusal would finish that option before it begins. But luck is on our side and Mélanie gets entry to *sixième* and David to *CE1*. Next, we need to find somewhere to live; do we buy in Lyon and take a mortgage or do we rent? Time is very limited to attempt to buy and so we rapidly opt for renting since, at this stage in our lives, we cannot imagine that we will not all be off abroad as a family in a year or so, once the Gambian contract is completed.

The International School is located in the suburb of Gerland, right next door to the ground of *Olympique Lyonnais* (the number one French football team, according to David) and just across the road from the old abattoirs!

The school is almost brand new having opened its doors just the previous year. However, local people and parents tell us that it is already proving to be a bit of an architectural nightmare (except, that is, for the two architects whom I presume were paid handsomely to design it).

First, they had the imagination to grow grass on the roof! Yes, local people ask the same question: 'how can the poor gardeners get up there to cut it?' Well, looking on the bright side, it does not need cutting during the summer because high temperatures and drought mean that the roof turns from green to Sahelian brown. It then becomes a bit of an eyesore and, not to mention, a fire hazard. And in the spring and autumn, I suppose that they could always tether a few mountain goats up there.

The next problem is that the school is built around a broad and high, central walkway called '*le Centre de Vie*' (the centre of life) which is very luminous thanks to numerous skylights. The only issue is that some of the metal frames expand too much in the heat and (*watch out below kids*) some glass panels have apparently fallen out and crashed to the floor. Local wags suggest that perhaps the walkway should be renamed '*le Centre de Mort*' (the centre of death!). The problem was 'solved' (if that is the right word) by stringing up fishing nets that are supposed to catch falling panes of glass before they attain the kids below.

Finally, the architects in their wisdom – modernity? – decided to leave the walls '*brut*' and so the building has an unfinished look (well, for me, it really is unfinished) because the walls are in bare breeze block and cement. Sometime after completion, a bright spark at the *Academie de Lyon* decided that the bare look was a bit depressing for the pupils and so commissioned an artist to paint a number of canvasses that would partially cover the breeze blocks. But in my opinion the saga then goes from bad to worse because some of the paintings seem to bear a passing resemblance to the '*Scream*' and, at best for me, can only be described as pupil inmates of a Russian *gulag*. Why did they not use paintings of many of the brilliant artists that the city and its surrounding villages has bred? Why not instead hang paintings by Seignol or Appian or Ravier or Henri, and so on?

One architect, whose design for the school was not accepted, was Santiago Calatrava Valls. More the shame because he is an architectural genius and, in my opinion, would have created a far more respectful environment for school pupils. Am I exaggerating? Just take a look at the fantastic train station at Satolas (now renamed Saint-Exupery) Airport, the image it conjures up is of a swan taking flight (this is an airport after all). No grass on the roof and no reminders of a death camp adorning the walls.

Once our children have received admission to the school, we look for and find a perfect apartment to rent in the Point-de-Jour area of Lyon and move in just before the start of the autumn term, and before I go off for my first trip to Banjul with the new project.

Sadly, we soon have a run-in with the school. After only two weeks I am called in to speak with David's class teacher, a young, unshaven and bespectacled gentleman.

His side of the conversation starts with "David is immature and has many *lacunes* and will need to repeat the year." (the word '*lacunes*' translates to gaps in his knowledge or academic shortcomings).

"OK," I reply, "but you do realise that he has just entered the French system after two years in an American school and he has only been living in France for a couple of months?"

"I still have no doubt that he will have to *redouble* (redo) this academic year" insists the teacher.

"Before proposing such a drastic decision, I would prefer that we look at the issues together and in more detail," I state. "First you say that he is immature. Tell me, if at seven years old he cannot be immature, at what age do you consider that a child can? Do you have children of your own?"

"No, I do not have children but he does have *des lacunes en français.*"

"Fine. Tell me how is he doing in other subjects like maths, English, art and so on?"

"All those are good. He is doing really well in those subjects."

"Right, so the crux of the matter is that he has gaps in his French. I presume that you will not tell me that he cannot speak French fluently so rather, as a seven-year-old, those gaps are in his grammar?"

"Yes, precisely and the reason that he will certainly have to redo the year!"

This response, short-sighted in my opinion (and to many French parents too), annoys me no end. But that is the sad reality of the French educational system at this time; numerous Ministers of Education have tried to change it over the years while the Unions stubbornly pull the many willing teachers out on strike (usually within a day or so of a new school term beginning). During these frequent strikes, parents struggle to get their children cared for, so that they can continue to go out to work. In contrast the striking teachers pull out their well-used banners and spend strike days gathered around mobile barbeques, eating grilled sausages, in the middle of the main thoroughfares.

At school in France at this time, you can be a brilliant pupil in biology or the arts but if you do not know your *subjonctive* from your *conditionnel* you are considered by the system a failure ... 'and you will redo the year until you do learn *la différence mes enfants!'*

"I hear you *M. le professeur* but I do not understand you. I, too was a teacher and when a child in my class had *des lacunes,* part of my job was to help them *combler leurs lacunes.* Does this not occur in your class, do you not help pupils overcome such having difficulties?"

"M. Marks, *vous pouvez critiquer* but, despite your criticisms, we have the best educational system in the world."

At this point, do forgive me for such a lack of respect, but I burst out laughing.

"*M. le professeur,* do tell me how many other systems you have worked in or even studied. From my side, I have worked at three levels in the English system, was president of the International American School of Dakar, taught in a Nigerian University and am now encountering the French system. And the last thing, I promise you, is that my son will have to *redouble* this academic year because YOU will be there to help him. Do I make myself clear?"

"*Oui, M. Marks, parfaitement. Merci.*"

And for the record neither of the children are ever obliged to redo an academic year in the French system.

It is now late-September and our project in The Gambia is about to start, with the exception of my component that does not begin until the coming January. However, I am asked to fly to Banjul for an initial week or so to be part of a team-building exercise. My official title for the trip is 'consultant' since my long-term assignment as the

Information Specialist on the project is not to begin officially for a further three months or so.

I find that there are few air routes available to reach Banjul. Basically, I can either go via London and take a flight from Heathrow or go via Brussels to pick up a Sabena flight. The latter is my preference as the timing is better and the tickets are also considerably cheaper. Tickets are purchased by the US company and DHL'ed to Cordon. I catch the flight and arrive in Banjul at around 8 pm.

How strange it feels to reach The Gambia by air. On many occasions in the past, I have driven into the country from Dakar both for work visits and holiday excursions but have never before had the opportunity to fly into Yundum Airport. The airport is tiny, efficient and peaceful. The Arrivals Hall is quiet and 'well-behaved'; certainly not like my first trip into neighbouring Senegal five years earlier where I was obliged to fight off taxi touts to keep my suitcases from disappearing in umpteen different directions! Similarly, at passport control, where a friendly officer welcomes me to the country, stamps my passport and wishes me a pleasant stay.

I am met at the exit gate by one of the project driver called Lamin (meaning 'first born'). He chats to me in English as I wheel my suitcase out of the terminal building and on to the gravel covered car-park. Our car, the usual project Landcruiser, awaits us and we are soon heading northwards in the direction of Banjul, that sits on a natural promontory on the south bank of the Gambia River, some twenty-five kilometres due North of the airport. However, while Banjul is the official country capital, and most of the government administrative buildings are located there, it is nowhere near to being the main population centre. That prize is claimed by Serrekunda that lies some ten kilometres closer to the airport and is also close to the epicentre of the tourist trade. The whole team has been booked to stay at the Senegambia hotel, located in the sector called Kololi.

The hotel sits across the road from a small forestry reserve, run by the Forestry Department with assistance from a German consulting firm that I am destined to link up with. Staying in the Senegambia is a first for me, since Véro and I have always preferred the more laid-back, and less pricey, Bungalow Beach Hotel.

Lamin drives into the grand setting of the hotel arrivals and a uniformed young man rushes over to the car to collect my suitcase. Formalities are quickly completed at reception and I am handed a note with my keys. The note is from my young American friend who was responsible for recruiting me into the team. The note says very simply that the team is gathered in the gardens behind the hotel, close to the outside bar.

Once my case is safely locked in my room and I have washed a little of the travel grime from my hands and face, I go down to meet my new bosses and the project's three other team members. The party in the garden is highly eclectic. I am introduced by my young friend to a Norwegian, a French, and a Pakistani; all US passport holders. These are the company hierarchy, based out of Washington DC. Then I meet a Kenyan, my new team leader, a young American lady, his deputy, and finally a chubby young man who seems to have rather a lot of beer cans in front of him. These three comprise the rest of the in-country technical team.

Introductions over, the company chairman, the aforementioned American of Pakistani origin, calls the waiter for another round of drinks while he slips off to smoke a cigarette. The drinks arrive rapidly at our table, strategically placed under an impressive 'sausage tree'. The tree is covered in large, red flowers and we can smell the fragrant blossoms from our seats several metres below. And so can a multitude of large bats that continually visit the tree to drink flower nectar and, while doing so, ensure the pollination of the flowers.

We pass a pleasant ninety minutes or so in the gardens. I find my new team mates and the company hierarchy both friendly and committed to our new project. After a hidden yawn, I make my excuses to leave for bed, and this signals the end of the evening for everyone else. We will meet up again for breakfast at 7.30 in the hotel restaurant and then have an initial meeting at 9.30 am to introduce ourselves to the government and to the US officials working in-country for the donors.

The donor team is led by a young woman who seems smart, committed and a lover of The Gambia. That is already a very good start. We then meet the senior government representatives who will work in support of the project. The first person I am introduced to is the Senior Secretary of the Ministry of Natural Resources. He is the most senior civil servant in the ministry and second only to the minister himself.

"We meet again Malcolm. Do you remember that we met briefly a couple of years ago when you made a courtesy call on the Minister during a mission from Senegal?"

And indeed I do remember because the minister had played a trick on me. "Errr ..., yes," I reply, "but luckily I did not fall into his trap!"

"What happened then, Malcolm?" asks an eavesdropping company chairman.

"Well, while I was trying to drum up work in The Gambia for the ecology centre in Senegal, I paid a courtesy visit to the minister. While waiting in the reception area to meet him, a youngish man came and sat next to me and started to really bad-mouth the minister. Of course I was a bit shocked and so replied in all honesty that I had only heard good about him and that I was keen to meet him for the first time. When the Senior Secretary here escorted me to the minister's office, I found the minister was none other than that young man. And, as I said, luckily I did not fall into his trap. It was the minister himself that told me about our project and advised me to try to apply for a position on it. Here I am!"

"And," says the Senior Secretary, "I hear that we will be working together on developing the Ministry's Strategic Plan."

This is total news to me but seeing the chairman's surreptitious nod, I reply "with much pleasure, sir."

"I look forward to seeing the terms of reference that you are developing," he replies. Nice to meet you again Malcolm but let me spend time with the other team members."

The company chairman apologises for not telling me sooner about the strategic plan but thanks me for keeping a calm head. Later that day I spend time with the Norwegian colleague from head office drafting out the terms of reference for the work on the strategic plan.

He tells me "I think that eight weeks should be adequate and, if you come back to Banjul in a couple of weeks' time, to begin the mission, you will finish up this piece of work just in time to get home for Christmas!"

This extra work is very welcome to our household budget and means that my full-time assignment in Banjul does, in financial terms, start in October and not January. Perfect for our Christmas finances.

2 |

Making of a Window Cleaner

A week goes by quickly during a consultancy mission but the experience gained from working with senior-level professionals always proves valuable; especially, during this trip. The time I spend with my Norwegian-born colleague and the Chairman of the company are particularly useful as they manage to make difficult (for me) topics sound simple; that is a real skill that every consultant must quickly learn. But soon Lamin is driving me back to Yundum and my return trip to Lyon via Brussels.

My stay at home in the apartment in the Point-de-Jour is very short-lived since a little more than a week later I am once again packing my suitcase and taking the aeroplane back to Banjul, this time as a consultant in Strategic Planning!

Should the question arise of how an ecologist can become a specialist in strategic planning, the answer is relatively simple. The work is to be carried out in the Ministry of Natural Resources (as an ecologist, I can tick that box), it requires someone who is familiar with the four components of the ministry (forestry, fisheries, etc.) to sit with each department (tick) and get them discussing and noting their priorities (tick), and it needs, especially, someone who has the time available to pull all the details together (tick).

And, truth be known, dedicated time is often the crux of a consultant's work. Often the people in a company or project or ministry needing the assistance have the in-house capacity and all the knowledge to do the same work as the consultant but they simply lack the time to dedicate fully to it. I have eight weeks to concentrate solely on the plan and can call on senior ministry staff when I need advice, information or finer details.

This mission has two additional positives. First it allows me to get to know the other members of the team as well as the senior members of the minister's cabinet and departmental heads across the different structures where I will eventually be working, well in advance of starting my long-term assignment. Second, it should allow me to begin trying to source a vehicle and find a furnished home to rent.

The other nice feeling about this work is that it is all carried out in English. Now that I am working in an English language environment, I find the work far less stressful than I did while in Senegal and where I was obliged to work and write exclusively in French. There is something comforting about using one's mother tongue and especially that I do not need to concentrate as hard as I do in French to pick up the nuances of the language!

For this eight-week stay, I have chosen to rent a studio apartment within a hotel in the area, near the coast, called Bakau, close to Cape Point. My logic is simple: I do not enjoy long stays in hotels at the best of time and certainly do not wish to be obliged to eat in restaurants for two or three meals in the day. Better that I purchase groceries from the nearby supermarket and fruit and vegetables from the local market and then prepare my own meals in the evening and morning. Otherwise I would be tempted to eat delicious local dishes like *mafé* (mutton stew in peanut sauce) and *thieboudienne* (fish and rice often called *bena tchin* in The Gambia). Worse still, I could eat fish and chips and other British 'delicacies' in the hotel restaurant where I am staying. I am not only worried about the calories from the food but that I would also be tempted to drink too many pints of beer at the bar during the hot Gambian evenings. Since I left Senegal, less than four months ago, my weight has shot up by more than five kilograms, much to Véro's displeasure, and certainly due to evening after evening of aperitifs with lovely friends in Cordon!

So the apartment it is. And, on the days that my workload becomes too heavy to spend time cooking, as it often does for consultants, I can simply order room service (or slip down to the bar!).

The hotel is popular with British tourists, and the clientele is a real eye-opener for me. This Friday evening, since I have made some good progress with my work, I decide to eat at the bar, relax and watch 'Old Man Peulh and his Troop' repeat the same act that I have witnessed several times in the past couple of weeks. 'Old Man Peulh' is a rotund gentleman of advancing years with a gleaming, hairless skull. His troop, composed of various members of his family including grandchildren, do traditional dances while he looks on with his beaming smile. He has his own act which is to dance around the floor with an earthenware pot on his head!

The hotel also has a Compere who swears to me that he is Gambian but since he retains a broad Scouser accent, I do wonder (and do not really care) if that is true or said for the benefit of the tourists. I have tried speaking Wolof to him but his proficiency is even less than mine! His time comes at the end of the evening when he sings old Nat King Cole and Harry Belafonte numbers including 'Oh Island in Sun'. That one takes me right back to my childhood vacations at a holiday camp on Hayling Island where it invariably rained for the entire week!

This particular evening, I am sitting at a long table with several British holidaymakers. I notice that the young man placed opposite me has not joined in the conversation with the others at the table, so I assume that he must be on his own. I make small talk and find that his name is Owen, and indeed he is in The Gambia on his own and hails from South Wales. He is here for a two-week package holiday.

"Would you like a refill," I offer, gesturing at his empty pint glass.

I am extremely surprised when he replies "I prefer to buy my own, thank you very much."

My quizzical look brings out an explanation "I am unemployed and have been saving small amounts each month for three years from my benefits to afford this holiday. I have two pounds per day of spending money, so I can afford for example, two pints of beer in the evening. If you buy me a pint, I have to reciprocate and that will mean I will have less money to spend tomorrow."

Now, there have been moments in our early adult life when Véronique and I have been really short of money but never so short that we had to calculate a daily expenditure, especially when on holiday. How can I get around this problem, and at least buy the poor guy a beer, without him feeling obligated to buy me one in return?

I pull a folded twenty Dalasis note from my back pocket and say "just by chance, as I came into the hotel from work this evening, I found this note laying on the floor. Now, it's not mine so can we let it serve to buy a couple of beers for us. Are you in agreement with that?" A smile and a nod and we are served our refills.

Owen asks about my work in The Gambia and is surprised when I tell him the string of events that led to me obtaining my current position. He shakes his head in denial when I tell him that I had started my working life as an Ecology lecturer at the University of

Calabar in Nigeria. That a chance dinner party there led to me meeting the head of a private Swiss consulting firm and, five years later, he had phoned me out of the blue to offer a consulting mission to the deserts of Chad. How, while in the small town of Bol, near to Lake Chad, I had practised my French swearwords on a particularly annoying French aid worker and that this had led to me being offered a senior position in Senegal. When working in Senegal, my project had an important target that was to switch its financing from donor-funding to earning its own living. This led me to explore market opportunities in The Gambia and, while on that trip, I had met a minister who had suggested that I look for a job in the country. So I joined an American team and we won the contract for the project I am now working on.

Owen looks at me and shakes his head slowly. "I am impressed at how lucky you have been for all those events to align to bring you here. To tell you the truth, I've always wanted to be a plumber but I am too old to get an apprenticeship and no one wants to employ someone like me who has been on the dole for so long. I cannot imagine ever getting away from benefits. But you started off lucky because you have the right accent. I bet your parents already had money and that is how you went to university. There is no one to help me."

I do not want to tell him that there are many poor people in the south of England too! Nor that my dad once worked breaking rocks in a quarry and that we lived in a tied house until the quarry owner kicked us out on to the street. I was only four years old at the time.

Instead I ask "Owen, can you afford to buy a bucket and a ladder?"

He looks at me and laughs "why the f*ck do you ask such a silly question?"

"Answer me and then I will tell you."

"Of course I can but I don't need to because me mum has the bucket and me da' has the ladder already."

"I bet your mum moans that she cannot clean the upstairs windows and can't find anyone to do them for her!"

"For love or money, she says," laughs Owen.

"Have you yet worked out why I asked about the bucket and ladder?"

"F*ck me, excuse my Welsh, are you serious? You are, aren't you?"

"Try it, Owen. Give it a fortnight to see if you can make a living and start picking up a regular round of customers. You don't have to tell Benefits about the work until you see if you can earn enough. It would help if you have an old bike so you don't have to lug your ladder around but can tie it to the crossbar."

Owen left The Gambia a few days later and went back home to South Wales. I only heard from him once, several months later. The envelope that arrived at my home in France was postmarked Swansea and contained a single item, a Polaroid photo of a smiling Owen. Held up in his left hand was a bucket, on the wall behind him next to a window was a ladder. There was an old bike propped up on the kerb by a pedal and his right hand was raised in a thumbs up gesture. He wrote a single word on the back of the photo 'thanks'.

My other team members have all found homes in and around the Serrekunda area while the project is renting offices in the Standard Chartered Bank building in the centre of Banjul; about fifteen kilometres away. The young man in the team has his house just down the road from my hotel and so he has been asked by the team leader to pick me up each morning for the drive into work. He seems a nice, friendly guy and we always chat easily about work, life in The Gambia, and life in general. However, what does surprise me is that every morning at eight when I climb into his car, I see two open cans of Heineken in the cup holders. These he swigs from as we drive towards the office. I like a beer or two in the evenings but certainly not in lieu of breakfast!

Soon after I start working out of the project office on the ministry-wide strategic plan, the team leader and his deputy speak to me about their concerns over our colleague's alcohol consumption. More bad news arrives as senior members of the government team that I am working closely with on the strategic plan also start to make comment about him drinking during office hours. Next, I begin to hear other stories from the ministry heads and departmental directors that I am cooperating with. They tell me that my colleague has shipped a large number of computers, keyboards, hard drives, printers, etc. in his container of personal effects. They add that they believe these items were not properly declared on his customs inventory. On the positive side, however, he is allowing ministry colleagues to use his equipment until purchases made by the project arrive in country, thus speeding up the work of his component. Still, I believe that he is sailing dangerously close to the wind but, as I am still officially a consultant and not yet a 'full' team member, I feel that it is not my place to get involved by saying too much.

That sentiment is rather taken out of my hands. One morning as we are driving into the office, he tells me, between swigs of beer, "do you know that I have lent several computers, screens, printers and other equipment to the ministry?"

"Really?" I say.

"Yes, and now I want to bill the project for the rental; what do you think?"

"Did you get prior approval for the rental and the fees involved?" I ask quite logically.

"No," he replies, "but at least with the equipment I am using in the ministry, my activities are able to move forward more rapidly."

I tell him, quite frankly, that in his shoes I would have sought approval to rent the equipment first and then, if approved, he could now be billing.

"Bugger that, I am giving the team leader a bill today."

"I would be careful if I was you," I reply. "You are going to put the team leader in a difficult position and he will be obliged to send the bill to head office for approval. I would be concerned about their response to any unapproved expenditure."

But, despite my warning, he sends in a hefty bill to the team leader. And, as I predicted, it is transferred immediately to head office for treatment and they are not amused by his little business side-line. He receives a stiff warning from Washington both for taking it on himself to rent out his equipment without prior approval and for shipping in the equipment without the correct custom's documentation. The following morning during our drive to the office he relates this latest news and I advise him that it would be better to 'eat humble pie' now and apologise to the government and the company for his actions. In response he tells me that either they pay up or he will quit.

Eventually, he does not need to go that far because senior government officials, concerned by his actions, use his excessive drinking as the pretext to ask the US mission to remove him from the project. What a foolish outcome for the young guy. By poor judgement he is obliged to leave his job and the country soon after I come back to start my full-time project post at the start of 1994.

Late in my eight-week stay for the strategic planning process, the team leader agrees that it might be sensible to start looking for a home to rent from the following month, January 1994. I have been recommended a rental agency by the young lady who is the deputy team leader. She is married to a Gambian and knows a lot of Gambian business people, including, it seems, an estate agent.

I have a good amount of dollars on my housing budget line and tell the agent that I require a furnished house with garden, even if small, plus a lockable garage. He picks me up in his car and tells me that we have four properties to visit. Unbeknown to me as I enter the car, he has decided to take me to visit the cheapest rental first and end with the most expensive. Immediately I enter the front door of the first building, I am obliged to tell the agent that we can forget this house straight away. It is filthy, needs totally repainting, has hardly any furniture and that present is stained and broken. There is no cooker or fridge or air conditioners, so the house is hardly furnished. The rent is very cheap but that does not negate all the work and purchases that would be necessary; and my furniture budget line does not contain adequate funds to cover all that is missing. We drive to the second, and here the house is in a bit better order but there is no garage or garden. Strike that one too. We go to the third and I feel that I could live happily in the house. It is a bit on the small side with only two bedrooms, and I really need three for when the children visit. But promising.

Finally, we drive into a small residential housing estate and up to a house, let me call it 'a home', that has well-tended gardens at the front and back, three bedrooms and excellent furniture with the contents going down to teaspoons and table napkins. I make the remark to the agent that the house and furniture look unused, and indeed this proves to be the case because the house is none other than the estate's Show House and, now that all houses on the estate have been sold, the owner wishes to rent it out. The rent is marginally over my budget but since I will not need to buy any furnishings or household equipment, I can certainly get approval to move funds from my furnishing budget line to house rental.

That evening, I take my Kenyan team leader back for a final viewing and he simply says "Go for it."

I feel pleased to have found such a beautiful place to stay, just off the Kololi Road. The beach is only a ten-minute walk away and there are several restaurants and mini hotels cum guesthouses in the vicinity. I know my family will love the house and its location.

The second thing I need to sort out is a car. And this sorts itself out in a relatively less pleasant manner. I receive a command from a senior functionary in the US mission telling me to come to their house at 7 pm on Friday evening. I arrive and am met by the spouse who shows me an old and slightly dented Renault.

"This is our car that you are going to buy for four thousand five hundred dollars. Here are our bank details so that you can transfer the funds to the US."

"This is all a bit fast," I reply. "First I want to go for a test drive and also would like to bring a mechanic to look it over."

"We can go for a drive, if you insist," replies the spouse, "but you do not need to bring a mechanic because the car has been looked after by the mission's mechanic. Unless, of course, you do not trust us."

What a nasty position to find myself in. The owner of the car – being very senior – could make my work life a misery if I refuse the purchase or play hardball over the mechanic. But then again $4,500 is a lot of money to hand over on a single person's word. I decide to push forward with the test drive and note that the car handles well and the engine sounds OK. I test the brakes and they work well too. After a quick drive around the block, I test the suspension, they are fine, look inside the oil cap and there is no 'butter' to indicate water getting into the engine block. Finally, I look at the mileage and the gauge indicates around 130,000 miles.

"I think $3,500 is a fairer price," I attempt to negotiate.

"Four thousand is as low as I will go," is the response I receive.

With a certain amount of regret, I shake hands. My only very small victory is that I leave the car seller with a right hand covered in engine oil.

My next set of negotiations are altogether more satisfying. I know that I will be going back to France on three or four occasions during the coming year and I will be obliged to cover the cost of tickets on all but one occasion. Logically, so I cannot complain, the project only pays my ticket at the start and end of the year-long contract plus one return ticket each for the family. Thus I will have to buy two or three return tickets each for Véro and the children plus a couple for myself. That works out at rather a lot of return tickets and a very considerable outlay. I wonder, then, if I might negotiate the ticket prices?

Since Sabena is already the cheapest and most convenient airline, I stop by their office which is only a few minutes' walk from my new house. At the door I meet a very pleasant Belgian guy, who is about my age, and chat with him about ticket prices. His name is Jean-Pierre and he turns out to be the airport manager for Sabena. After a moment chatting, he excuses himself and goes through a door marked 'Manager'. A few minutes later, he reappears and tells me that the manager would like to talk with me.

I knock on the same door, enter and find myself face-to-face with a pretty Belgian lady who introduces herself by her first name. She tells me that she is the manageress of Sabena in The Gambia, and how can she help me?

Out of politeness, I explain, *en français*, that I will need to return to France every two or three months and that my wife and children will be coming out to The Gambia approximately midway through each of my visits. "Is there anything you can do with ticket prices?" I ask.

"Will a 40% discount be OK?" she replies immediately. "Jean-Pierre told me that he has seen you a couple of times at the airport, taking our flights, so we are happy to help a frequent passenger."

Am I delighted with a 40% discount? You bet I am!

Later that week, I go to the bottle store that it is conveniently situated just outside my hotel and buy six bottles of a Côte de Rhône wine that I know well. I have been popping into the store on several occasions, always chatting to the Gambian store owner. On this occasion he tells me that once he gets to know expatriate Brits he is happy to accept payment by UK cheque. He also tells me that he is willing to take a larger denomination cheque and return cash in Dalasis; giving a very honest exchange rate. This is a perfect arrangement for me at a time when cash machines do not exist and large amounts of money have to be brought in as travellers cheques or cash.

Once the wine is safely in the car, I take a drive over to Kololi to check on my new house. I have the keys already but have promised that I will not move in before January when the rental contract officially begins. However, I am allowed to leave luggage and personal effects inside. I have already started to purchase a few canned goods which are locked into one of the bedrooms and I want to add the wine and a box of canned beers to my stash.

As I leave the main Kololi Road and drive along the dirt track that leads into the estate, I spot a European man just getting out of his car to open his gate. I recognise Jean-Pierre from Sabena and find, by coincidence, that we are to be neighbours.

I stop to greet him, repeating my thanks for helping to get me the ticket discount, and hand over a bottle of wine "from *chez-moi*," I add.

"That's really not necessary" he says "but come in and we can drink some together."

Two weeks later, I am headed again to Yundum Airport to catch the long first leg back home for Christmas. As usual, the airport does not seem very busy and so I am soon through formalities and on to the departure gate. The plane is ready to leave on time and I follow the other passengers boarding into Economy. As usual, I have an aisle seat.

A few moments before take-off, Jean-Pierre comes up to me and says in French "Excuse me sir, but you are in the wrong seat. Would you follow me to the correct seat please?"

Of course, by now being a very frequent flyer, I do not tend to get my seat number wrong. And I soon realise that Jean-Pierre is showing me yet another kindness as we pass through the curtains that separate Economy from Business.

"Here's the correct seat Malcolm. Have a lovely trip home and I'm looking forward to meeting the family soon. Merry Christmas!"

And, indeed, he is right. Today is the 14th December, the children are on holiday in a couple of days and Christmas *en famille* is beckoning.

The holidays pass with a lot of happiness, too much eating and (according to madam) too much drinking as well. But then again, as I frequently have to remind her, I have a growing responsibility to help the French economy in every way possible!

Soon I am again packing my black suitcase and note that it is collecting a fair number of customs and security stickers. Back to Lyon Satolas, on to Brussels and then the long haul to Yundum. After disembarking, I pass first through passport control and then into baggage collection. I note Jean-Pierre busy with a customer that it seems has lost his suitcase. I give a quick wave and a mouthed '*salut*'.

I find Lamin waiting for me in arrivals. He has a broad grin of welcome on his face. He knows that I will have brought a few packets of duty-free cigarettes for him and so he always volunteers to make the airport runs to pick me up.

As we travel back towards Kololi – yes, I will be sleeping in my new house for the first time tonight – Lamin tells me that the team leader has just recruited a new driver. Interestingly, the new man was previously a sales manager with the local brewery, Banjul Breweries. I quip that that is great news because he can keep us stocked in JulBrew (the local beer) but express surprise that he would have left a good job with the brewery to become a driver. Lamin explains the simple reason: our new driver realises that he can earn far more as a driver on a development project than by continuing to work for a local company, even in a position as good as sales manager.

This is one of the problems with development projects. Local hires generally earn far more, even in relatively modest jobs, than they could ever hope to earn in more senior roles with a local company. I experienced just this situation in Senegal where donor agency contract hires would earn two or three times the salaries of the local civil servants seconded to the same projects and often doing similar work. Invariably, rather I should say inevitably, this leads to jealousy and trouble down the road.

I often wonder if development agencies, like the World Bank and the UN, are not doing the country a disservice by paying such high salaries and that rather they should set local-hire rates closer to in-country market levels.

Of course, the local hires would vehemently disagree with me, so I will keep quiet!

3 |

Want a drink, Mr President?

Finally, I am a fully paid-up member of the project team. My title is 'Information Specialist' and I have two main tasks. The first is to work as an adviser to the newly created National Environment Agency or NEA to support them in developing a cross-ministry 'Environmental Information System' and the second is to lead on the development of large scale Natural Resources maps of The Gambia based on aerial photographs.

The first role, to help develop the EIS, is my current main function because we await the arrival in country of the hundreds of aerial photos that were taken at the tail-end of 1993 during a countrywide aerial survey. These will ultimately be our base material to develop the maps but there is considerable preliminary work to undertake before we can make a start on the photo-interpretation and map-making; not least being to find a team of volunteers from the ministries ... and then to train them!

Developing the EIS is also easier said than done. The Agency itself, being only recently formed and institutionally housed in the Office of the President, retains little of the available environmental information in its own offices, rather it seeks to be a clearing house of information for any structure – government or non-government – that might wish to contribute or source relevant environmental information.

After setting up an office within the NEA headquarters, I attend our first steering committee meeting with the relevant staff of NEA and other lead ministries (Natural Resources, Land Resources, Agriculture and so forth) who are backstopping the EIS. With them, we agree the outline of a strategy for developing the structure of the EIS, within which we begin discussions of how to identify, obtain and share relevant environmental information. We also set some tentative end-dates for achieving the different parts of the strategy. At all moments as we discuss and plan, I try hard to ensure that the majority of initiatives proposed seem to come from the senior civil servants and scientists present. I have always found that this is the best method to gain civil service buy-in and therefore ensure national ownership and sustainability. After all, at this point in time, I only have a one-year contract before leaving the country.

As a final point, before the meeting breaks up, we agree that my NEA counterparts and I will draw up a proposed structure for the EIS as well as methods to collect existing information, and present them at the next steering committee meeting to be held in two weeks' time. The committee also proposes that a couple of other committee members be charged with drawing up plans for a national information workshop, to be held in a month or so in Banjul. We consider this workshop to be an essential part of getting our plans off the ground and will, hopefully, be attended not only by Gambians but also by many from the overseas donor community that work with The Gambia.

After the meeting ends, I make my way back to our project office in the Standard Chartered building and walk straight into a blazing row. The proverbial has hit the fan for the beer-guzzling, computer-renting colleague. He has just received his marching orders from the company in Washington and these are being delivered by our poor, gentle team leader. And the outgoing gentleman is not happy, to say the very least. His shouted threats of court action and worse are for all in the office and many street passers-by to share and appreciate.

Finally, he calms down a little and I persuade him to come with me to his office so he can tell me his side of the story. But nothing I say can make this bitter pill taste better. He made unwise moves, refused to apologise, and is now paying his dues. He leaves the office ten minutes later and this is the last time I ever see or hear from him. But what a foolish end to a nice professional position in a lovely country?

His expatriate replacement arrives in the office the following day. Yes, really, the changeover was that rapid. Our new colleague is called Frank and he has been working in The Gambia on and off for several years and is currently in-country completing an assignment for the World Bank. Not only does he slot straight into the team as though he was always with us, he also slots straight into my affections as a very nice guy and soon to become a great friend.

Frank is some ten years older than me and confesses to having a very serious affliction: he is sadly a member of a worldwide fraternity that contains only 'Drinkers with Serious Running Problems' (his words!). To translate this into non-medical terms, he is a paid-up member of the Hash House Harriers. And not just paid-up for he is also the Hash Master; not quite equivalent to the Grand Master of a Masonic lodge, but pretty close!

Meeting him and having him as a colleague is a real God-send. I have now been married for almost seventeen years and so, for at least that long, I have been used to making friends as a couple with Véronique. And she is far chattier and open than me. Suddenly,

I find myself a geographic bachelor and now have to try to make friends as an individual. This invariably means that when I do get invited for drinks or dinner, I am the odd one out at the party.

Thinking to broaden my contacts I recently joined the Fajara Club, a private members club, mostly for expat Brits but also hosting a good number of Gambians and expatriates of a multitude of other nationalities. I had thought that the club might function like the Palm Oil Club that Véro and I had joined in Calabar, so many years ago. But while the Calabar club was the only place in town where expats could meet, the Fajara Club is just one of loads of places to socialise in The Gambia. Many evenings when I drop into the club for a meal or a beer after a late day in the office, I find that I am the only person present. But that is not always the case!

The day after I hear that my membership to the club has been accepted, I drop in at around 7 pm to pay my subscriptions and have a quick beer. The place is almost entirely empty with only a very large man sitting at a side table and an elderly Gambian gentleman standing at the bar, drinking from an almost empty glass. The barman greets me with a friendly smile and so I ask for a pint of lager for myself and a top up for my bar colleague. When the drinks are served, the gentleman moves along the bar, we chink glasses and I say 'Malcolm' and receive in return 'Dawda, and thanks for the drink'.

I assume that Dawda must be a regular at the club because he immediately says that he believes me to be new in town as he has not seen me here before. We chat easily about my work and life in France and many other trivia that people use when getting to know each other. He seems a nice chap and tells me that he works for the government. I feel pleased to have met a pleasant person on my first trip to the club. Soon we are sharing a second drink and I notice the time has just passed 8 pm.

As we finish our drinks, Dawda tells me that he really should go home as his wife will be wondering where he has gotten to. As the toilets are near to the exit, I start to accompany him across the room until I come to a firm stop thanks to the large gentleman who has placed himself very carefully in my passage.

"Please wait sir and let the President leave before you go to the toilets."

Welcome to The Gambia where ministers play tricks on unsuspecting visitors to their offices and the President leans at the bar without any pretension. This type of gentle behaviour appeals to my sense of proportions and is one of the major reason why I come to look on my time in The Gambia as one of the nicest interludes in what will prove to be a very long expatriate life.

Monday late afternoon comes around and the Grand Master has persuaded me to try my hand at the Hash. I have my trainers and running kit in the car, so we go off together for my first meeting. As we drive the ten kilometres to the start of the run somewhere inside a dense forest on the outskirts of Banjul, I confess that I have done little exercise since leaving Nigeria; more than ten years ago. This was not quite true because I did infrequently play squash during my recent time in Senegal with a young Danish colleague. He made up for his very serious lack of skill in squash by insisting that we keep playing until he could finally win a game! But again, Senegal is almost a year ago.

I learn that the Hash, run in dozens of countries around the world, is a multi-layered affair. For a start, there are usually at least two different circuits: a longer one, typically around ten or twelve kilometres, where runners and joggers can go at their own speed (often pretty slow!) and a shorter one of about five kilometres, targeting the walkers. The two circuits generally share the same start and end points and are calculated to end approximately at the same time. I choose to be brave and take the longer circuit. My calf muscles will likely complain tomorrow!

By the time we arrive at the start point, that sits several kilometres down a long straight forest trail, there are already seven or eight cars parked on the side of the road and fifteen or so 'hashers' of various shapes, forms and ages chatting together. The eldest person must be in his late fifties but he is accompanied by a pretty, young woman of exotic appearance, I later learn from Mauritius, no less. The youngest is a boy of about six and he is going to run with his dad. The Grand Master tells me that when the little boy gets tired, he climbs into the special backpack that his dad has strapped on his back and then his dad starts running again. Not surprisingly, his dad is a former rugby player from Wales and this, at a time, when Welsh rugby sweeps all before it in the northern hemisphere.

I am introduced to the other runners and then off we go for my very first Hash. I have decided to run until I am out of puff, then walk until I stop panting and then try to run again. Despite being ten years older than me, the Grand Master goes storming off in the company of two young stags that have shown up to run with us, I should say: in front of us! I was a little concerned that I might get left behind and lose the trail; not a good thing in the heat of a tropical forest, but I need not have worried – the Hash has thought of that. Every week, someone raids the offices of the US Embassy and of USAID and empties the paper shredding machine of its tiny pearl-shaped pieces of paper. Ahead of time, these are gently sprinkled along the trail we are to follow. At intervals are slightly larger piles of pearled paper and, as I approach the first one, I can see everyone ahead has stopped. Ah great, a chance for a breather as I chug up to the others with a smile on my face to have gotten this far.

"On-On" shouts the Grand Master as soon as I arrive, and the wretched stags and hares go charging off along the 'sprinkles trail' of paper making me wonder if I should change my brand of soap. After a few sweaty kilometres, we enter into a village and the children run with ease alongside me. They laugh and giggle as I try to speak to them in Wolof, that is until an elderly gentleman calls out to me in English and says "they do not speak Wolof, only Mandinka!" Well, at least I tried.

Ten long kilometres, lots of sweat, and a fair amount of panting later I spot our parked vehicles in the distance. My first Hash is coming to an end. And what a sight awaits me. A rather rotund gentleman, by the name of Peter, is standing at the back of a beaten-up, old Austin van and is handing out cold, very cold, bottles of Julbrew beer to all the runners. Heaven in a small bottle.

The Hash Master comes across to me and offers his congratulations for finishing the run; and I did not even come last (actually second to last but shhhh!). He is at least as sweaty as me and his glasses are steamed up making me wonder how he can see through them.

The next item on the agenda, after the cold beers, is the raffle draw. I buy two lots of tickets and they go in the hat along with the tickets bought by the other runners. The winning tickets are drawn out of the hat by the little boy who was running with his Welsh dad.

First prize is a bottle of Portuguese wine – and I win it! Second prize is a couple of cans of tinned fruit – and another of my numbers comes out of the hat; accompanied by much booing and shouts of 'fix, fix' from a Brit called George. I, of course, decline the second prize. Later in the draw, yet another of my numbers is drawn and again the audience, led by George, accuses the Grand Master of being in cahoots with his work colleague. The Hash Master gently explains that I had bought twice as many tickets as everyone else while, to keep the peace, I kindly decline this prize too (since it was a bottle of lady's cream and I did wonder what I could do with it).

The field ceremony over, we make our way back to our cars. I take the Grand Master back to my house and we quickly shower and change out of our sweaty gear. Back in the car, and he guides me to the next part of the Hash evening which he tells me is to share a 'Runners' Meal'. That sounds quite civilised; big mistake Dr M.

The Hash club tries to spread its custom around half a dozen or so restaurants; mostly run by expatriate Brits who lower their prices for the evening in exchange for considerable extra custom. Tonight we will be eating at the restaurant owned by Peter (he of the old Austin van and the cold beers). He takes orders from the fifteen or so members that have made it to the restaurant with the choice being either 'Fish and Slips' or 'Bangers and Hash'; the names keeping right up with the gravity of the event!

Before the meal is served, I am told in all seriousness by the Grand Master, that we are going to turn to the highlight of the Hash ceremony: the 'Down-Down'. I do not have to wait overlong to find out what that means.

He stands up and the room goes instantly quiet, after all this is the Grand Master of the Banjul Chapter of the Hash House Harriers.

"I call Malcolm and Tony to come forward," he says sternly.

I instantly wonder if I should roll up my trouser legs but then again, I am only wearing shorts, so Tony and I simply step towards the Grand Master.

"Stand on the stools," he commands.

We obey instantly.

"Bring forward the libation," he commands again.

Peter comes from behind the bar and hands each of us a pint mug filled to the brim with lager and then we are told 'wait-wait'.

The Grand Master begins to gently hum "ummmm, ready Hash?"

"Ready, ummmm" sings the assorted gathering standing before me. They then break into song:

"Here's to Malcolm and Tony, they're true blue. They're now Hashers through and through. They're drinkers and runners, so they say. Tried to get to heaven but went the other way. Drink it down, down, down, ..."

As the song hits 'drink', the Grand Master mimics to us to begin drinking. Before the end of the fifth 'down', my glass is already empty while Tony is only halfway through his.

"On your head" shout all the hashers in unison while the Grand Master mimics that we should upend our glasses over our heads.

Poor Tony is absolutely drenched by the half pint remaining that cascades over his long hair and soaks his t-shirt and jeans. My glass provides two or three drips that make no impression on my shining locks.

A round of boos breaks out from the audience, directed rather unfairly, I am sure you will agree, at me. After all, I served a long apprenticeship in beer drinking while playing rugby for Queen Mary College, London. And we were always taught never, but never, to waste beer; certainly not to pour it over our heads.

"Next," says the Grand Master, "is this week's nomination for the Hash Sh*t. Now, I had thought to give it to George over there, who I caught moaning about the raffle draw. But now, we have just witnessed extreme bad sportsmanship by Malcolm. Can you believe that he finished his beer before we had finished the 'Down-Down' song? Hash Sh*t this week is therefore accorded to Malcolm."

The audience roars its approval.

He hands me a toilet seat and tells me "for your sins, you must wear the Sh*t trophy for the rest of the evening. Now back on the stool."

I climb back on and am handed another pint glass. This time the song is cut short to a single 'down' giving me time to swallow about a third of the glass before I have to play to the audience and tip the remainder on my head.

The Grand Master hands me a towel and says *sotto voce* "well done buddy, and welcome to the Hash."

Now, for me, the Hash serves several useful functions. First, I get to make quickly a host of new friends of all ages and backgrounds. Second, I get to visit several out of the way bars cum restaurants that I might never have found on my own. And third, believe it or not, I get to enjoy running all over again! And run I do. Not only with the weekly Hash but also on my own, along the beach in the early evenings.

For the first of these runs, I leave my house at 5 pm, cross the Kololi Road, run in the direction of the Senegambia Hotel before turning right along a dirt-track and out on to the beach. The beach at this point is pristine sand and seems empty while the sea looks inviting although the Atlantic on this coast is a dangerous place to swim alone. I run north thinking to do five or six kilometres before turning back south and leaving via another dirt-track that goes past a little restaurant cum bar cum guesthouse owned by the other new Hash member called Tony. For several weeks I have been promising Tony that I would drop in for a chat and to drink a beer with him. This evening provides the ideal opportunity ... but first the run.

As I jog up the beach, relishing the feel of the sea breeze on my already sweating body, a young man with Rasta dreadlocks starts to jog beside me.

"Hi bro" he says.

"*Nan-ga-def gorgui*" (how are you doing chum), I reply in Wolof hoping that he then understands that I am not a tourist and wish to be left alone.

"Heh, I'm fine man. I just wanted to ask if you want a pretty girl to give you a massage. She is just up there by the palm trees."

"*De-dit, jere-jef* (no, thanks), I'm trying to run, as you can see".

He continues to run beside me as I move further up the beach, and then suggests "perhaps you would prefer a man instead, I can bring you one too, no problem."

"*Gorgui, demalle tuti*, I really am trying to run would you kindly go away?"

He stops running beside me and announces with no real conviction "I can bring you younger girls if you wish." I ignore him and keep running and after a few moments he shouts out a question towards my back: "*Gorgui*, why on earth are you running in this heat?"

Good question! And the simple answer is to build up a proper thirst by the time I get to Tony's bar.

The Hash is also the cause of my first return trip to Dakar since I left Senegal the previous year. Our Grand Master and the hash master in Dakar have organised a run sponsored by the two clubs. This will be the Banjul club's first ever visit to my old haunt. Rooms have been reserved for us in a hotel called the *Croix de Sud* (the Southern Cross) that sits conveniently in the town centre. We leave Banjul in several cars first thing in the morning and arrive in Dakar in the early afternoon. My work colleague, Frank the hash master, suggests a stroll around the Place de l'Independence; fine by me. It feels good to be back in Dakar and to revisit places that had become so familiar during my four years plus living in the city.

We leave the hotel and head south towards Avenue Sarrault. But some things have changed since I left Dakar in the summer of '93, particularly the city's young villains. As we walk down the quite afternoon street, two young men, boys really, start walking towards us; and they have the ominous pink tissue paper held in one hand.

"Incoming Bandits," I say to the Grand Master, "watch out, one will go after your wallet and the other will be after mine. They will try to distract you either by waving the pink tissue paper with fake jewellery in your face or by going after your shoelaces, so get ready."

I need not have worried. These poor guys thought that they were dealing with two middle-aged tourists not with a seasoned former resident of Dakar nor a battle-hardened US veteran.

The bandit who is coming at me, waves the tissue paper in my face and at the same time tries to get his hand in my pocket. As he twists slightly to go for my wallet, he exposes the side of his right knee. Perfectly placed now for me to give it a hard kick. Down goes bandit number one.

The second suffers an even more painful experience. He foolishly goes for the Grand Master's shoelaces which means that his head and neck are left exposed at waist level. One solid left-handed rabbit punch leaves the second bandit sitting rather surprised on the tarmac.

We '*high five*' and continue our stroll down the road, chatting as we go, as though nothing has happened.

Sadly, this was certainly not the bandits' best day because by coincidence two patrol policemen at the bottom of the street have witnessed the proceedings! They pass us with broad smiles on their faces and go to collect the youngsters for an uncomfortable night in the cells.

We run the hash with the Dakar pack, composed mostly of Americans and many known to me from my time in the town where

I had served as the President of the International School of Dakar of which many of their children are students. My grand presidential title does not save me. During the down-down, the Dakar Hash call me out for harsh punishment because they consider me a traitor for having never run the hash in Dakar. Their torture is terrible. No, not having to drink cold beer during down-down but having to sit in a bucket of ice while doing so!

I am starting to get excited because the family is due to arrive for a three-week stay at the end of next week. I have been scoping out places to take them for day trips. After all, in The Gambia, every-where can be reached in a couple of hours. The Grand Master has recently told me about the Bamboo Lodge that sits out in the man-grove swamps just to the south of the airport. I consider it better to go and see it before taking the family there; one never knows. The directions he has given me are easy to follow so that after a thirty-minute drive, I arrive in a small car park cut into the outer ring of the mangroves. I park, get out of the car and lock the doors.

Out of nowhere I hear "Hello *toubab*" (white man). I look around and can see absolutely no one. "I'm here," the mysterious and obviously female voice says, "in the shop."

Now that I am less surprised, I can follow the voice to a small wooden structure by the edge of the mangroves and, out of curiosity, I walk across. What I find in the shop leaves me very marked. There is a young girl, perhaps fifteen or sixteen years old sitting propped up in an ancient wheelchair. The top of her head does not quite reach the level of the counter; the reason that I could not see her until I approached more closely. She has the most angelic face that I have ever seen. Pretty, beautiful are simply not the right words to describe her. She is lovely with the sweetest smile one could imagine. She also suffers from horribly disfigured legs that are bonelike, twisted and deformed and keep her trapped in the wheelchair for life.

"My name is Sophie, what's your name? I cannot call you *toubab* every time you visit here! Would you like to buy anything? I have vegetables and fruit that my dad grows and these small baskets and trinkets that I make to help earn money for my family."

After buying several articles that I think my kids will like and putting them in the trunk of the car, I go back to Sophie and ask for directions to the Bamboo Lodge.

"Just follow the trail over there and you will eventually come to the Lodge. I will be gone when you come back because my brother is collecting me soon. You are nice, so have a lovely time and bring your family to visit me when they get to The Gambia."

The loveliest souls often reside in the most tormented frames.

The lodge is amazing. It is built almost exclusively from bamboo, hence its name, and looks rather like a large, multi-legged scaffold. There is an enlarged room at one end, next to a kitchen and a bar. Here, the customers sit less than four feet above the water. Then there is a ladder made of bamboo and recycled wood that leads to a similar room upstairs. I decide to stay in the lower room, near to the water, and order a sandwich and a cold beer. As I look out of the glassless window and down into the relatively clear water, I spot a number of small fish and, as I throw in crumbs of bread, more break the surface in a feeding frenzy. Many look like some sort of tilapia but others are pipefish that belong to the same family as seahorses. Magic.

Looking across to the muddy side of the mangrove swamp there sit dozens of mudskippers seemingly sunbathing but really on the lookout for any foolish flies that might come down to the mud to feed on detritus thrown up by the last tide. But the mudskipper is quite capable of swallowing a smaller skipper if the fancy takes him.

This fish is an interesting fellow. While most fish breath uniquely through their gills, these chaps can also get oxygen across their skin and the mucous of their mouth lining; providing they stay moist.

In the child-rearing arena, the ladies are put to real shame for it is the males that build the home (tunnels in the moist mud) and protect the eggs, once laid, from predators. In the meantime, the gentler sex goes off on other pursuits. Ah, that's the life ladies. You sunbathe while the men look after the kids!

For me, their most remarkable features are their modified front fins (pectorals) that are able to function as 'legs' and propel them rapidly across the mud. Could the mudskipper have been the fore-father of amphibians that millions of years later eventually evolved into *Homo sapiens*? I have no idea, but nice to let the imagination run wild.

My reverie is disturbed by the lodge owner who comes to sit with me for a chat.

I ask him "in a week or so when I come back with my family, may we fish from the platform of your lodge?"

"Of course", he replies "but why not take a *pirogue* (canoe) and go further into the mangrove? You can catch bigger fish there."

"Can you arrange that for me, I am free tomorrow and would like to try the *pirogue* before I take my children out in it?"

"No problem, the *pirogue* owner is the father of the girl you must have seen when you parked your car. He knows the waters around here well and can take you to good fishing spots. He only charges three pounds for a morning or an afternoon of fishing."

I book the *pirogue* for the following day, to leave the lodge at 9 am. I want to see which fishing methods work best before I take the children out to fish. After all, there is nothing worse for impatient kids than a fishless fishing trip.

The following morning, I arrive at the lodge early enough to eat a simple breakfast and drink a coffee before Sophie's dad arrives with his gear: two paddles. It looks like this fishing expedition will not be quite as adventurous as the ones I used to make during the five years or so that I spent in Senegal. Then, various of M. Sène's multitude of sons would take me out to sea off the Nature Reserve of Popenguine in their *pirogue* driven by an outboard motor. During those trips, we invariably caught many different species of fish, even once an octopus, while my dad, visiting from the UK, had a close'ish encounter with a hammerhead shark (it bit in half the fish he was just reeling in!).

I greet Sophie's dad with a 'a *salam malikum*' and '*nan-ga-def*' and receive a 'good morning sir' in reply. He helps me to place my two rods and fishing bag into the *pirogue*, waits until I have climbed in and am sitting comfortably and then pushes off. He paddles us gently to the middle of the rather large creek that runs beside the lodge and then we head downstream towards the open sea. Since the second paddle is sitting idly on the floor of the *pirogue*, I pick it up and begin to paddle in unison with him. He turns his head and flashes me a broad smile as we move faster towards our destination.

Some twenty minutes later, after turning a few times right and a couple of times left – meaning that I am totally lost within the mangroves – he drops a breeze-block tied with rope over the side. We have dropped anchor.

I bait my three hooks with pieces of prawn and let them sink rapidly into the murkiest water I have ever fished. I offer him a hand-line and several raw prawns, thinking he would also like to fish but receive a polite 'no thanks'.

No time to worry because my rod end kicks and I am soon reeling in two fish, catfish to be precise. Each weighs around the half-kilo mark and, unlike the catfish that my children catch at the 3D-lake in Cordon, these do not have nasty spikes coming out of their pectoral and dorsal fins.

I go on to catch about twenty catfish over the course of the next hour and a half but nothing else. I indicate that we should weigh anchor and go closer to the bank. I want to try some float fishing to see if I can catch some of the tilapia-like fish that I saw the previous day. That strategy is a failure. It seems that it's catfish or no fish today.

My time is almost up and so we start to paddle towards the lodge. The paddling is rather harder and progress slower now that we are going against a receding tide than when we left with it. I get back to the lodge at just after 12 noon, hand half the fish over to the *pirogue* owner and arrange to meet him the following week once the family arrive.

The lodge owner kindly brings me a bowl of water and a sliver of soap so that I may wash the rather heavy odour of catfish slime of my hands and then takes my lunch order for a plate of *mafé* (mutton cooked in peanut sauce accompanied by three or four types of vegetables all laying on a bed of rice) – my favourite – and a bottle of beer. Heaven in the mangroves.

As I eat, far too much (if I am honest) of this delicious dish, I reflect on the beauty and importance of the mangrove swamps the world over. My very first job, soon after leaving London University with a brand new PhD in Ecology tucked in my back pocket, was at the University of Calabar in southeast Nigeria. At the age of 26 I was the very first plant ecologist to have ever worked at this new university and I threw myself into designing and leading the teaching of several beginner and advanced ecology courses. My enthusiasm was noticed by the university hierarchy because very rapidly I was offered the directorship of the university botanical gardens and research site as an additional job on top of my teaching and research duties. While the botanical gardens were most certainly not akin to Kew Gardens, by any stretch of the imagination, the research site proved to be an enormous area of forest, wetlands and hundreds of hectares of prime mangrove swamps.

Senegal also claims some mangrove swamp, mostly in the areas called the Sine Saloum and Zinguinchor. I had visited these areas several times during family holidays or fishing trips.

Mangroves are fascinating and important areas made even more interesting and perhaps surprising when it is known that the mangroves across the entire globe can boast only a very small number of different tree species; far, far less than any other type of forest. But the tiny diversity of trees, hides the importance of those species in many parts of the globe. They protect against tidal erosion – just look what happens to the coastline when the autochthons decide to chop down their mangroves – and they provide a rich source of nutrition for marine life, as well as important spawning grounds for fish and crustaceae. Woe betide a nation that decides to destroy its mangroves.

The family travels out to The Gambia at the end of the week and the three of them awake on Saturday morning to an extended holiday in the country. Although we had previously spent long weekends in The Gambia when we lived in Senegal, this is the first time that we are together in our own home and for several weeks.

At seven a.m. master David, now aged eight, thunders through our bedroom door for a cuddle followed fifteen minutes later by a more respectful Mélanie, aged twelve and "I'm really too old for a cuddle dad but I missed you".

Véro and I have already chatted through an agenda for the next few days. Today, Saturday, we will take a picnic to the beach at lunchtime, have a siesta during the heat of the afternoon, and then go to Tony's restaurant for dinner. He has promised to have some lobsters ready for us; always one of Véro's favourite dishes, and some real fish and chips for the kids who miss this British delicacy now that they live in France. *Poisson pané et frites* does not have quite the same ring to it, you must agree. Plus, there will be lashings of HP sauce (a delicacy *introuvable en France*!).

Tomorrow we are off to the Bamboo Lodge for a fishing trip and lunch. Véro offers not to overcrowd the *pirogue* and rather will remain with a book at the Lodge. None of us is fooled because we always knew she would find an excuse to wriggle out of the fishing trip. While Monday afternoon is the Hash, of course, but I do not give away too many of the details or any of the Hash secrets. The three of them will find out what is in store in their own good time!

We arrive at the Lodge parking and as we get out of the car, I call out "Good morning Sophie."

The kids spin around in surprise as a young voice calls back "Hello Mark, I see you have brought your children!"

I take them over to Sophie's shop and introduce them to the young lady. Mélanie is soon chatting with Sophie about her life in France, Véro is sorting through the baskets while David turns to me and says in French "dad, her legs are like my friend in the market in Senegal."

And he is right. In Marché Kermel, there was a young beggar that we all became very fond of who also had a twisted spine and withered legs. Every Saturday morning when we did our food shopping, he would come to greet us and receive alms, often handed over by a slightly younger David.

Sophie's dad is waiting for us by the *pirogue* and has kindly brought two very old, sun-bleached but functional lifejackets for the children. Both our children learnt to swim at a very young age and indeed they are both better swimmers than me but I am concerned that if an accident happens and one of them falls in or the *pirogue* overturns, they might panic. The jackets remove that worry.

We all climb in the canoe with David taking a seat near to the captain and Mélanie sitting near to me. We follow the same route as previously with the children taking it in turns to paddle and, within twenty minutes, the three of us have our lines in the water. Both my children are becoming competent fishermen with Mélanie catching more because she is more patient but with David rapidly catching his sister up.

"Dad's luck" chimes David as I reel in the first catfish but, not to be outdone, he is soon pulling one into the *pirogue*.

"You two are so lucky", moans Mélanie, "I haven't had a bite yet."

"Reel in," I say, "let me check if your bait is still on the hook." Since the piece of prawn looks a bit ragged, I take it off and put on a fresh piece. "That's for luck Mimi, try again."

Almost immediately Mélanie is striking into a fish and pulls out the biggest so far. She replenishes her bait and sits patiently, then starts to mutter and finally to complain as David and I pull out several more fish.

"Dad, please, can you put on some more bait and give me a little more luck?" asks my girl. Sooner done than she is again pulling a fish into the *pirogue*.

The penny finally starts to drop. Every time I put bait on the hook, Mélanie catches a fish. Each time she baits the hook, nothing. Why could that be? The mangrove water is very murky and full of sediment so the catfish must be finding the bait ... by smell.

"Mimi have you put anything on your hands this morning, cream or something?"

"Yes dad, I put suntan cream on my face and arms and on Dave's face too."

And there we have the reason!

The time on fishing trips always seems to go fast and we are soon heading back towards the Lodge. But not before we see a family of otters playing on the edges of the mangroves and a pair of pied kingfishers trying to catch mudskippers off the muddy bank.

4

A coup, map-making and bananas

Although the family may be on holiday, I still have to work at NEA. Today's major task is to write terms of reference (we call them ToR) for two sets of consultants. The first consultant is to come out to The Gambia and train a (still to be assembled) team of national civil servants in aerial photo-interpretation. We have heard that the photos have now been developed and will arrive in country around the start of June. My company has already identified a well-qualified and experienced technician from the Netherlands to undertake the training and the ToR is required mostly to formalise the recruitment process. Training in the photo analyses is to begin, hopefully, in late June.

The second consultancy is to follow a few weeks after the initial photo-interpretation training, with the task then being to train the team in how to digitise the interpreted photos and, from there, build natural resources maps of the country in a software called ArcInfo. I have requested my company to offer this work to my old project in Senegal. They have agreed to send two of their experienced technicians to work with the Gambian team. My reasons for insisting that the contract be placed with the Senegalese team are very simple. First, I have incredible faith in the capacity of my old colleagues (and as we say 'better the devil we know'); second, the technicians will be able to explain to the Gambian team the more complex parts of their work both in English and, if necessary, in Wolof; third, and very importantly, I wish to show my technicians and their ministries just what serious technical capacity lies just over the border. Too frequently expertise is brought thousands of miles when equally qualified personnel can be sourced quite locally.

As 4.30 pm arrives, the Grand Master comes into my office and asked if I am ready to leave for the Hash. The run today is to start close to my house on the Kololi beach and so, after a detour home to change and pick up my family, now resplendent in running gear, we go off to the meeting point. David declares to 'uncle Frank' that he will be running with his dad while Mélanie volunteers to keep her mum company on the walking circuit.

At exactly 5.30, the Grand Master declares On-On and the keeper of the trumpet blows a quick blast. The Hash is underway. David runs alongside me for a couple of kilometres but then admits that the run is longer than he thought, especially as it is hot and sticky today. By chance we arrive at a point where the runners' circuit overlaps with the walkers' and where there is a pile of sprinkle paper signalling a spot for a breather. We wait a few moments for some of the slower runners to catch up and, while doing so, hear the unmistakable 'chatter-chatter' (well, this is the Hash, remember) of our two ladies approaching. David goes off to join mum and Mélanie leaving me to call On-On and torment the slowest of the runners who have only just caught up and who thought they might be able to stop at the sprinkles' pile for a breather!

The end of the Hash is signposted, as usual, by Peter's white van and ice cold Julbrew beers. I give the children a few Dalasis each so that they can go and buy raffle tickets while the Grand Master delights David by selecting him to draw the winning tickets.

After a quick shower and change of clothing (I tell my family to wear only old clothes), we go off to the restaurant; let the ceremony begin!

The Hash Master stands and calls out "come up here David, Mélanie and Véronique."

"What's this about?" queries Véro.

"You'll see!" I reply.

This week the Grand Master has decided to dispense with the stools but not with the drinks. Véro is giving a pint glass filled with water and the children each receive a half-pint glass of water too.

The Grand Master begins the humming "ummmm, ready hash?"

"Ready, ummmm" we all sing before breaking into the Hash song:

"Here's to Véro, David and Mélanie, they're true blue. They're now Hashers through and through. They're drinkers and runners, so they say. Tried to get to heaven but went the other way. Drink it down, down, down, ..."

The Grand Master mimics to them to begin drinking and allows the 'downs' to run a bit longer than usual. But finally he is obliged to say "On your heads."

This is the moment for crass indiscipline to break out. After all we are dealing with Frenchies here, and there is no race more undisciplined than our adored cousins from the other side of the channel!

Véro simply empties her glass on the concrete terrace and mutters "I am not going to ruin my hair that I just spent 300 francs getting styled before I came to The Gambia!"

David and Mélanie smile at each other and then both simultaneously throw the water out of their glasses and all over poor uncle Frank. The Grand Master of the Gambian Chapter of the Hash House Harriers has never been so insulted, and likely never so soaked.

Uproar ensues with half the hashers cheering for the kids and the other half, the older ones mostly, muttering about the young no longer respecting tradition.

The Grand Master calls the riot to order by pulling out the infamous toilet seat that represents the award for the Hash Sh*t. "I am going to award the Hash Sh*t this week to Malcolm for daring to bring such a riotous family to the sacred Hash ceremony."

Between giggles and guffaws, David pipes up in his squeaky voice "... and Uncle Frank, dad told us to throw the water over you."

Which was certainly not true! Would I show such disrespect?

The Grand Master stands flabbergasted "what? You are telling tales on your dad? Never in my time as the Grand Master have I ever changed my mind about the Hash Sh*t but tonight is a first. Malcolm give me the trophy back because David Marks, you are the new Hash Sh*t for this week."

The good fun stops soon after the meal is finished with Véro dragging the three of us out of the restaurant for the drive home. The kids loved the experience but I do not think that French ladies are yet quite ready for the Hash House Harriers!

The following day, just after lunch, I am working in my office in the Standard Chartered building when Amadou, a young man that works as a 'shoeshine boy', comes in to the office and takes my shoes for their daily polish. I can hear him through my open door brushing the shoes and chatting with Lamin, the project driver.

I am concentrating hard on writing my sections of the project's quarterly report and do not notice the swift passage of time.

At three-thirty, our secretary pokes her head around my door and tells me "the ministry has just phoned and the senior secretary asks that you go over to his office to provide some technical guidance in a meeting of senior staff."

"OK, thanks. Where did Amadou put my shoes, Mary?" I reply to our secretary.

"Didn't he give them back?" she asks, "he left at least thirty minutes ago."

And yes, the boy who has been polishing everyone's shoes in the office for the last several months has decided today to steal my best pair of black leather shoes; and just before I am to go into a meeting with the ministry hierarchy!

I walk downstairs in my socks and climb into Lamin's car for the trip to the ministry. Lamin explains that the Eid festival will start in a few days and he can only think that the 'shoeshine boy' needed money to buy his bus ticket home and so decided to nick my shoes. They will already be on sale in the market ... at a knockdown price.

Nothing to do but to climb the steps into the Ministry of Natural Resources, enter the large conference room and take my place at the front of the meeting. I say nothing, none of the audience says anything either, and the meeting proceeds with me standing at the white board in my socks explaining the technical issues at hand. At the end of the meeting, the senior secretary thanks the audience, composed of all the directors as well as other very senior members of the ministry, for their attendance.

He then turns to me and says "Malcolm, thanks for your valuable contributions. Before finishing the meeting, we would all like to congratulate you for making today's fashion statement; especially with the hole in the toe of your sock!"

The audience laughs vigorously and then laughs even more when I explain that our 'shoeshine boy' had just stolen my shoes. The good-mannered teasing lasted for several more months of my stay in The Gambia and even becomes something of an urban legend. That is because, many years later, while I am working in Guinea-Conakry, an expatriate technician hailing from Senegal asked me if, during my time in The Gambia, I had ever heard of the story of the *toubab* (the white man) that had to attend a ministerial meeting in his socks because his shoes had just been stolen!

Finally, the lovely time with my family comes to end and they have to return to France. School beckons for the children. I get Véro and the kids to Yundum in the early evening and they receive their boarding passes for their economy seats. Big hugs and see you soon and the family goes off towards passport control and finally on to the plane.

Step up dear Jean-Pierre. "*Madame Marks, mes enfants. Je suis vraiment désolé mais nous n'avons pas assez de repas en économie. Veuillez me suivre s'il vous plait ?*" and he kindly leads them through the dividing curtain and into the business class section because there is supposedly insufficient food for the passengers in economy!

Final word from master David "Mum, great, now you won't have to pay for your champagne!"

With some delay, the aerial photos finally arrive in Banjul and there are a surprising number of boxes. But perhaps not so surprising since they are at a scales of 1:25,000 and 1:50,000 in black and white and colour respectively. There are two sets of each so that we can use stereoscopy during our analysis. Now the photos are in place, my Washington office has been in contact with the consultant from the Netherlands, and he is due to arrive in Banjul on July 21 and start the training the very next day. Due to the delay in the photos arriving, I realise that we are now three weeks behind my anticipated schedule. Nonetheless, that does now give me a couple of extra weeks to get a team of civil servants together and to fix the date for the Dakar technicians to begin their input some two weeks after we start the photo-interpretation training.

To gather a local team, the lady director of NEA sends a note to the senior personnel in affiliated departments requesting volunteers to report to my office at the Standard Chartered Bank building in one week's time. For the Dakar input, I telephone and spend a long time chatting with the Technical Director. That part is easy.

What is not quite so easy is the meeting the following week with the 'volunteers'. Sixteen warm bodies turn up; some are really keen to be there while others have clearly been ordered to be present by their departmental heads. Nonetheless, I start by providing a very in-formal presentation on what we hope to achieve (the first ever Natural Resources maps of The Gambia) and the means to achieve that result: training in photo-interpretation followed by training in the GIS software ArcInfo. The two periods of training will be provided on-the-job as we analyse the photos and build the maps together. We estimate that the work will take five months full-time.

Among the volunteers is a very sparkly young man, named Stanley. He is a born leader and a born comedian too. He is clearly excited by the tasks that lie ahead and keen to get started on the training which he sees will enable him to progress his career in the Land Surveys Office. He speaks up for the rest of the team, many of whom sit in silence.

After the presentation is made and Stanley has said his piece, I ask if there are any questions. One of the obviously less keen volunteers, sitting slouched in his chair at the back of the room, raises his hand

and asks "what salary top-up will we receive and what is our *per diem* rate?"

First I have to silence Stanley who is less than happy with that question and then I answer very calmly "the work we are all to carry out is first and foremost for The Gambia. It is not for me nor is it for the USA. It is for your country. It will be hard but interesting work, it may well require working longer hours than usual, we may be under stress and so, on occasions, lose our tempers. But at the end of the work, you will have developed an amazing resource for your country while each and every one of you will receive unique training in photo-interpretation and GIS in the context of The Gambia. There are no salary top-ups, there are no *per diems*. There are only volunteers from the Gambian civil service. If any of you are unhappy, there is the door ...".

Surprisingly only the gentleman who asked the question about money and one of his cronies get to their feet and sheepishly leave the room without a further word. Over the next couple of days, Stanley – who seems to have taken on the role of leader of the team of volunteers – informs me that a couple more are obliged to drop out of the team for other, more legitimate reasons.

On July 21st, I accompany Lamin to Yundum Airport to meet the Dutch consultant off the Sabena flight and take him to the Senegambia hotel where he has chosen to stay. The next morning, we meet again in our offices in the Standard Chartered Bank building and spend an hour looking at the photos, the equipment and the training schedule that is to begin in a moment. As we finish our initial briefing, the first of the volunteers walk into the conference room, led by a very cheery Stanley. All twelve of the volunteers arrive and get settled at their places.

The consultant closes the curtains in our conference room and begins his initial PowerPoint presentation at 9.30 am sharp. By 10.30

am we all start to practice laying out twinned adjacent photos and attaching tracing paper over the top of one of the pair and measuring out the critical area for analysis. These we place under stereoscopes and begin to learn and practice selecting out areas representing different types of features (roads, rivers, towns/villages, etc.) and vegetation (marsh, mangrove, forests, agricultural fields and so on). The work is fascinating, everyone is concentrating hard, trying not to make mistakes. Our consultant is also very patient with his team of novices!

At around 11.30, I give up my place at one of the stereoscopes to another technician and make my way to our project toilets. On my way out of the room, I peep through the blackout curtains to the street running two stories below. I am immediately shocked by what is missing: there is absolutely no one walking in the streets and this, in an African capital. That is unheard of.

Next, I notice a soldier in uniform and carrying a rifle walking slowly down the street. This is the first time in Banjul that I have seen a soldier with rifle in the streets. What is happening?

I do not need to wait long for the answer. Mary, our office secretary, tells me that there is a call from the US Embassy, a first for me.

"Hello, Malcolm Marks from the ANR Project," I say.

"Malcolm, this is the Ambassador's Secretary. His Excellency has asked me to inform you that the junior officers of the Gambian National Army have launched an attempted coup. They are already in command of the Presidential Palace and Sir Dawda Jawara, the President, has taken refuge on the USS Moure County. H.E.'s instructions are for you and the rest of the team to stay put in your office and not to attempt to leave until we give the all-clear."

'Blast' is all I can think to say. This will certainly put a very large cat among the pigeons.

I go back to the conference room and wait twenty minutes for lunchtime to arrive then I break the news to the team members. Everyone is shocked. The Gambia is a calm country and coups belong to more turbulent places like Nigeria and Guinea-Conakry. But no longer, one has landed on our doorstep.

Since the US embassy has advised us to stay put until they give the all-clear, we agree that we might as well continue to work until the normal 5 pm office closure or until we receive other orders from the embassy. In the meantime, it is lunch and hungry workers – coup or not – have to be fed.

Luckily, I had the foresight a few days ago to arrange food for fourteen people with a lady called Urmi, a Senegalese woman who runs a small restaurant near to the port where I often take lunch, and to bring the food to the office.

A shout from Mary declares that Urmi and a couple of her sons and a daughter have arrived with two enormous pots of food and a crate of soft drinks. The largest pot is filled with *thieb* (rice) and the slightly smaller one with a mix of fish, vegetables and hot, hot chillies. This meal was to have been a gesture of thanks to my new team and, when I put in the order, I never realised that the food would be delivered and we would eat it in the midst of a *coup d'état*!

No matter, today, despite whatever is occurring outside, we will all eat a big plate of *thieboudienne* or *bena tchin* as the Gambians will insist on calling Senegal's national dish.

After serving the team, our consultant and myself, there still remains sufficient food in the pots to feed the three project drivers, our accountant, and the secretary plus two of the technical team who happen to be present. Twenty or so very generous portions cost me the grand sum of £12!

We try to continue with the training as though nothing has happened. But of course it has. Listening to a little transistor radio as he works, Stanley – now officially elected by the team as the leader of the photo-interpretation work – provides us with a running commentary. It seems that the coup started as a rowdy protest, a minor mutiny.

The senior officers had left the previous day for military exercises on the American ship leaving the junior officers, the lieutenants and captains, in charge of the barracks. And these junior officers were beginning to moan. The international media tells us that problems have been fomenting for several months but one of my team announces that his brother, who is in the army, has told him that the anger stems directly from the failure to pay a promised salary top up for UN *casque bleu* services in the Liberian civil war.

It seems that the junior officers decided to take their case directly to the President and so took a military vehicle and then stopped and 'borrowed' a four-wheel drive owned by an international NGO. They travelled to the Presidential Palace hoping to discuss their problems with the president but he had gotten word of the mutiny and escaped by helicopter with his family to the US ship. When the young officers arrived at the palace, no senior person was present to receive them and so they simply walked through the front door.

Even at this time, the junior officers apparently had no thought of declaring a coup. What is said to have happened, is that Lieutenant Yaya Jammeh, only 29 years old, jokingly sat on the president's chair and declared it very comfortable and, from now on, it would be his. A minor mutiny thus evolves into a full-blown coup.

The leaders of the coup are quickly announced on the radio: Yaya Jammeh, Sana Sabally, Edward Singhateh, Basiru Barrow and Sadibou Hydara. The coup leaders declare a three-day lockdown of the country: 'everyone should remain at home'.

Home is exactly where we all wish to be but we patiently await the US Embassy call. Finally, at around 5.30 pm the call comes through and I am told to go directly home and to let the training team members find their own way back. There is no way that I would ever leave these colleagues to their own devices; that does not belong in my definition of teamwork. Nonetheless, better not to argue at this juncture and so I say simply 'OK' and hang up the phone.

Back in the conference room, I get everyone together, including drivers, and announce "we have three project vehicles and drivers while Stanley came with his own car. Please sort yourselves into groups of individuals who live close to each other. Ensure that we fill each car. I do not want anyone left behind in Banjul. We are going to proceed in convoy at a slow pace, no faster than 50 km per hour. I intend to travel in the front of the first car. Should we get stopped at a checkpoint, please allow me to do the talking. Once we get to Serrekunda, the cars will split up and deliver each person to their home. Drivers, then please drive back to my house in Kololi where we will park the cars. All clear?"

My car is driven by Lamin, of course, and we also have three technicians and the Dutch consultant squashed into the back seat. Stanley is in the second car and his old Toyota is followed by the two other project four-wheel-drive vehicles. We have agreed that we will keep in close formation until we reach Serrekunda.

Banjul is totally empty with not a soul walking in the streets or driving a car. At each corner we see soldiers with rifles or machine guns. I wave at each of them as we drive past and receive salutes in return. With the roads empty, we are soon leaving the outskirts of Banjul driving along the South Bank road and heading towards Denton Bridge; so far so good.

As we near the bridge, I can see a soldier on my side of the road rise from a chair, rifle at the ready in his hands. Other soldiers are in the centre of the road, two with grenade launchers. Serious weaponry and a barrier blocks the entrance to the bridge.

Lamin offers to speak with the soldiers but, knowing his rather tempestuous character, I refuse and say better that I do the talking.

We slow the car right down as we arrive at the bridge. The soldier holds up his hand. We come to a complete halt with our three other cars tightly positioned behind.

The young soldier, for he is extremely young, barely more than a recruit, stutters as he asks "sir, sir whe ... whe ... where are you going. You should be ho ... home already."

"At ease soldier," I say and immediately he seems to relax. "We are a technical team from the US Embassy."

"Thank you, sir, please go straight home and stay there. Your team should go to their homes without you."

"I will see them home first soldier, but thank you for the advice, and good luck."

"Thank you, sir," and I receive a salute that I return. He then turns and orders the other soldiers to open the barrier. We are through and have only ten kilometres until we get to our homes.

Lamin, cheerful as he always is, queries "doctor, were you ever in the army? That young boy showed you military respect when you spoke to him."

"Of course Lamin. I served for two years ... in the Combined Cadet Force at my school when I was fourteen. I made the rank of Lance-Corporal!"

The passengers in the car join with Lamin in roaring with laughter.

I arrive home safely after dropping off my colleagues. The other two cars are already parked in my garage and this third one can stand in the driveway. I shut and padlock the driveway gates and wish Lamin a safe walk home; he only lives a few hundred metres away. The other drivers soon phone in to tell me that they have reached their homes safely.

All looks good for the three-day curfew. My freezer is well stocked with meat because I recently bought and butchered a good-sized piglet from my housemaid's family and, of course, I have frozen fish plus a few small lobsters. There is lots of rice, potatoes and noodles in the pantry plus a good stock of fresh vegetables with plenty of bananas ripening in the garden on the trees that I had planted. My beer and wine stocks also look healthy. I could certainly withstand an enforced three days or so at home without too much discomfort.

Just after I have kicked off my shoes and put on the TV to follow the latest news, I hear the outside bell ring. On looking through the door, I see a young man, obviously of eastern Asian origin.

"Hello, my name is Dick," he calls from outside my locked gate. "Excuse me for bothering you but I just moved into the house across the road from you," and he indicates his house where the removal men were busy over the last weekend. "I heard about the coup and I'm a bit worried about how events are going to play out. I'm scared that foreigners may be targeted, what do you think we should do?"

"Come in Dick, better that we chat inside." I let him in through the locked gate, lead him to my sitting room and then open two bottles of beer and hand him a glass. "I wouldn't be too worried if I were you. The Gambia is a nice little country and the armed forces and police officers always show foreigners a lot of respect; after all tourism is a big money earner here. Do you want to eat with me this evening? You can even stay a few days if you are really worried. I have two house guards and my generator has plenty of diesel if the electricity is cut. No problem."

Dick stays with me throughout the three days of curfew and, not surprisingly, we become great friends. Dick is a star. He speaks impeccable English and hails from China, not from Hong Kong or

Taiwan but from the People's Republic of China itself. During our three days together he tells me his unlikely story.

He was an uneducated and unemployed youngster until recruited in China by a businessman who trades in The Gambia. He and a dozen or so fellow Chinese were employed on pitiful salaries, not even pocket money as he tells me, and shipped over to Banjul on a steamer. The trip lasted several weeks and during that time he shared a tiny cabin with the other recruits while their boss and his grown-up daughter had a suite of rooms.

Dick took one look at the boss's daughter and fell in love with her. He told his fellow workers that one day he would marry her which caused great mirth and teasing because of his lack of education and lowly social status. But the teasing did not discourage him, indeed it had the opposite effect. Dick realised that he could not gain an education very easily but he could learn English, and learn English he did.

Once arrived in Banjul, two years before our meeting, he had worked much harder than the other workers and was quickly appointed the foreman both for his work ethics and obvious intelligence ... plus his now excellent English language skills. Just to make sure of his place in the owner's respect, he also quickly learnt Wolof so he became the chief intermediary between his boss and the market community. The company trades in textiles and garments and Dick helped it to prosper.

The owner's daughter saw the impact that Dick was having on her dad's company, the respect that the other Chinese and also their Gambian partners and clients had for him. She liked his witty remarks and confident manner. He shone, like a star, among the dull Chinese community that she lived among in Banjul. And you have already guessed, she fell in love with him and they got married.

His wife is away in China at the moment on a buying trip for the company. I will have to wait to meet her.

The three days go quickly and pleasantly before Dick moves back to his house over the road. From that moment on we remain great friends and Dick nurtures my love of Chinese food by preparing a range of incredible dishes from very simple, local ingredients. Who would have thought that fried cucumber with a handful of minced meat could taste so delicious or a fried pumpkin plant that he happened to see growing on the side of the road and liberally doused in soy sauce would prove so mouthwatering? On several occasions, I tell Dick that he really should open a Chinese restaurant in Banjul, but to no avail!

All is quiet in Banjul but the US Embassy informs all American nationals plus third-country nationals like myself that we should not yet return to our offices. Instead we are told to remain at home for another week while instituting a 'buddy system'.

This means that when we are obliged to go out of our homes, to buy necessary food items and so forth, we should phone our buddy, stating where we are going, the time we are leaving and the estimated time we should return. On returning home we must then immediately re-phone the buddy to say that we have arrived back safely. If the second call does not come through within fifteen minutes of the anticipated time of return, the buddy is supposed to press the alarm bell by calling the embassy.

My buddy is, of course, the Grand Master. He calls me on the third day of our curfew to ask if I am bored.

"Of course I am," I reply.

"I'm working at the embassy, wanna come over for a chat? Tell them at the door that you have come to see me. I'll leave your name with the receptionist."

I drive up to the embassy gates where the armed Marine guards on duty pass inverted mirrors under my car and, once satisfied that I am not a threat, usher me into the compound where I park. I am then escorted in through the bomb-proof front door that leads to reception. I see a lady on duty behind a glass panel and say. "Good morning, I work for the ANR Project and I've come to see my colleague, Frank."

"Good morning you must be Dr Marks, and you mean that you have come to see the Colonel!"

I vaguely remember that the Grand Master had told me that he was a military reservist but I did not know that he was so senior. "Yes that's right, I would like to see the Colonel if you please."

I am led through a number of impressively thick doors, up a flight of stairs and along a corridor before we stop in front of a blank door.

"The Colonel is working here," I am told.

I knock and enter and am flabbergasted by what I see. My buddy is sitting behind an enormous desk in an enormous room and has at least a dozen separate telephones arranged in front of him. I begin to say something but catch my tongue at 'C.I.', thinking that an embassy is perhaps not the best place to start saying anything foolish.

"I'm helping out at the embassy and I'm, errrr, in charge of organising transport," I am told by my smiling friend.

"Okayyy, I will not say anything further." I reply.

Of course, being so close to the lines of power, he has learnt far more about the situation than me. The coup has been successful, the old president has fled to Dakar in neighbouring Senegal and the coup leaders are cementing their powerbase. The embassy believes that if all remains calm for a couple more days, we should be able to return to the office and restart work.

The following day, the embassy calls a 'town-hall' meeting (I am beginning to get used to American jargon) where the entire US community, some forty persons (plus me), turns up at the embassy to receive an update. The young Ambassador himself leads the meeting and I am impressed at this first official gathering that I am attending just how down to earth and friendly he is. Firstly, he provides us with the same news that I had earlier received from Frank. He goes on to tell us to continue being careful, avoid crowds and retain the buddy system but we can start to go back to the office the following day. The second item on the agenda is that the embassy has developed a 'Plan B' in case the situation deteriorates rapidly. The plan is built around an orderly, motorcade evacuation via the south of the country and into the Casamance of southern Senegal; thus bypassing the ferry crossing that would have been necessary had we gone northwards.

The Ambassador states "we aim to get all Americans out of the country rapidly and safely. Any questions?"

Now, I realise that I am not American and frankly I am not too concerned if the US does not take responsibility for me. After all, I am a UK passport holder and so can simply go to the British High Commission that lies within walking distance of my house. But it turns out that I am not the only one who realises that I am the odd-man-out in the room.

Frank raises his hand and receives an invitation to speak from the ambassador.

"Ambassador, If I am not mistaken, we have an important person in the room who appears excluded from your evacuation plans."

"Hold horses Colonel, I know you are talking about our British friend over there. I forgot to say that he will be in the lead car … in case we get stopped by military roadblocks!" (*pause for people to stop laughing*) "we need to take him with us because he is going to be our official translator in Senegal" (*more laughter*) "and I hear he knows the best restaurants and bars in Cap Skerring." (*small round of applause*).

Suddenly I feel more like a member of the US community in Banjul!

Soon after I arrive back home in Kololi, Stanley rings to tell me that the civil service has been instructed by the new government to go back to work. He has spoken to the entire team and they will arrive at our office at 9 am sharp to re-start our training activities.

I make a quick trip to the Senegambia Hotel to provide our consultant with the news and it feels good to know that we can get our work underway again; despite having had more than a week taken out of our work agenda.

Time goes quickly as we begin the photo-interpretation in earnest. And so quickly are we working our way through the first boxes of photos and making short field expeditions to 'truth' (verify) our analyses that I have to request my old project in Dakar to send their technicians a.s.a.p. Moctar, a very old colleague and friend, and Ba, a newer recruit but known to me from my days at their flagship project, arrive the following day driven by my former driver, Malick.

Straight to work! Both Senegalese trainers speak passable English and, when their English fails, they switch to Wolof. Listening to them speaking in their local language and understanding quite a lot of what is being explained, I have to laugh at how bastardised the language of the cities has become. Fully ten or fifteen percent of what Moctar is saying uses French words; of course therefore not always understood by my Anglophone colleagues. At such moments, Stanley calls out 'Malcolm?' and I translate the French into English. Equally, when my Gambian team ask questions in Wolof, an equal part of their words is in English, cue for me to translate the more difficult words into French. At least my new translator role means that I am obliged to listen carefully to the explanations throughout the training sessions!

My former Senegalese colleagues are excellent trainers and they quickly have us understanding the importance of the initial digitisation process where we enter *points* (small towns, villages, etc.), or *lines* (roads, streams, power lines) and *vectors* or polygons that encircle the different features on the ground such as marshland, forest of different types, plantations, agricultural fields or water bodies. Entering these features into the computer is performed on a 'digitisation table' and uses a clicking device (a little like a mouse but with crosshairs for greater accuracy) to insert the points. We are warned to be extremely careful when digitising vectors and ensure that the points that we add to create the required shape close the vector (basically this requires re-clicking on the starting point). If not, we leave the vector open and the computer will automatically give the neighbouring label and map colour to the unfinished shape.

After we have digitised the first two aerial photos, Ba demonstrates how the two files of digitised information (for photo 1 and photo 2) are combined to begin the map formation. This requires a sub-programme within ArcInfo to be started. After only a few seconds of clicking and clunking by one of our three 386-computers, the calculation is complete and we have the first part of our map generated, covering two adjacent photos.

Over the next couple of weeks, the team enters a steady routine. We are making good progress in photo analyses, a couple of team members have become proficient at digitisation, and others at combining them into the growing map files. However, as our map files grow in size with more and more photos being added via the digitising table, so the speed of our 386-computers gets slower and slower to such a point that Stanley makes a decision: we need to break into teams and try to work around the clock otherwise we will never get the maps completed by year-end. I am absolutely and pleasantly flabbergasted (and so proud) of this decision that I am, for a change, lost for words.

Soon after this decision, we receive potentially bad news via US-AID. The US government in Washington DC is reviewing the case for continuing to provide technical and financial assistance to The Gambia. The logic is clear: the US only provides development aid to democratically elected governments. The coup and installation of a military government is, of course, highly undemocratic and therefore likely to force a stop to all USAID assistance. But what a blow such a political move would be to my super team of Gambian mapmakers who started from nowhere only a few months ago and are now blossoming in their work and even taking it in turns to work through the night to keep our programme on schedule.

Luckily, their diligence has not been overlooked by either USAID or the US Embassy for, I hear, that a request has been made to Washington for a special dispensation to allow us to continue our work. This, is received soon afterwards, thank goodness.

Not so good news for my team leader. His activity of trying to advance natural resources policy within the ministry has ground to a halt following the coup. He is, sadly, given notice to leave the project. Similar notice is given to the assistant team leader. Only my buddy, the Hash Master, and I remain on the team.

As soon as this news breaks, I am called to the donor's office and informed that I am to become the Team Leader for the remainder of the project. An honour, for sure, but one I wish I did not have to assume in this manner. The only other downside of the new position is that I have to deal with an odd-John representing the donors. Let me call this person 'Cyril'.

The highly intelligent, devoted and likeable lady who was the original technical lead for the donors of our project has been recruited by an international NGO and left the country. She has been replaced by 'Cyril'. I have met him on a couple of occasions in the past but not had to work directly with him. That changes now as I receive a request to go and meet with him at 11 am!

I enter his office and the first thing he says to me is "Mr Team Leader, every morning when you wake up, ask yourself 'what can I do for 'Cyril' today?'."

What a silly thing to say and how does one respond to that? I look at his desk and see that he has three empty banana skins lying next to his elbow. "Cyril, tomorrow, I recommend that you buy a few more bananas."

The meeting ends with nothing achieved. I avoid 'Cyril' like the plague for the rest of my assignment in The Gambia.

We are coming up to the autumn half-term in France and so I request approval from both my company and the donors to travel home for a ten-day break, covering two weekends. It is nice to get away from our hothouse of photo-interpretation and digitisation warm in the knowledge that they are in Stanley and the team's safe hands. Two or more of the technicians are now taking turns to spend every night at the office to keep the computers running. As we merge larger and larger photo files within ArcInfo, our 386-computers are really struggling and click and clunk for up to eight hours at a time to get their calculations done and combine the files. Stanley and I realised a while back that if our computers go down during the night – for example if there is a short electricity cut – having no one around to reset them will mean that we lose up to half-a-day of computer time on each terminal. Time is more and more of an essence as the end of the year approaches, and so the night shift has become a permanent feature.

My ticket with Sabena is purchased and Jean-Pierre is there to greet me as I approach the aeroplane steps. No more joking about 'lack of meals' or 'wrong seat', I am simply handed a business class boarding pass as we shake hands and say '*à bientôt*'. See you soon.

I find the whole family well and, since the last time I saw my daughter (only a couple of months previously), she has blossomed into a young woman. David on the other hand has not changed too much except for a few more freckles on his nose and a slightly less squeaky voice.

And Véro is making a great success of her new venture. By one of those odd coincidences, some of the American parents with children at *La Cité Internationale de Lyon* school had heard her speak French with one teacher and then switch seamlessly into English with another.

"Véro, we need to speak to one of the French teacher but cannot find the words to explain ourselves or understand his response. Can you please help us, by perhaps being our interpreter?"

Always a helpful person, she agrees of course. This leads to requests for her to help them become more proficient in French. First by providing coffee mornings in the guise of French conversation classes and, as that proves a bit boring and the Americans generally admire the way the French cook, it morphs into Teaching French via Cooking Lessons! But not just the cooking, rather the whole razzamatazz: how to lay and clear the table; which sequence to serve dishes; what wine to serve with which dish and so on and so on; even how to carve a roast chicken! She starts with three or four American ladies meeting once a week but this soon expands, by popular request, to three times per week with up six anglophone ladies of diverse nationalities per session.

Véro's entrepreneurial streak is assisted by an outgoing Californian women called Leslie. Leslie is a lovely lady and does not like the way some of the other ladies drop out of sessions without notice and without paying so she has installed, in Véro's name, a 'pay-in-advance' policy. But even she was not quite ready for a couple of ladies who 'sold' their attendance on to strangers when they could not make a morning session!

Another financial tip from Leslie was to use Véro's logo (I had found it on Word Perfect!) to generate an array of logoed kitchen items ranging from aprons to tea-towels and on to oven gloves. Her mark-up is not quite as much as the famous crocodile but every little helps.

But the final genius move from Leslie is to suggest a range of ideas for Christmas gifts. The idea for the most popular gift arrives during my leave from Banjul and sees us buying a 25 kg bag of mixed herbs from a wholesaler in Lyon, lots of metres of material that looks suitably Mediterranean, and plenty of yellow ribbon. One afternoon, Véro knocks up a few hundred bags on her sewing machine while I weigh into each one hundred grams of mixed herbs. Mélanie completes the task by tying a neat bow of ribbon around the neck of the bags and attaches a hand-painted label bearing the cooking logo. The two hundred and fifty bags sell like hotcakes and the vast majority end up under American Christmas trees on the other side of the pond.

We are spending half-term in our home in Cordon where our builders, the lovable Franco Brothers, have recently converted our fifty square metre loft into two additional rooms, a proper bedroom for Mélanie with the other room being a spare bedroom that will eventually house my office. They also lower the ceiling and pack it with insulation.

We use the occasion of this vacation to talk through all things financial. The previous year, just before leaving Senegal, I had clicked over 40 and Véro passed the milestone earlier this year. Suddenly 65 and retirement age does not seem as far away as it did only a few years back. We both understand that my career path is likely to take us away from Europe for long periods and remove the opportunity to contribute to a pension in a national or company scheme. And so the emphasis is firmly on our shoulders to design our own pensions. We lay out various possibilities and come up with a mixed pension plan using the analogy of a wall composed of different bricks. The first foundation brick is to make voluntary contributions to the UK government pension. Despite UK pensions not being particularly generous, voluntarily buying years while outside of the UK is cheap. At this time in 1994 I will likely have to contribute around £30 per month. Of course, I made contributions for several years while living in the UK but now send off a request to purchase as many missing years as possible as well as set up a standing order scheme at my UK bank to pay for future years.

We agree that a second brick in our pension wall should be related to property. While UK house prices have soared year after year, those in France – especially in the countryside – remain stubbornly anchored to the floor; mostly due, we believe, to the horrendous tax that the state imposes on every purchase. When buying a property, one must add close to 10% in taxes and fees on top of the purchase price. But this can also play to our advantage if we try to buy cheap properties, renovate them as needed and rent them out. The rent should cover any mortgage or loan that we might need to take to cover the purchase or the repairs. And, during rental, the cost of repairs can be offset against tax on the rental income. Since, hopefully, we will only need an income when we eventually decide to retire, any rents received can be ploughed back into adding more properties to our scheme.

Our own house in Cordon that we had purchased at the tail-end of 1981 cost only £6,000 (as a ruin) and now, more than ten years later, must be worth at least ten times more; mostly due to the extensive renovation that we have undertaken over the years. Equally, in 1991 while we were still working in Senegal, we had purchased another small house in our courtyard for £9,000. At the time of buying, the roof of this second house was structurally more sound than had been the roof of our home. But, in contrast, it had been used as a holiday home for decades and still had a floor of beaten earth and no proper sanitation. During my stay in the Gambia, we had borrowed from the bank and used the cash to invest small amounts in the 'Little House' by getting the Francos and other artisans to undertake a multitude of renovation work. So far so good.

The problem with paying money into the UK pension is that the cash cannot be accessed until one retires. Similarly, by purchasing and renovating property, the money is effectively tied up for a good number of years; Capital Gains Tax (the French *plus value*) takes care of that. So how else to invest for our future while still having access to the money in emergencies.

We discuss which other bricks we can use to build our 'pension wall'? Bank accounts generally allow rapid access but offer so little interest that never manages to beat inflation. So we put that idea to one side. Then Véro logically suggests that I should consider investing more in shares since I enjoy the challenge and we can get at the money relatively quickly if we need to. Share investment then become another of the bricks in our retirement savings plan.

My holidays go too quickly, as always, but this is likely the last vacation I will take from The Gambia given that my contract is due to complete immediately prior to Christmas, and that is only about eight weeks away. With sadness, I say farewell to my little family and make the now familiar journey to Yundum Airport via Brussels, courtesy (of course) of Sabena.

The following morning, I drive early into the office and am met by three of the photo-interpretation technicians who are just finishing the nightshift. They give me a quick run through of progress before excusing themselves to go back to their homes and a well earnt sleep.

Our secretary, then arrives in my office with a few items of accumulated mail. After we finish chatting about the family and my vacation, she moves a concealing pad of writing paper on my desk to reveal a small package, a little box. Inside lies an American Embassy 'thingamajig', I am not too sure what it is. Is it a paperweight, a medallion, a desk ornament or, well, a thingamajig? The bronze medallion reads 'American Embassy Banjul' and it is fixed to a base of white Italian marble. Pretty, but I notice straight away that the top right hand corner of the marble base is chipped.

The secretary also sees that I have noticed the chip and says "one of your outgoing international colleagues was unhappy that you received the medallion and grabbed it out of my hand when it was delivered by the embassy messenger to the office. The medallion dropped to the floor and see what happened? I am sorry but it wasn't my fault. She was angry because her work was not recognised in the same way by the embassy."

"No matter, I am pleased for my team that their hard work has been recognised. Don't worry for the medallion."

A few days after my return to the office, senior representatives of the embassy and of the donors come to see our work in progress for themselves and to meet and speak with the photo-interpretation team. The whole team receives hearty congratulations for their dedication and hard work and we are thanked for our extraordinary efforts during this time of continued crisis in the country. Certificates in each team member's name, including mine, signed by the American Ambassador, are handed out. The certificate states that the US Embassy wishes to recognise the outstanding work of the photo-interpretation team during such a difficult period in the country. After the certificates are handed out, little speeches are made by several of our visitors, including of course by 'Cyril'. I am next and finally Stanley. A proud moment for us all to receive this unexpected recognition.

As a final comment, the head of USAID adds that the Washington office has also been impressed to hear about our activities and dedication and has decided, after approval from the appropriate US Undersecretary of State, to extent support for the interpretation and map-making activities, including my own time, in Banjul. We are to get financed for a further couple of months, taking our activities through to March 1995. This extra time should enable us to finish the first draft of the natural resources maps. The extra time and wages is also an unexpected financial bonus for me!

Today is November 5 and, of course, Bonfire Night! The Fajara Club holds a party and fireworks display that, we later hear, frightens half the population of Serrekunda who fear that a new military crisis has broken out. But no, it was only a few bangers and rockets courtesy of the Standard Fireworks Company!

The approval for my extension comes through just in time because, a couple of nights later, on 11 November, I awake in the early hours of the morning to repeated cracks of gunfire in the distance. What is happening, I do not know, but it does not sound good.

The Grand Master arrives, rather later than usual, to the office the following morning and explains that he was delayed by two roadblocks on the road towards Fajara. With the help of what he gleaned from soldiers manning the roadblocks and what Stanley can add, it is rumoured that there was an attempted counter-coup led by one of the initial coupists, Basiru Barrow. It is said that some twenty or so soldiers were killed in the gunfight that put down the supposed coup.

(Many years later, the country's Truth, Reconciliation and Reparation Commission (TRRC) will hear that there was no counter coup rather a mass execution of dissenting soldiers leading to the largest loss of life in The Gambia's short military history).

However, for the majority of the ordinary residents of The Gambia, the military shenanigans of the junior officers impact relatively little on our day-to-day lives. Yes, the tourist trade dries up for many months and, yes, many donor agencies decide to curtail financial support to the non-elected government. However, it is still possible to go out and about with no checks or disagreement, just a simple late-night curfew. Shops, restaurants and bars stay open until 11 pm, the usual goods can still be found in the shops and markets, and the ferry across the Banjul River still breaks down every other day!

One or two of the young coupists do let power go to their heads. For example, one likes to have two motorbike outriders in front of his official SUV. The 'clowns-on-the-bikes' as they become known crack whips at anyone or any vehicle that fails to get right out of their way, and quickly. But since the cavalcade always drives with sirens blaring, everyone has the good sense to pull off the road before the clowns arrive.

In contrast, most people have only good things to say about Captain Edward Singhateh. Almost every morning, as I drive into Banjul for work, I see the captain pull his SUV over to the side of the highway and pick up as many school children who can squeeze into the back of the pickup for a lift into the town. (Years later I was therefore immensely surprised to learn that Captain Singhateh was described at the TRRC as 'a sadist').

Christmas comes with the family safely arrived in Kololi and just as quickly it is gone and the children have to go back to school for the January term. I cannot believe that they have now been more than a year in the French system while we continue with our rented apartment in *Point de Jour* on a hillside overlooking central Lyon.

My work remains pretty much monopolised by the maps but I have not totally neglected my other activity of working with the NEA on developing the Information System. During one morning in my little shared office in NEA, there is a knock at the door and two Europeans, that I have never seen before, walk in.

"Hi, you must be Malcolm. I am Michael and this is Henrik."

We shake hands and Michael tells me that he is from Germany, the head of a brand new project, financed by GTZ (the German Development Agency) and that he is now based within the NEA. The two men are trying to set-up their office and equipment and have hit a snag with getting their printer to work from their computers. Can I help? Of course I can, and I do, and the printer is soon working.

Their thanks extend to an invite to eat at the restaurant with them this evening; and just like that I make friends with Michael and destiny has decided that our paths are to cross in the future.

As the end of my extension nears, we make a final effort and get the last few aerial photos interpreted, digitised and combined into a final, but still draft, map file. Ba comes back to Banjul for a final few days and helps us set up the map legends, and add lines of longitude and latitude, scale and other necessary items that will assist in reading the maps after printing.

My time is up, my work is finished, my container for France is packed, sealed and shipped out direction Cordon. I have sold my car to a recently arrived Indian gentleman who intends to rent it out as a taxi. I feel sad to leave The Gambia and my national colleagues that have become great chums, especially Stanley. The work has been fascinating, the country welcoming – notwithstanding the coup.

Before returning home, the company asks that I fly out to their Washington office for a week or so bringing copies of the different digital map files with me. These are to be used to print off a set of draft maps to be presented to USAID. By preference and with a little more time, I would have liked to check visually the draft prints for errors that should be corrected before they are mass produced. But our time is up.

My company has also received a request from the World Bank that I should go to their Washington offices and provide a lunchtime presentation about the information management and map-making work in Banjul during a quaintly named 'Brown Bag' seminar. This basically means that I talk while everyone else eats their lunch (from brown bags, of course).

Lamin drives me for a final time to Yundum and gives me a big hug of farewell while Jean-Pierre is at the foot of the stairway into the plane with my new boarding pass. This gives me a chance to say a last thanks and goodbye. I step into the business cabin, take my seat and we are soon airborne to Brussels. However, on this occasion I am not due to take the Lyon flight; first I must go through to American Airlines and take my flight to Washington.

The flight from Banjul to Brussels is over six hours, followed by an extended wait for my connection in Brussels, then the trans-Atlantic flight to Washington of around another six hours. Pretty much a whole day of travel and what I do not need is to arrive in Washington and find that my suitcase has not kept pace with me. After waiting for more than an hour for the luggage carrousel to stop turning, I join the queue of similarly misappropriated and tired travellers to declare my luggage missing. The gentleman taking my details does not seem overly concerned, why should he? After all I am only a passenger. He takes the telephone number and address of my hotel and says that the suitcase will be delivered to my room as soon as it arrives. In the meantime, since I have travelled business, I may spend up to $500 on replacement clothes and personal items and bring the receipts to his office for reimbursement on the day I leave the country.

My only pieces of luck are that I wore a good jacket and trousers on the plane and so have suitable attire for the office tomorrow morning plus I was given a 'goody bag' on the plane that contains a toiletry set; at least I can shave before going to the office.

This is my first visit to Washington DC and it is vastly different to my only previous trip to the US that was to New York when I worked for another international agency. Of course Washington, as the capital, is a big town but it has none of the neck-twisting features that the Big Apple offers, and I certainly feel more at home here.

This is also the first time I get to meet many of the staff that have been my administrative back-up during my extended stay in The Gambia. I also get to see the seniors that had come out to Banjul for the team building exercise, fully eighteen months ago.

On hearing of my lost suitcase, one of the ladies in the office suggests a particular department store that is known for selling good quality clothes at knockdown prices. After work in the late afternoon, I walk to the store that sits conveniently near my hotel and purchase trousers, shirts, underwear and a pair of good quality shoes, for the grand total of $350. I am particularly taken by the shirts that are monogrammed YSL and indeed they last me for at least ten years (when sadly I become a little too 'generous' to continue wearing them!). But now at least I can look presentable when I stand up to give my presentation at the World Bank.

The following morning, I am called to chat with the big boss, in the presence of some of the other seniors. The managing director congratulates me for the good work in Banjul and says that the company is proud to receive such excellent reports from the donors in Banjul and Washington about how well the photo-interpretation work in particular has gone. Like everyone else, it is nice to receive praise, but I do insist that the praise and thanks really belong to Stanley and his team.

The next item on the agenda of our meeting are my future work plans. I explain that in the absence of a new long-term posting, I have decided to become a freelance consultant based out of France.

"And that is exactly what we hoped to hear from you. While the company does not want to lose your skills and experience, we currently do not have sufficient work to offer you a full-time job on a permanent basis. But we would like to offer you a consultant's contract guaranteeing you, let's say, one hundred days of work over the next twelve months. Would that be acceptable to you?"

Well of course it would because one hundred days of consultant's pay provides an excellent basis on which I can begin to build my future consulting business.

Today is my last day in the States. My new clothes are packed neatly into my trusted holdall that has travelled with me back and forth to many countries in Africa. I have also purchased a new Toshiba laptop; my first ever. It is quite chunky and the screen is black and white. I will have to wait several more years for the slim-line versions with colour screens to start appearing in the shops!

A few moments before leaving the hotel to take the bus to the airport, the telephone in my room rings and I am talking to a representative of American Airlines.

"I'm pleased to say that your suitcase has arrived at Dulles Washington Airport. We are about to send it out to your hotel. Sorry it has taken so long to arrive but it got sent back to Banjul by error"

"Great! Keep it there please, I am due to fly out on your 12 noon flight to Brussels."

I arrive at the airport and make my way to the American Airlines office. There, outside in a long queue of lost luggage, sits my black hardback suitcase fresh from its trips to and from Africa and now sporting a few additional security stickers!

Into the Wilderness

For the first time in several years, I feel that I do not have a proper job; that I have just entered the work wilderness, so to speak. Yes, I know that I have the offer of one hundred days per year from the company that sent me to The Gambia, I even have a signed contract, but I only get paid when I have completed assignments, and they are slow in arriving. At the moment I have been back in France for a couple of months but have only been able to bill a single half-day of work. That does not pay too many bills, especially since I have had to add a dedicated business phone line in my attic office in Cordon and purchase a modem to dial into the new-fangled internet and email. The extra phone bills alone have easily swallowed what I earned for that half-day.

But finally I have a few assignments to carry out for the company. The first is to take me to Rabat in Morocco. I am so excited to get underway that I arrive at Satolas Airport a day early; that explains why the flight is not showing on the 'departures' board, *durr* Malcolm! Luckily the drive to and from the airport only wastes an afternoon.

I eventually do spend a small week in Morocco with the main objective being to collect information about an upcoming US-funded project that my company wishes to bid on. Sadly, the USAID mission in Rabat have put down the shutters and no one from their office will speak to me except a single person who feels sorry for the fact that I have flown in to the country for nothing. He offers to have a short chat over an aperitif (I think he was more interested in the aperitif!). What I am able to glean during that meeting is exactly the same as I obtained reading the USAID published information pre-visit; so almost a wasted trip. However, this being my first trip to Morocco, I am able to do some sightseeing over the weekend and pick up some info about a private oil and gas company that is looking for a reputable company to carry out an environmental scoping study. Perhaps something will come from that.

The second mission is to attend the annual geographic information conference in the Ivory Coast where I make a presentation of our photo-interpretation and map-making activities in The Gambia. Stanley comes out for the trip too, as he is my co-author. By chance we also meet up with several colleagues from my old project in Senegal, including Moctar and Ba who trained our photo-interpretation team.

The third mission takes me for a few days each to the two West African Guineas: first to Guinea Conakry, a French-speaking country, and the second to Guinea Bissau where Portuguese is the official language but many educated people speak passable French, luckily!

At the airport in Conakry I am met by a local contact for the US company who takes me off to the hotel he has reserved in advance. Ummm, doss-house would be a better description run by two dubious characters who manage to steal a few of my traveller's cheques, but how they could ever cash them in beats me. I get to meet with several donor agencies and pick up the information I need and then have the hotel call a taxi to take me to the airport for my late evening flight over the border to Bissau.

The yellow and black taxi is waiting for me outside the hotel door, and I notice that there is the driver and another person sitting in the front passenger seat. Being quite used to shared taxis, I am not surprised and think nothing of the second person.

We set off towards the airport and all around is in darkness; there is an electricity outage in this part of Conakry, but the driver picks out the dirt road towards the airport thanks to his headlights.

After a few minutes, the other passenger turns to me and says "Do you remember me, sir?"

"No, I'm afraid not", I reply.

"I was the customs officer who helped you at the airport when you arrived. Now I am going to work at the airport, is it OK if you give me a lift there?"

I have absolutely no recollection of anyone helping me at the airport when I arrived in the country but reply "if you need a lift to the airport, I have no problem with that."

"Thanks, that's nice. But I have to tell you that my child is sick and I need money to pay the hospital for her care and medicine. Can you help me with money and then I will help you get through the airport, so you will have no issues with any officials?"

I lived in Nigeria long enough for Véro and I to have heard almost every trick in the book, and we even fell for a few in the early days. The line about a sick child and bills to pay was one of the tricks we had fallen for.

"I am sorry but I have no money to give you."

"Then I will make sure that you have lots of trouble when you get to the airport" he threatens.

"That's easy to solve" I state. "Driver pull over to the side of the road please." He obeys and I confess to being nervous at this point because the two men are certainly in league. "Driver you can either take me to the airport and you know I will pay the fare and give you a tip or I can get out and you can take this gentleman instead."

The driver turns to the other passenger and shouts "OUT" at the top of his voice.

He obeys but before leaving the car asks me "how will I get home from here?"

"Your problem buddy," I retort.

The taxi pulls back on to the road and the driver says "thank you, sir, for dealing with him like that. He told me that he knew you and so I had told him where you were going. He is a bad man and I was frightened."

"I was a little frightened too, look" and I show him the open *Opinel* knife that I usually keep in my suitcase for cutting fruit or *saucisson*! We laugh nervously together but get to the airport without further incident.

Conakry Airport is very small, as is the aeroplane from Air Guinea that will take us across to Bissau. In the waiting room we are only about a dozen passengers, including a couple of Portuguese expatriates. Fifteen minutes before departure time all the passengers are led through a room where there are several armed guards.

"What Guinean money do you have?" I am asked by one of the guards.

I put my hand in my pocket and come out with the equivalent of about £2.

"You cannot take that out of the country with you, it is an offence to try" one of the officials says with a certain amount of threat.

"Would you like it?" I ask him with a smile on my face.

He returns my smile and holds out his hand. I hand the folded bills over to him and these slip rapidly into his pocket.

"You can go. Next" he says.

As I walk through the open exit door towards the plane, one of the Portuguese passengers says to me in English "you did the right thing to give him your Guinean Francs. On my last trip out of Conakry, I saw a Russian gentleman get angry with the guards and rip up the few bills he had with him. He was arrested for defacing the president's image. I often wonder what happened to him."

The squalid hotel where travellers' cheques were stolen from my locked room and locked cupboard, the attempted scam in the taxi and this incident at the airport all combine to leave a bad taste in my mouth. For several years I considered Guinea to be the worst country I have visited, and that includes my time in Nigeria. However, several years in the future I go back many more times and have a totally favourable experience in this beautiful and ecologically important country.

But tonight it is a relief to leave Conakry and make the short hop on the Air Guinea flight to the city of Bissau. We arrive at the airport late in the evening and, after collecting my small suitcase, follow the signs in Portuguese indicating 'taxi' (yes, same word). Just outside the terminal sits a single vehicle, an old, dented and yellow Toyota Corolla. The colour and the mark (and the condition) are ubiquitous of taxis right across West Africa. I know that my hotel is only a five-minute drive from the airport but I speak not a word of Portuguese and so I simply read out the name of my hotel and the taxi driver indicates with his thumb that I should climb into the back while my suitcase goes in the boot. He climbs behind the steering wheel ... and we continue to sit there. Odd? But no, just like taxis in Calabar, he will not move until he has a few more passengers.

These eventually arrive and we move off with pop music blaring from the radio.

In the car is a sign declaring that a taxi ride is 3,000 Pesos, my mind boggles for that is about one French Franc or ten pence! After around three minutes we pull into my hotel, at which point I realise that I have no Pesos and so hand the taxi driver a one thousand CFA note, equivalent to twenty times the fare. I pick up my suitcase and say '*senhor obligado, no pesos*'. He follows me into the hotel, clearly not happy with me until the receptionist explains to him that he has hit the jackpot with this ride but if he is still unhappy, the CFA can be changed for 60,000 Pesos and then I can pay him the 3,000 Pesos fare. Strangely he prefers to keep the CFA!

The following morning after breakfast, I need to find my way to the World Bank office for a meeting that the company has set up in advance. Not wishing to make the same mistake as the previous night, I ask at the reception if they could change a $100 bill into Bissauan Pesos; no problem. The receptionist then seems to disappear under the counter and the absence extends to five minutes or more – but I can hear much shuffling, so he is under there, somewhere. Finally, he reappears with a breakfast tray loaded with more bundles of notes than I have ever seen in my life. He plonks the tray on the counter and takes my $100 bill in exchange.

I know that I stare with an open mouth for a good moment at the pile of money until finally, I remember my manners and say "thank you but what is all that money?"

"Well sir, it's your Pesos in exchange for the dollars" he replies.

I can think of nothing more to say than to ask "what can I do with all that?"

What I really mean is how can I carry that load around with me but he interprets my question to mean how can I spend it.

"Well, sir," and he moves a few bundles across the tray, "this pile will pay your taxi into town and get you back. These two will buy you lunch in a local restaurant" and so he continues.

"Would you mind looking after the money while I get a bigger bag please?" I ask trying not to laugh because I have just remembered the joke about hyperinflation in Zaire where money is moved around in wheelbarrows and robbers will steal the barrow and leave the money behind. Perhaps I should have told him to look after the tray!

I return with my sports holdall and load the pile of bills in, go outside the hotel with the receptionist who hails a taxi and gives instructions as to where I need to go.

As we set off to drive towards the centre of Bissau City, the taxi driver speaks to me in Portuguese. Sadly, I cannot understand a word he is saying. I try French, English, Wolof and even a little Peul/Fulani that I had picked up during many missions into the Ferlo in Senegal. Nothing works. He repeats the same phrase on two or three occasions and then finally a light goes on in my brain. He must be asking if he can pick up other passengers along the way. Now how do I answer 'no'?

Finally, I say *"O sole mio"* which most people will recognise as coming from a song that Pavrotti often sings. I am assuming that 'sole' must mean 'alone' as in sole or solitary while 'mio' must mean 'me'. Wouldn't you agree?

Well that seems to work because he says "ahh Spanish, OK *senhor, sole*" and we continue into town.

(As I am writing these words, I think that it might be a good idea to do a Google check about what I actually did say to that driver. Imagine, to my great surprise, that I learn that 'O sole mio' is actually Italian, not Spanish, and it means 'My sun or sunshine'!! Thank goodness the driver understood what I *meant* to say and not the proper translation; I might well have been left standing on the side of the road!).

My meeting goes well with the Bissauan representative of the World Bank and a few of his colleagues since we are able to speak together in French. Our meeting breaks up just before lunch, and once the more junior colleagues have left the room, I invite the representative to lunch. We go out of the office building and I find my taxi driver waiting for me outside. That was unexpected but the driver tells my lunch colleague that he will wait for me and take me back to the hotel when I finish work. I pass a small bundle of bills to the World Bank representative and ask that he tells the driver that the money is for his lunch. The driver responds with *'obligado senhor'*.

The World Bank representative takes me to an unpretentious restaurant for lunch and, once we have said our goodbyes, I return to the hotel with my personal taxi driver.

Last night when I arrived at the hotel, it was too late to try to get my bearings and this morning, apart from entering the small restaurant for breakfast, I did not have the time to explore. Since it is early afternoon, I wander around the hotel checking out the small gift shops. I always try to take small, local presents back for the children from each country I visit. That is easy for Mélanie, I can invariably find locally made items of jewellery like the silver bracelet I obtained in Guinea-Conakry, but a bit harder for David.

I notice there is one shop bearing the sign 'Air Europa' and that is precisely the company that will fly me back to France the day after tomorrow. Unfortunately, it is closed but I note there is a mention in the window saying that the agent will be back at 4 pm; in thirty minutes or so. On the dot a European lady unlocks the door and sits behind her desk. I enter and get out my plane tickets so that she may reconfirm my flight. I am certainly not expecting what she has to tell me.

"Dr Marks, I am so sorry to tell you that Air Europa has just declared bankruptcy and will no longer be flying from Bissau or anywhere else."

"Great, what are passengers supposed to do then?" I ask with a fair amount of exasperation.

"We are talking with Air Guinea to put on a special flight from here to Dakar in Senegal. It will be much easier to get a flight home from there. But you will need to go to the Air Guinea office in town and book your ticket. And you should do that now because there will be very few seats available."

"*Merde!*" I say under my breath, "where exactly is the Air Guinea office located?"

She hands over a business card with the logo of Air Guinea and its coordinates and I leave the hotel straight away, finding my taxi still waiting outside. I show him the card, he nods and we drive to the address indicated.

There are already a handful of passengers of different nationalities from my cancelled flight inside the office, queueing patiently to get their replacement tickets. My turn arrives and my seat is booked.

"That will be $135 US sir. The plane leaves at 8.30 tomorrow morning but best to arrive two hours early at the airport."

Luckily, I have just sufficient dollars in cash to pay the bill and strangely I am looking forward to getting back to Dakar; a city I know like the back of my hand.

My wind-up alarm clock goes off at 5.30 am giving me time to shower, get down to the reception to pay my bill and outside to find a taxi. We drive into the airport compound at 6.35 am ... and there are no lights showing in any of the airport buildings. However, there is a solitary fellow traveller and early riser standing outside a door marked '*Entrada*'. I stand behind him thus creating a queue of two.

Little by little others begin to arrive and join the queue. The sun starts to make a gentle appearance on the eastern horizon and that is the cue for a number of cockerels in neighbouring villages to awake and sing their welcome to the new day; at least it is not raining.

The hands of my watch pass 7 am and not a sign of life inside the terminal building, 8 am arrives and is left behind and still nothing, 9 am passes and although the sky is now bright and the sun shining down on our queue '*entrada*' remains stubbornly '*fechada*'. By now there are around a dozen people in the queue and most have taken to sitting on their suitcases, me included.

At 10.30, a lady arrives and unlocks the door. We all try to shuffle forward to follow here inside but, false alarm, she is the cleaning lady I am told by the head of the queue. At least a few lights go on inside the building suggesting that there is some life in there.

Midday is now here and finally two uniformed officials arrive at the door and go inside. As they pass, one tells us that we can start to enter in around an hour; oooph.

True to his word, at 1.15 pm, the doors are opened and we are allowed entry, passing our suitcases and bags through an antiquated x-ray machine. By 1.20 pm, I am sitting on a very hard chair in the departure room (lounge would be a mistaken use of the word). The room fills up progressively with expatriates and local families so that I estimate that there must be around fifty people in the room. This is a bit worrying since I had been told that the plane would be maximum a 32-seater.

At 4.30 pm, a young hostess comes up to me and says very quietly in my ear "are you Mr Marks?" after I nod she continues "you see the door over there to the right of the toilets?" I nod again "let me speak to the Portuguese family over there and to the French couple next to them, then when you see I have finished, please walk leisurely through the door I have indicated. Do not say anything and do not hurry. Is that clear?" I nod again intrigued, and she moves over to the Portuguese family and then on to the French.

Once she has finished her subterfuge, I pick up my bags and, as instructed, go through the door next to the toilets. The Portuguese and French follow close behind plus a few more people who were obviously given their instructions before me. We find ourselves in a small room with a door opening to the outside where the runway is situated and a quick count shows sixteen passengers.

The hostess then comes into the room and locks the door through which we had passed only a couple of minutes earlier. She informs us that Air Guinea is only sending a sixteen-seater plane, a Cessna I think I hear her say, for the flight to Dakar. The airline has decided to fly out of Bissau only those passengers with onward flights and that is the reason she spoke individually to us. She is worried that the passengers left behind will not be happy and, true to her word, there follow bangs on the locked door and shouts of protest from the neighbouring room.

We hear the plane as it arrives at the airport for landing and again as the twin propellers whiz round to slow the landing speed. Soon the plane, and it is very small indeed, pulls up in front of the terminal and we walk out carrying our cases and bags. I am amazed to see the logo on the side of the plane declaring that it belongs to Air Europa. Here I am, like all the other passengers, with a paid ticket to France that has been cancelled and having to purchase another ticket with exactly the same company to get me to Dakar. Something very odd but at least thirty minutes later we are airborne, direction Senegal.

We fly due north, hugging the coastline and at a very low altitude, certainly no more, I would guess, than a thousand metres. The view is sensational as we pass out of Bissau and into the Casamance of southern Senegal, across The Gambia and back into Senegal at the Sine Saloum. As we fly up *la Petite Côte* I can clearly see the town of Saly Portudal, near to where we once had a lovely beach house, while in the shallow waters a few metres off the shore, I can make out three large, guitar-shaped objects in the water. I assume that these are guitarfish, a quite rare sighting if true.

Soon after leaving *la Petite Côte* behind I can make out the Dakar lighthouse off the Point des Almadies flashing a welcome as we make our approach to Leopold Senghor Airport. We land at 7 pm. Daylight is gone as quickly as it had arrived this morning and I must now try to book an onward flight to France. First I try the Air France desk and a lady kindly enters my details into her computer and informs me that a flight has indeed been reserved for me but with Air Afrique. I move along the counter and am told by a smiling Senegalese lady that I am booked on their flight for tomorrow morning so I must try to get accommodation in the airport hotel aka the fleapit.

After those trips to West Africa, not much happens with my one-hundred-day contract during the following three months. There is a little work writing sections of proposals for contracts that the company is bidding on and I do get asked to go back to Senegal to teach a course on Monitoring and Evaluation (M&E) for middle managers of various donor agencies, many coming from USAID offices in a number of West Africa countries. While teaching this activity is enjoyable, less fun is to hear the participants continually bickering at me about the level of *per diems* they have been allocated by their employers. Everywhere in the development community, *per diems* are seen as salary top-ups and not payments to cover out of pocket expenses, as is their intention.

By the end of this, my first year as a consultant, I have been paid for eighty-seven days of work. Not too bad but not as much as I would have liked. And I know that I really must work hard at expanding my list of clients if I am to succeed as an independent consultant.

Now that I am living in France, I know that I will need to make a tax declaration in the coming April, of my earnings for the current year. I have never had to make a declaration in France before and so have no idea what is required. Véro is as equally clueless as me having left France as soon as she finished school.

Best we believe, therefore, to take an appointment at the local tax office to get their guidance. I am interviewed by a very friendly gentleman who shares a surname with a popular brand of French alcohol and is the most senior of the tax inspectors in the office.

I explain my work and that my income will likely vary from year to year and he tells me "Since you are working predominantly out of the country, I do not think that you need to declare your income in France because you do not really qualify as a resident for tax purposes."

I find the response difficult to understand and so state "while I do work abroad, my wife is a French national and resident in the country and our children go to a French school. I do want to do things correctly."

"So you wish to pay taxes in France? That is the first time I've ever heard anyone declare that!" and he laughs out loud "but what you say does make me question my first opinion. Let me call in my colleagues and get their opinions too."

In troop three additional tax inspectors and he explains my situation. Two agree with me and one with the chief tax inspector.

"That makes two-all on our side and so, M. Marks, I decide that you shall have the casting vote," he says trying not to laugh too loudly!

"Logic and morality tells me that I should be declaring my income in France," I state with all honesty. And so I do. And, since I have earned relatively little in that first year, the tax I must pay following my first declaration is minimal. But the income declared annually will eventually help me when I need to get a mortgage.

However, that does not stop my French friends from teasing me no end about 'the Brit who wanted to pay our income tax!'

The New Year of 1996 begins while my contract with the Washington company ends. I am therefore now a fully freelance consultant. During the first few months of this year, I have billed a few days of work for a UK-based company that has asked me to help them develop a marketing strategy in West Africa with the work including a trip to Brussels to meet with the European Commission. But nothing much else has come up. However, I have not been sitting idle for those first months of the year. I learnt after I left Nigeria back in 1983 that the best way to get another job is to play the numbers game. What I have done is to set myself a target of sending out a minimum of ten curriculum vitae per week, mostly by post, not only in response to job adverts but also to any consulting group I can find: in the US, France, Germany, UK, wherever. I occasionally get a reply along the lines of 'thanks for your CV, we currently have nothing ... but if a suitable ...' heartbreakingly slow but just as I expected. Who knows something *might* just come up one of these days from all those CVs.

However, my luck begins to change in late March when my old, Washington-based company contacts me to ask if I would undertake a six-week mission to Niamey, Niger for one of their partner organisations. The objective is to help a large agricultural development programme, again funded by USAID, develop a Monitoring and Evaluation (M&E) training programme with an accompanying training manual destined for small, local NGOs and village groups. The assistance programme is offering grants to these target groups to help them undertake small agricultural and natural resources projects. In order to be awarded such a grant, typically of a few thousand to a few tens of thousands of US dollars, the groups must pass several selection criteria. However, to date, no group has ticked all the criteria, and the one criterion that every group has failed to attain is the development of a small M&E plan for their proposed project. Hence the need for my input.

My terms of reference inform me that I will be working with a second consultant, a lady hailing from Canada.

I fly out to Niger with Air France in early April and meet up the following morning with old friends. The first person I see is a long-time employee of the company and the team leader in Niamey. We had previously met a few times at conferences during my work in The Gambia. He takes me to a neighbouring office and there sits a good friend that I had worked with in Chad, so many years previously. That mission to his project in Ndjamena had been pivotal in convincing me to move away from university teaching and into fulltime development work, starting as an advisor in ecology with a senior development agency in Senegal.

The first item I learn from the team leader is that the other consultant has been obliged to cancel at the last moment meaning that I am now to undertake the mission on my own. After a day of introductions to staff, including my local counterparts, the USAID technical officers and other development agencies in Niamey (including my old friends at Agrhymet), the team leader takes me back to his home for dinner. I get to meet his wife and three lovely kids aged from seven through eleven. I am immediately 'uncle' and plied with questions about France and my family.

I am now four days into my mission and my work is not going well, I have to admit. I just cannot seem to get my head around the training in M&E that I need to develop. It is not the training itself but rather that I have to develop a programme that can be delivered by others and to a particularly wide variety of audiences. These will range from professional NGOs with university level educations through to small village groupings who may have only received education up to primary level. Furthermore, the training will have to be presented in several different local languages by the programme trainers who will not be M&E specialists. They will need the contents of the training course to be spelt out in considerable detail. How can I get around these issues? I just cannot seem to figure out the means to do so.

That evening, while I am eating in the gardens of my rundown hotel, called rather hopefully '*Le Grand Hôtel*', I feel that tomorrow morning I must come clean to the team leader and admit that I have reached a mental jam. No consultant ever wishes to make such an admission but I feel it would be better to do so early in the work than string it out for a couple of weeks, worry endlessly and then still be obliged to make the admission to him. Once that decision is made, I feel more relaxed and sleep soundly.

During the night my mind enters dream mode and I dream of my four years spent in Nigeria, almost fifteen years previously. I dream of the period when I needed to take eighty or so ecology students, many from the larger cities of the south of the country, into the bush to see 'ecology in action'. My worries at that time were two-fold. The first was how to keep them safe, especially the 'townies'. And the second was how could I spread myself sufficiently thinly to help eighty students with work problems?

In British universities, such an exodus of students into the field would have meant that three 'demonstrators' (normally doctoral students or post-doctoral researchers) would accompany the lecturer.

Their role being more to help the students than to keep them safe. After all, the most dangerous animal to be encountered in UK is the humble viper while in Calabar, Nigeria there exist a multitude of poisonous snakes, spiders, and centipedes and one must not forget larger carnivorous mammals and the occasional crocodile. For the safety issue, I had made sure that we stayed on well-trodden paths and crossed my fingers that eighty boisterous students would make sufficient noise to keep any hunting animals at bay. But instead of having a ratio of one staff to twenty students, I had to work on my own since the department of Biology at the university had only a single postgraduate student and he was not for loan to ecology!

My dream of this conundrum, seventeen years previously, pointed out to my sleeping brain that, in order to cope with and help so many students, I had developed a book, a toolkit of ecological exercises to be carried out in the field. Each tool in my ecological toolkit was a standalone and covered a single field exercise. The students could use the tools on their own and only needed my help if I had not been sufficiently clear in my writing or they needed some additional information.

The recesses of my brain were reminding me that this had worked successfully in the forests of southern Nigeria, why not give it a shot in the Sahel of Niger.

And that dream that awakens old memories becomes the impetus for me to write the 'M&E of Natural Resources Management Activities at the village level: A Toolkit for the M&E of local interventions'. I heard, at a later date, that my toolkit had been translated into Spanish and used as far away as Cuba. As the French say *'pensez à tête reposée'* although this usually means to think things through when relaxed rather than learn from your dreams as I have just done!

Niamey is not over-endowed with restaurants although on a previous visit in the company of Senegalese colleagues, they had insisted on searching out the one and only Senegalese restaurant in Niamey. While I love Senegalese food, the distance from the sea does make getting a good *thieb* rather difficult! But my favourite restaurant on this particular trip is located a couple of hundred paces from my hotel's entrance. It is, in fact, located on a roundabout at the top of the hotel road but traffic is non-existent in the evenings when I eat there. The little place is run by two middle-aged sisters and they have placed a couple of tables at some distance from their shanty kitchen where their specialty (read: only) dish is chicken and chips served with ice cold beer.

During this six-week stay, I tend to eat twice a week at the roundabout rather than stay put in the hotel. One evening as I am tucking into a rather tough fried chicken, a gentleman comes up to my table and takes a chair.

"Do you remember me sir?" he asks

"No, sorry, I do not." I reply in all truthfulness.

And then the familiar story comes out: "I was the customs officer who helped you at the airport, perhaps now you remember me?"

"Really, when would that have been?" I query as I play him along.

"Oh, I do not remember the exact day but it was quite recently. Surely you remember me helping you," he insists.

"Sorry my friend but you have me mistaken for someone else. I drove across the border from Nigeria, I did not come through the airport," I lie as I continue playing him.

"Oh, then perhaps it was not you but someone who looks like you. However, perhaps you can still help me?"

Knowing what is coming next I say "are you the gentleman who has a child in the hospital and you need money to pay for the medicines and treatment?" I dangle the hook in front of him and he bites hard.

"Yes, that's it. My child is in the general hospital. Can you give me money to help with the bills for her treatment and medicines?"

"Mmm, you see those three men over at the table to your right," he swivels his head to look and then nods, "they are policemen and if you do not leave the restaurant in the next two minutes, I am going to call them over to arrest you for trying to cheat foreigners. So go quickly while I am feeling nice."

He gets up and leaves in a real hurry.

One of the sisters comes across to me and apologises for the man who has been pestering me. She tells me that he tries to hustle all foreigners who come to the restaurant. Then she asks how I had managed to get rid of him so easily.

"I told him that the men at the table over there were police officers and I would report him if he did not leave."

"Sir, how did you know they are the police?" she asks as she walks off to bring them more drinks.

That incident coming not long after the same story in Guinea and several years after a similar attempted scam in Nigeria, leaves me wondering if there exists a regional school for con artists in West Africa!

The weekend arrives and the team leader and his family have invited me for lunch but, before going over to their house, I drive across to a small 'antiques market', mostly out of curiosity, to see if I can find gifts for the family. I am a little disappointed because there are no real antiques just some rather tatty second hand furniture. However, as I wander from one little shop to the next, I spot something interesting peeking out from underneath some very dusty French novels; the point of, I believe, a stone arrowhead. I move the books, and I find that I am not mistaken. This is a real prehistoric flint arrowhead. The store owner sees me looking hard at the object and comes across to chat. He tells me that this part of Niger, now semi-desert – called the Sahel – was once a very fertile zone with a large hunter-gatherer population, at least ten thousand years ago. Then the climate started to change and became very dry as it is today. The population of the time had used stone implements for hunting and for domestic use and he brings out a drawer full of other stone tools and weapons. The drawer includes a few dozen arrowheads of different shapes and sizes. I learn that the long thin ones were for lancing fish in the rivers and ponds that abounded at that time. Others that are broader were affixed to arrows and used for hunting larger animals like antelope or warthog. He also shows me chunks of stone sharpened on one side and edged on the other to form a grip. These are hand axes and scrappers that could chop bone or be used to skin a dead animal. Fascinating. I also spot in his drawer some petrified wood plus some 'sand roses' and add them to a growing pile of arrowheads and stone implements. Gifts for my young son David.

We negotiate down from his starting price – which I already think is pretty cheap – and settle at a level where I am happy and he is very happy. As we shake hands and I say my farewell, he rather sheepishly brings out a cloth wrapped item from a drawer in his desk.

"Sir, since you are fascinated with these items from prehistoric Niger, perhaps you might be interested in this item that I received just this morning." And he shows me a little figurine, a fertility piece, carved out of hard clay.

"It's lovely," I state, "where does it come from?"

"My source opened an ancient tomb that he found in the desert and he asked me to sell this item for him. I am only asking thirty-five French Francs."

"I'm interested at twenty-five" I reply and we settle for thirty, or three quid, which is the same price I had just paid for all the arrow-heads, hand axes and petrified wood. That statue of a young lady still has pride of place in my souvenir cupboard as I write these words.

My M&E toolkit is finished; I have provided training courses on using the toolkit to the lead trainers who will then train further trainers before the larger team takes the message out to the small NGOs who aspire to receive grants from the programme. After a shaky start, I am very satisfied at how well the work has gone during my six weeks in Niamey. And I have really enjoyed my stay in the country. But time to make my way home.

I am flying home in a jumbo jet courtesy of Air France. We are travelling via Ouagadougou, the capital of Burkina Faso, and then on to Paris. The plane in Niamey is less than half full as we taxi down the runway. Slightly more than an hour later we touch down in Ouagadougou. This is only the second time I have been to Burkina Faso, if only to sit on the runway. Fully sixty percent of passengers disembark leaving just a handful of people still remaining on board the large plane. Our numbers are then swollen by the arrival of fifty or so passengers, mostly I presume Burkinabe, except for a young, bearded white guy who has been allocated the seat next to me. Since we are to be travelling companions for the next six hours, we say *'bonjour'* and introduce ourselves. His name is unknown to me although his accent suggests he is a French Canadian.

While talking about the reasons for our presence on the plane to Paris. He tells me that he has been working in Ouaga for an international organisation while I mention that I have just finished a M&E mission to Niger. He replies that his wife often undertakes such missions too.

I wonder if it is just possible that it is his wife that missed partnering with me for the work in Niger, although they do not share the same surname.

Curiosity gets the better of me and I ask "is it just possible that your wife is called 'Annick'."

I receive a look of surprise and the question "Have you met my wife then?"

"No, but she was meant to be working with me in Niamey but called off at the last minute."

We both laugh at such an enormous coincidence that sees us both take this plane towards Paris and find ourselves sitting side-by-side. And the coincidences do not stop there. We venture on to chat about hobbies and we find that both of us share a love for antiques; and he knows Lyon and the weekly flea market called '*Les Puces de Canal*' that Véro and I go to frequently. He tells me that he had gone there several years ago, found and purchased a very old book from which, sadly, all the engravings had been removed; probably for framing as pictures. Nonetheless, he tells me that he had set about trying to find copies of each of the missing engravings, a mammoth task that he recently completed. The old book and the missing engravings are, at this moment, with a bookbinder cum book repairer who has a workshop in a little village outside of Lyon.

As I question him further on the location of the workshop, he mentions the village of Lhuis. So here again is another enormous coincidence, because I know of the gentleman concerned, indeed he has recently done work for us too.

"Let me tell you a story about your book repairer," I say. "He used to rent a little house in the village of Rix, just down the road from Lhuis, and that was his vacation home for almost twenty years. Sometime around 1980, he had an old aunt who passed away and we heard that she left him some money with a single proviso: he could only receive the inheritance if he used it to buy a house, which he did in the neighbouring village of Groslée; a mill house in fact. He moved out of that little rented house in Rix in early 1982 and you will not believe it but we moved in just afterwards and stayed for the entire summer of 1982; a summer marked by the birth of our daughter."

Coincidences, coincidences but then again, I suppose, if you talk to enough people there will always be coincidences!

I arrive back in France in the middle of May and spend time at the apartment in Lyon while the children continue at their school. Once more I have no work on the horizon until I receive an email from the programme in Niger. My contract had stipulated that all texts that I develop should be in English, which had seemed a little strange to me given that the trainers are all Francophone. Indeed, the email requests that I now assist them by translating my reports, toolkit and training manual into French. I set about the work straight away, and as I finish up each mid-afternoon, Véronique takes over to correct my work. Spelling and grammar do not pose any serious problems, where I really need the help is translating expressions in the way that a French person would write them; not as an English speaker would. But all good stuff because I can bill an extra four weeks' work and now, by June, I have already billed over seventy-five days of work so far this year. Sound progress on last year.

The summer is here and the children are on vacation. We transhumant from Lyon to fresher pastures in Cordon where we will spend our summer. No sooner have we opened our wooden shutters, letting in some fresh air and sunlight, than we hear some of the village children arriving to get up to gentle mischief with Mélanie and David. During the summer, as with every vacation, several of them will pretty much be living with us full time, and it is a rare meal that does not see at least a couple of extra kids sitting at the table and helping afterwards with the washing up and tidying away. This is how life should be; the citizens can keep their cities, give me the relaxed countryside every day.

However, that does not mean deckchairs and novels for the adults. It means looking after my expanding vegetable plots which try to supply sufficient salads, tomatoes and the rest to hungry broods of kids. It means standing in the cool, cool Rhône with my schoolteacher buddy Gérard while we pull out countless tiny bleak, roach and the occasional perch to be fried as whitebait for the awaiting hordes. It means sneaking out of our courtyard early in the morning before the prying eyes of curious neighbours can spot in which direction I will go to my secret woodland areas to collect delicious forest mushrooms like ceps, chanterelles, and cornucopia (*trompettes de la mort*). These Véro will soon add to delicious, slightly runny omelettes made from our neighbour's free range eggs.

All four of us agree that our vacation time in Cordon is quite close to perfection. However, that does not mean that we do not go off for holidays. But our usual method for selecting holidays is a little atypical! It generally starts with one of us – often the children – saying 'I wonder how it is in the Massif Central or around Bordeaux'. Well, there is only one way to find out: get in the car and go take a look. This summer we have decided, in response to a question from Mélanie, to go off for a week to the Cathar country which means that we need to head in the direction of Albi, Carcassonne and Toulouse in south-western France.

To imagine our holidays of this period, one must forget all about the internet and booking rooms through AirBnB and setting the GPS to find the fastest route and the *Coyote* app. to warn about police radars so the speed limit can be broken with impunity. These do not yet exist. Guidance is via paper maps that once unfolded are impossible to refold, and wherever one wishes to travel the roads to be taken never seems to be on a single map sheet. We book accommodation on the day, or at best a day in advance, by checking through our '*Guide des Chambres d'Hôtes*' (guide to bed and breakfasts). We usually select a couple that are close to the places we wish to visit and have nice photos and descriptions. Then, a quick stop at a public telephone and, with a little luck, we can make the reservation. The added bonus is if our hosts also offer '*table d'hôte*' since we know we will enjoy fresh local produce and undiscovered local wines during the evening meal. The perfect way to finish a long day as tourists.

Over the years we have stayed in dozens of B&Bs across the length and breadth of France. Many have been highly memorable and very few disappointing. The only one that stands out in our minds for a 'never again', and is remembered even by the kids, now adults, was in northern France as we made our way across to the UK. We stayed in *La Vielle Poste* (the old post office) with a charming couple who tried their hardest to make us welcome, along with their several other guests. The only problem was that they possessed three absolutely enormous Great Danes, and they stank (the dogs that is!). These dogs liked nothing better than to be petted and so would not leave us alone for a moment. The owners had placed single beds at the back of their lounge cum kitchen and the dogs slept on them. Those stank too, so the whole house was pervaded by the odour of wet dog. Yuckeee!

Since it was early September and the evenings still warm, we tried to avoid the dogs by sitting outside in the little walled garden of the B&B. Not to be ignored, the dogs found a way to join us via an open door. There followed a scene that we still laugh about *en famille*. I was relaxing in a chair, reading the local newspaper and sipping a glass of wine when the largest of the dogs decided to join me. We all watched transfixed as this enormous beast took position in front of me, facing away, and then carefully walked backwards until his bottom hit my knees. He then sat down on my lap, all fifty kilograms of him!

The fun and laughter around the silly, smelly dogs and the stinky house came to end when David developed an intense allergy and the poor little fellow had to be dosed with antihistamine to get him through the night. I do hope that eventually the health department closed down that establishment!

Our vacation to Cathar country means a couple of days getting there so that we can explore interesting places on the long journey across France. We avoid motorways as much as possible and, in preference, go along small country roads that invariably lead to interesting discoveries.

Today is an exciting day as there will be an impressive, almost full eclipse around midday. As an added incentive, we are allowing the children each to choose an activity for the day. Mélanie wishes to visit Cordes-sur-Ciel, an ancient Cathar stronghold, and see the eclipse from the top of the hill where there are several restaurants and the church. David spots a sign at the bottom of the hill to Cordes that simply states 'Maze of Maize' and says 'let's check it out dudes' (we cross our fingers that the Ninja Turtle phase will end soon!).

We are obliged to park at the bottom of the steep hill leading to Cordes. As we walk up the narrow road that winds its way up the hill, we window-shop through the glass fronts of innumerable tourist shops selling trash (my word). But halfway up the hill we spot a glass workshop and go in to look at the products. David receives a sharp warning (*pun intended*) to be careful and not to touch. We spot a beautiful glass vase that had recently been blown in the workshop and make the purchase. Little David always adored that vase – and the childhood memories that went with it – and it now has pride of place in his adult apartment in Barcelona. Of such simple things are memories made.

At the top of the hill, all of the restaurants are packed but we manage to buy some sandwiches and bottles of water from the bakery and take our places ready for the eclipse. At 12.45, we sense a slight dulling of the daylight and a small chill in the air. Looking down to a distant field at the foot of the hill, see two donkeys slowly trudge their way across the field to their stable for the 'night'. The eclipse begins to occur and we view the scene with fascination through the special eclipse glasses that *papy Belou* (Véro's dad) has given to the children for just this event. Although the sun is not totally obliterated, enough disappears to place us into darkness for several minutes. As the moon completes its passage in front of the sun, full daylight begins to return to this beautiful hilltop village and the surrounding countryside.

We watch as the donkeys emerge from their stable and again take up their places in the field. As Mélanie says through a cloud of giggles "donkey one to donkey two: 'how did you sleep?' donkey two replies 'like a log, the night seemed to go so quickly'!".

Eclipse over, our little man insists, quite rightly, that is now time to go to the maze of maize. I suppose we have to. On arrival at the farm, we receive a presentation about the events of the afternoon. Until then we had naively assumed that we would simply be turned loose in the maze, cut out inside a field of maize, and told to find our own way back. Not at all, there are surprise events every fifteen minutes or so with jugglers, story tellers and even a maize demon. But once the events are completed, we are left to our own devices to find our way out. Before being abandoned we are all told to shout if anyone gets lost and really cannot find their way out. Someone will come to find you.

While the two ladies chatter, David asks me in all seriousness if there are any tricks to getting out of a maze of maize. And indeed I believe there are. I read somewhere that if you follow a single wall and do not deviate from that wall, no matter what, you will almost always find your way out.

"Mum / Mélanie, let's have a race to see who can get out of the maze the quickest," says David.

And off he goes like a little whippet, sticking closely to the right hand wall while I try to keep up with him. The two ladies simply smile and continue on their way, with a tremendous amount of chatter.

After seven or eight minutes of hugging the right hand wall, we see a clear space ahead and David informs me "that looks like the exit ahead dad. That was easy-peasy."

But actually not so easy as we have only managed to arrive in the very centre of the maze. About turn and off we go again. Finally, we come to the exit and find our two ladies sitting on the grass verge.

"What kept you?" queries Mélanie of her little brother.

"Dad told me that if we stick to one wall, it would bring us outside, and it did, see? But how did you get out more quickly?"

"We followed the little signs on the ground that showed the way out, of course!"

Holiday time is over, and just in time, for I receive a call from the German company that had begun working in The Gambia just before I left. The caller informs me that the NEA have requested that the draft natural resources maps that I had been developing with my local team should now be corrected and published. Am I available to undertake a mission to The Gambia to do the work? Of course I am!

That is the good news. The less good news is that the company cannot provide an exact date for me to carry out the work, and it looks like it will be in the last quarter of the year, i.e. in a couple of months' time. However, in the meantime, am I available to help them develop their company publicity material? They are in the process of producing flyers, brochures and a catalogue of their capacities, activities and experience. What they are proposing is that the text will be written by their staff in German, and translated in-house to English. I am required first to correct the English text and then to translate the English into French. By the volume of material, it looks like I have work for two weeks or so. The deal is sweetened further by them asking me to develop a plan and methodology for the updating of the Gambian maps in advance of my mission to Banjul.

Summer finishes and the children go back to the apartment in Lyon to restart school. I split my time between Cordon and Lyon, staying in Cordon when I need to work and going to Lyon during my downtime. Finally, in late autumn, I get the call I have been waiting for and catch the plane back to Yundum Airport. This trip is pleasant because I get to see my old friends at NEA and also Stanley and several other members of the original map-making team. My old colleague, Colonel Frank, the hash master, is also still in the country. I am being accompanied on this trip by George, a young member of the German company team, who is being sent with me to learn about and assist with my consulting work.

We pass through Yundum Airport, as easily as always, are picked up by the project driver and driven to the Senegambia Hotel where we are to stay. As we drive in the darkness towards the hotel, I spot a new building off to the left of our road. It has a very bright sign outside bearing its name, Yasmin, and the words 'Chinese Restaurant'.

For what reason, I cannot say, I tell George that the restaurant is new and must belong to my buddy and former neighbour, Dick. We will test the veracity of my statement the following evening.

And it is true, for after work we walk to the restaurant, go through the front door and I am immediately swept into Dick's arms. What a surprise for both of us. Dick's wife, Yasmin, is also in the restaurant having just arrived back from one of her frequent buying trips in China.

We are sat at a table and Dick joins us, explaining to George the circumstances of our meeting during the coup. No need to read the menu; Dick instructs one of the waiters in Chinese and plate after plate of delicious food arrives at the table until we are obliged to say 'enough!!'

Then the difficult moment arrives: the bill. Dick refuses to give us one and simply tells George that Malcolm is my family and my family does not pay to eat. How do I deal with this?

I take Dick off to one side and tell him two things. First I cannot come back if he will not let me pay and his food is great and I am so happy to see him and his wife again. Second, we are not really paying anyway because the company gives us a *per diem* but if we do not submit bills we will not get the money. Grudgingly, for that evening, he allows me to pay, at least, for the drinks.

A few days into our mission, an old friend, another German but working in the Forestry Department for a different German company, comes in to say hello. He has a problem. He has a visitor, called Jorgen, from the company's head office in FeldKirschen working with him at the moment. Jorgen wants to go sea-fishing and has asked my friend to organise a trip for him this Saturday, in just two days' time. My friend has no idea how to organise a trip but had heard from the Gambian forestry staff that I went fishing often when living in the country; please help!

I make a call to an old Gambian contact who has a boat moored at Denton Bridge, asking him to be available the whole of Saturday afternoon and to bring fishing equipment for barracuda fishing.

"That's settled then. Tell Jorgen to come to pick me up at the Senegambia at 12.30 sharp on Saturday. He needs to bring a hat because it will likely be hot."

On the Friday evening my consulting team mate, George, implores me to go back with him to eat at Dick's restaurant. This time we refuse to order until he agrees to let us pay for our food. As usual, Dick comes to sit with us and eats along with us. In conversation, I mention that I am taking a German colleague fishing on the Saturday afternoon.

"Malcolm, as soon as you finish fishing, drop the fish off here on your way back to the hotel. I will prepare a meal based on the fish you catch and Yasmin will join us to eat with you and your friend."

And that is exactly what happens. My boatman is waiting for us on the Sarro Bolon (river) just downstream from the Denton Bridge. He has brought two hefty rods sporting large lures with two sets of triple hooks tied by a length of fishing wire; barracuda gear. The barracuda looks and behaves rather like a very large saltwater pike, a ferocious carnivorous fish. The boat chugs into the bolon and I show Jorgen how to cast well clear of the outboard motor, set the reel to give out line should a fish take the lure, and trawl behind the advancing boat. We chatter as the boatman covers the short distance from the landing point towards the sea but instead of going into the sea, he takes a left along another wide bolon. We manoeuvre like this for about forty minutes and, just as I am getting concerned that we will have no fish to take to Dick, I get an enormous pull on my line with my reel squealing in protest. I put the brake on the reel and strike back against the tugging fish. I can feel the hooks set hard.

I have caught barracuda several times in the past, first in Nigeria, where we used pieces of raw meat as bait, and more recently in Senegal and then in The Gambia. Jorgen has never known that excitement and so I pass him my rod saying "you take it."

And he does. He plays the fish like a professional and fifteen minutes later we have a beautiful eight kilo fish lying at the bottom of the boat.

I then explain the offer from the local Chinese restaurant to cook it for us. Jorgen replies that he has had a lovely day and so the restaurant bill is on him.

"If you can," I reply.

The evening is perfect, the food so varied and divine and everything is based on our barracuda; including the sushi as the starter. Dick and Yasmin join us from time to time but for most of the evening have to leave to serve other customers. We chat about simple things: work, family and ambitions. Eleven o'clock arrives and we agree that this perfect evening must come to an end. Jorgen waves at Dick who comes to our table with his usual smile.

"Can I have the bill please Dick?" he asks.

"Nope!" says Dick "it's on the house."

Jorgen turns to me and asks if I have somehow already paid causing Dick to come into our conversation insisting, once more, that I am family and so do not pay. Embarrassing. Jorgen insists on paying, Dick refuses saying that we had provided the fish anyway. Finally, I ask that we be allowed to pay for the drinks which compose a hefty part of the bill.

Jorgen pays for the drinks and then adds a large 50% tip on top. We have just found a way of getting around Dick's refusal to let us pay for our food: add an enormous tip!

Back to work on the Monday and a visit for morning coffee from a grateful forestry colleague.

"Malcolm, I cannot thank you enough. My boss loved the afternoon fishing, being able to catch his first barracuda and the perfect meal that you arranged at your friend's restaurant."

"What do you mean 'your boss'?" I query.

"Oh, didn't I tell you? He is the owner of the company I work for in Germany and he told me this morning to get a copy of your CV as he thinks the company can make use of your skills."

My trip is soon over and we have made good progress with correcting the maps. Our local counterparts can finish up without further assistance and so George and I make our individual ways home, to Essen for him and Lyon for me. Christmas is coming and we have to get ourselves busy at Cordon.

Dense snow welcomes in 1997. Once again, I have little consulting work on the horizon despite continuing to send out letters and CVs. However, we decide not to get too worried (what would worrying achieve anyway?) by the fact that I have earnt almost nothing during the first four months of this new year. Rather we decide that I should make use of my free time by doing two useful things. First, to expand and intensify my vegetable gardens. While the aim is not to be self-sufficient, if I can grow most of the vegetables and salads we need for the summer months, that is less of our savings that we need to spend on fresh food. The second item on my list is that I should do all those jobs around the house that have been put off during my time working in West Africa. First on the work list is a fitted kitchen for Cordon.

We make a trip to IKEA and find just the perfect kitchen for our home; and it is on special offer because IKEA is discontinuing the model. Why people have not appreciated the beautiful solid cherry wood doors, we cannot imagine. But they are perfect for us and, due to the sale, well below the budget we have allocated.

I can fit all the flat packs for the cupboards and trimmings into the back of my Citroën BX while our friendly carpenter has agreed to knock up a solid wood work-surface with cherry wood trims to match the cupboard doors. We recently purchased a new, top class oven from a departing American family, and buy an end-of-line gas hob in Morestel while the double basin sink and mixer taps also come from IKEA. We already have the washing machine and dish-washer. To set it all off, Véro finds some Mexican tiles somewhere in the backstreets of Lyon.

Fitting kitchens is a job I enjoy because it needs a lot of thought and logic to ensure that electric points, water and waste pipes are all in the right places. I spend a couple of days getting the electrics and water pipes just right and then build and fit the cupboards. The carpenter is true to his word and delivers the purpose-built work surface on the promised day which permits me to take a jig-saw and cut out the correct sized holes for the sink and the hob.

This morning I awake with everything fitted with the exception of the sink; my task for the morning. I am under the sink with my arm bent at a crazy angle trying to bolt the mixer tap in place before I solder on the water pipes. As I concentrate hard on my task, I realise the phone is ringing and in my hurry to untangle myself from under the sink, I bang my head and stumble across to the phone.

"Malcolm? It's Emilio. Do you remember that we met in Abidjan a couple of years ago?"

And indeed I do. If the truth is known we met in an airport hold-ing cell along with around twenty other foreigners that, like us, had just flown into the capital of the Ivory Coast for the GIS conference in 1995! Why a holding cell? Well, we were criminals of course!

What had happened is that the very day we flew into Abidjan from Europe, the country had brought in a law that entry visas could no longer be obtained at the airport on arrival as had been possible for umpteen years previously. Now, apparently, visas had to be obtained pre-departure but none of us had been informed by the conference organisers or by the airlines. Thus pretty much all the foreigners on our flight were illegals and found themselves in the holding cell while the authorities decided what to do with us.

And Emilio? Well, he is a likeable but sometimes rather 'emotional' Italian, a couple of years older than me. He also speaks excellent French and was letting the guards know, in no uncertain terms, what he thought about them holding us in the cell.

Something that I learnt at the sharp end in several countries when dealing with officials is to remain calm and polite. To this end, I asked this angry foreigner to quieten down and let me talk with the guards.

"I apologise on behalf of everyone that we violated this new rule but please realise that the fault lies squarely with the airline, Air France, that just flew us all in from Paris. Why on earth did the airline let us board the plane if we were all coming into the country illegally? Really, it is disgraceful and so disrespectful of your amazing country."

Well, that change of tone left the guards scratching their chins and clearly now feeling a little awkward to have twenty European scientists of seven or eight different nationalities held in a room at the airport.

Sensing their change of attitude, I continue "we have all come here to attend the Africa GIS Conference and the organisers will be feeling worried if we do not soon turn up at the conference hotel. I would imagine right now that they will be phoning the keynote speaker, your Science Minister ..."

Name dropping appears to work for they take a photocopy of our hotel details, ask us to leave our passports and promise to get visas affixed and the documents back to the hotel by that evening, which they do.

I find Emilio a great character and we spend the four or five days of the conference going to the different presentations together and chatting about our interests in developing information systems. In the evenings we visit various Ivorian *boui-boui* (local restaurants) that serve excellent African food and cold beer. My favourite among the restaurants has to be *La Bâche Bleue* where they serve an amazing *'poulet bicyclette'* (the chicken so named, not because their muscles are stringy like professional cyclists, as popular opinion insists, but because they are brought from the countryside to the markets tied and hanging upside down from the handlebars of bicycles).

Now, with my mind back in Cordon, Emilio is on the line and he explains that his little company has recently won a contract with the European Union to design an information sharing project across fifteen countries of West Africa. There is to be three months of work, much based in Niamey at the Agrhymet Centre; a research unit I know well from my days at the Ecological Centre in Dakar. When not in Niamey we will need to visit all fifteen countries involved to discuss local requirements as well as build national and regional ownership. Among the countries to be visited are some Anglophone (Gambia, Ghana and Sierra Leone), Francophone (Chad, Niger, Burkina Faso, Benin, Togo, Ivory Coast, Guinea-Conakry, Mali, Senegal and Mauritania) and even two Lusophone (Guinea Bissau and Cap Verde).

"Are you interested? We really need your experience in information systems and, of course, your English language skills. I have Moussa from Brussels in the team too."

What can I say, I have been sitting around since I left Banjul waiting for just such an opportunity?

"Great, Emilio, sure you can count me in."

"Malcolm, that's one hundred percent sure? I have to submit your name to the EU for approval and there can be no going back. We need to mobilise in a couple of weeks' time in early May"

"One hundred percent, no worries."

After our call ends, I phone Véro to give her the good news about my upcoming work plus a resume of progress in fitting our kitchen.

After a quick cup of tea, I am once again playing the contortionist under the sink trying to complete the fixing of the mixer tap. And, of course, the phone rings again!

"Hello Malcolm, Michael here from the GTZ project in The Gambia."

"Hi Michael, don't tell me that the printer is not working again?"

"No, no, it's fine" he laughs "and everyone asks me to send their best wishes, they miss you."

"Me too, Gambia is a great place to work."

"Yes, I agree and that is the reason I have phoned. Would you like to come back for a few months? I have to return to headquarters in Germany and we need someone to hold the fort. NEA asks that it be you."

My head is spinning a little, perhaps due to getting out from under the sink a little too quickly but more likely due to this feast of offers that is now following a famine of work.

"Michael, I do have other commitments so what period are we talking about?"

"We need you for three months," that sounds familiar, "and we would like you to arrive early next week."

"I can manage about a month now but then I am fully booked for the following three months, and I can't be flexible on that, sorry."

"Heh, that's bad news for us. I'm sorry too. Looks like this is a no-go then."

What a crazy morning but at least the mixer tap is fixed and working. Now to start tiling with those Mexican tiles ...

We all meet up at Roissy-Charles-de-Gaulle to take our flight to Niamey. Emilio has come in from Nice, Moussa from Brussels, and me from Lyon. All of us have visited Niamey on several previous occasions so we all know the town and the *'Hôtel Terminus'* where Emilio has booked us. He has also hired a car, so we are mobile.

The following morning, we drive over to Agrhymet and meet up with the Bissauan head of the establishment as he will be making inputs to our work and is to host our conference that will take place in a week or so. Before that conference, to be attended by senior scientists from the fifteen countries as well as representatives of several of the major development agencies, we have to start developing the broad structure of the future programme to present to the audience. Since Moussa and Emilio are both Francophone, we decide to develop our presentations totally in French and use a local company of professional translators to translate them into English; one less job for me, I believe.

The morning of the conference arrives and so do the translators. During the day, they will do simultaneous translations (mostly from French to English for the far fewer Anglophones in attendance) but before we start at 11 am for the first session, I have a couple of free hours. Enough time, I feel, to sit down with the translator who has translated our texts into English and review the quality. I receive a shock. My pet parrot could have done a better job! The text is gobbledygook. He has obviously used a translating software – and they are very primitive at this time – and put together a total mess.

I have to tell him "I'm sorry but your translation contains too many errors and inaccuracies. We cannot accept it as it stands and so

cannot distribute it to the participants, they will simply not understand it."

He snaps back "I am a professional translator and stand by every word I have translated. Give me a single example and I will defend that example!"

I look at the first paragraph and see the word 'dashboard'. "OK, describe to me in French what you understand is the meaning of '*tableau de bord*' in the context of this text and specifically this paragraph."

"*Mais monsieur,*" he starts, "*c'est une référence à un tableau qui résume les données.*" (it refers to a table that summarises the relevant information).

"*Et je suis d'accord avec vous.*" I reply that I agree with him but then ask "*donc pourquoi vous l'avez traduire en anglais* as the 'dash-board' of a car? I know that both a summary table and the dash-board of a car translate from English to French as '*tableau de bord*' but they do not translate that way when you go back to English from French. Your translation software has let you down and clearly you did not check your work afterwards."

He mutters something that is incomprehensible because on my first go, I have found a very silly error that should not have gotten into the text and that he cannot defend. I then point out several more grammatical and more serious errors, and receive a stumbled apology about lack of time. Sadly, that apology does not correct the English text. I have just over ninety minutes to edit it as much as I can before we need to start handing the text out to the Anglophones in the audience.

The participants start to arrive in the large lecture theatre where we will be working. Like birds of a feather, all the Anglophones sit in a group. That makes my next task easier, especially as I notice that I know all the Gambian contingent and one of the Ghanaians.

I give them our written translation in English that I have hurriedly corrected as time has allowed and explain that we had experienced problems with the translators and that later today I would give them a replacement text. All good.

The week-long conference passes well with no serious issues raised by the invited participants although we do have three consultants employed by the Food and Agriculture Organisation who seem to be intent on creating trouble until one of them accidentally lets slip that the FAO, in cooperation with the World Bank, is considering to develop a very similar programme, also to be based in Niamey. The only real difference is that ours is to be financed as a donation from the European Union while theirs will be in the form of a reimbursable loan. Emilio and I consider that this contingent of expatriate consultants are looking to provide themselves with some future consulting work by trying to get our proposed project dropped. Yes, there is even competition in the development world!

The time comes for us to leave Niger and make our trips to the other fourteen member states. I have been allocated, in order, Benin, Togo, Ghana, Ivory Coast, Sierra Leone and Mauritania for a total of twenty-two days work plus travel time. The three of us will then meet up in Senegal following my Mauritanian leg, travel together to Ivory Coast for a sub-regional meeting and then all go back on the same flight to Niamey to continue our work. Emilio and Moussa have their own countries to visit, and our total mission is expected to take pretty much the entire month, and probably a bit more.

While my colleagues have rather complicated travel agenda, mine is even worse. I am leaving Niamey, direction Cotonou in Benin but necessarily passing via Lagos to catch an Air Afrique connection. After my meetings in Benin, I am to take a taxi overland the one hundred and fifty kilometres to the neighbouring capital of Lomé in Togo. Once work is completed there, I continue by taxi for the two hundred or so kilometres to Accra in Ghana. From Ghana, I am to take a Ghanaian Airways flight to Abidjan, and from there a long hop flight across to Freetown in Sierra Leone. From Sierra Leone, I am flying into Dakar, staying one day for a breather and then taking the small plane of Air Senegal that serves Nouakchott in Mauritania.

I am to spend usually three nights, occasionally four, in each country. Quite some travelling in view over the next month.

During the Niamey conference, all three of us are able to liaise either with the national point person or the assistant for each country we are to visit. All our contacts have been asked to help smooth our trips by, for example, getting us met at airports, booking hotels, laying on local transport and arranging meetings in their respective countries. Without that assistance we would never have been able to make our round trips in such a short period of time. But even then, life is not always easy.

My first stop is in Cotonou where I am met at the luggage conveyor belt of the airport by a charming but unknown gentleman. He greets me in a friendly but courteous manner and immediately grabs my suitcase and asks me to follow him to the car. I assume, as most people would, that he is a driver sent to take me to my hotel but when he tells me his name is Vincent, I realise that he is in fact the big boss of the national remote sensing laboratory in Benin. I quickly apologise for my lack of manners and grab my suitcase back, but not before he bursts out laughing at my embarrassment. That gentle first meeting is destined to seal a friendship that continues up to my very last visit to Benin many years later.

He takes me to the *Hôtel du Lac*, where he has made a reservation for me, saying that it is friendly, simple and reasonably priced. And indeed it is, because it becomes the place where I try to stay during many future trips to the country. The following day, Vincent takes me for a tour around the different ministries that will be cooperating with our programme and in the evening, he asks if I would like to try local food (of course I would) and so I am taken to a small restaurant where today's special is porcupine; now that is a first for me (and, yes, it is served without its prickles!).

The following day at lunchtime, it is my turn to take him for a meal having heard about a Senegalese restaurant not too far from his ministry office. We are served a genuine Senegalese meal by genuine Senegalese ladies who giggle as I speak to them in my less than perfect Wolof. The afternoon is taken up by a meeting at which I present our proposed project to an audience of around twenty and receive considerable constructive feedback and wishes of good luck with the rest of my trip.

The next morning, Vincent arrives at the hotel with a taxi driver he knows and frequently uses for personal trips. The driver speaks pretty good French and will drive me to Lomé in Togo, stay with me for the three days I will spend there and then drive me along the coast road, into Ghana and to the capital of Accra. Vincent kindly negotiates a good rate for the trip and tells me that I should give him a few dollars every day to cover his food, accommodation and fuel.

We say our farewells, knowing that we are to meet back in Niamey in a few weeks' time. I climb into the front passenger seat while the driver places my suitcase into the car boot, and off we go, direction Lomé about four hours away.

Cotonou is the only city in the world that I have visited where Honda 50s and the like are so plentiful that they cause traffic jams; especially at roundabouts. Honda 50s are also the most usual form of taxi on the Cotonou roads, with sometimes two or even three passengers tentatively hanging on to the backs of the young drivers, but one soon gets used to taking the motorbike taxis around the town!

We take the route RNIE-1 out of Cotonou and this is my first time to see Benin outside the capital city. Of course, it bears quite a resemblance to the countryside around western Nigeria. In both places the Yoruba are the principal tribe and provide the dominant language.

Before I know it, we are passing through Ouidah, a city infamous for the cruel slave trade that it housed so many years ago. Ouidah is also the centre of voodoo in Benin; best not to stop there too long!

A little more than twenty kilometres after Ouidah, we arrive at Lake Aheme, a most incredible place. Here live a population of fisher people who have built ingenious villages on stilts in the lake. Of course they use nets for fishing but they also have other ingenious ways of catching fish. One common method is to drive a ring of stakes into the lake bed, leaving a few centimetres between each stake. Food is thrown inside the structure which brings in hordes of little fish to gorge themselves. As the fish grow, there comes a time when the little ones are just too large to get back out through the gaps between the stakes, or so I am told, anyway!

As we drive, my taxi driver becomes chattier and tells me that the villagers along the lakeside, who grow maize as a stable crop, are experiencing trouble from rogue hippopotami who come from the lake at night to raid the fields. Some villagers tried to drive the animals away and one was bitten almost in half by these enormous herbivores. The government is trying to help but since the animals are protected, they can only try to scare them off and drive them back into the lake.

Soon we come to Aklo and the road turns south towards the border with Togo. I cross my fingers that there will be no issues at the frontier. And there are none. We drive along the narrow coastal strip that sees Benin appear to continue well into Togo before we arrive at a dirt road with a movable barrier that marks the border between the two countries. I leave the car, taking my passport and briefcase, enter into a rather dilapidated building and move over to the counter where two policemen are chatting. I say my good mornings, ask how they are and tell them that I have meetings with the Ministry tomorrow in Lomé. My UK passport is taken, stamped and I am praised on the quality of my French. No hassle, no problems and two minutes later we are driving in Togo.

Our journey continues for a further thirty kilometres until we reach Lomé. A quick stop to ask for directions to my hotel and I am soon checking in to a pleasant place with broad gardens to the front. I use the word 'pleasant' in relation to the quality of rooms and gardens, also the price, but not for the welcome. I find all the staff sullen; not rude but somehow sad, downcast. Quite a change after the friendliness, smiles and chattiness of people in Cotonou.

The following morning, I am phoned by a gentleman named Foly. Seemingly a strange name but one that I subsequently find very common here. He is my contact for Togo and we had met briefly during the Niamey conference. He picks me up in his official vehicle and we travel across Lomé to the ministry and our first meeting. This is the second time that I make my presentation of the proposed structure for the programme and so it is getting simpler and I do not need to think so fast on my feet.

We break up for lunch and then re-gather in the afternoon. Togo, as perhaps the poorest country to be involved in our programme, is anxious that it should go ahead. I receive full support from the gathered audience. In the evening, Foly invites me to go for dinner with him but I insist that it is on condition that I pay the bill. A short 'argument' ensues and I realise that I am hurting his pride by insisting on paying. A quick back step, an apology from me based around the fact that I am receiving a per diem for just such entertainment, and we head off to a quaint restaurant where I taste for the first time 'bush-rat' that tends to go by the name of Agouti and, before I shock too many people, the so-called rat is rabbit size, eats grass and does not live in the sewers! Indeed, it is delicious in a chili pepper sauce, accompanied by pounded manioc and ice cold beers!

The following day is Saturday. Foly tells me that his wife is away on business in Nigeria and would I therefore like to go for a drive to see the countryside. Of course I would. He picks me up early and we are soon leaving Lomé, heading due north. As we travel, he asks about my stay in the hotel where the ministry always places important guests. I mention that I find the hotel very pleasant and correct but that the staff seem distant, somehow sad.

Foly explains that their president is called Eyadema and he took power thirty years ago in a coup back in 1967. He did stand for election in 1979 and then again in 1986 receiving over 99% of votes cast (yeah sure!). Armed troops with support from Ghana had tried to overthrow him in 1986, just before the election, and then again in 1993, both times unsuccessfully. The following year there were civil disturbances against the president and, in response, the military supporting Eyadema, went on a rampage in Lomé, firing at civilians and killing many. This resulted in an estimated three hundred thousand citizens fleeing the country or moving into the countryside. Many have never returned to Lomé.

"All that to explain to you that our economy is probably the worst in West Africa, people are poor and suffering and can see no solution. There is no light at the end of the tunnel for the 'little guys' and the only way of surviving is to *se débrouiller* (get on with it and look for opportunities). I was lucky because a couple of year ago my ministry allocated me a stretch of forest to be cleared to allow the passage of this north-south road. I borrowed from the bank to buy two chain saws, hired two *boucherons* (woodcutters) and was paid by the government to clear my section of the forest. My *boucherons* put valuable timber wood to one side and made charcoal with the rest. I sold all the wood and charcoal to traders in Lomé. After paying back my loan and paying the *boucherons*, I made around $20,000 profit. That's how my family copes with life in Togo. Not many people have my luck."

We continue our drive northwards until the end of the morning, covering about one hundred and fifty kilometres according to Foly. We arrive at the town of Atakpane, getting close to the centre of the country. We take a right and soon arrive at a beautiful lake, called the 'Retenue de Nangbeto'. A relaxed lunch at a small *gargotte,* called Eric's, with a cold Togolese beer and we start to make our way back to Lomé.

It's Monday and so time to leave Togo and head along the coast in my *Beninois* taxi to Accra. Lomé abuts against the border with Ghana so within ten minutes I am walking into the frontier post and two minutes later my passport is stamped and we can leave; well not quite. A Ghanaian policeman comes out to inspect my transport and speaks – in English of course – to my taxi driver. The poor guy understanding not a single word of what the official is saying begins to move some CFA notes out of his shirt pocket; thinking the policeman must be asking for a bribe.

I quickly stop him from trying to pay the policeman by translating his words *"il te demande de conduire doucement au Ghana"* (drive carefully in our country)!

The road is long from the Togo frontier to Accra but we pass through such beautiful countryside that time seems to fly. The landscape and vegetation remind me a lot of my time in southern Nigeria. After only thirty kilometres, we come to the edge of the beautiful Keta Lagoon and follow the road to the south meaning that we have the lagoon on our right-hand side and the ocean on our left. What a beautiful part of the world with little fishing villages dotted along the shores and ladies hanging gutted fish to dry in the sun. Ghana was once called 'The Gold Coast' because of the incredible amount of the precious metal discovered there but it could equally be named after the beautiful sandy beaches that we now drive past.

As lunchtime approaches, I ask my driver to keep his eyes open for a restaurant. He tells me that he would like to eat attiéké but perhaps I would prefer something European. Attiéké is well known to me. It originated, I believe, in the Ivory Coast and is a type of couscous made from grinding fermented cassava roots and is served with fish or chicken and sliced tomatoes and onions. Delicious.

Once arrived at my hotel in Accra, it is time to say goodbye to my taxi driver. He leaves with a good tip in Euros and a big smile on his face.

I already know a few of my hosts in Accra as they made several visits to my old project in Senegal. They work for an organisation called 'RSO'; and only a drunken consultant with a weird sense of humour could have come up with that acronym. Indeed, for many project developers, dreaming up the acronym of the title of a project can often take more time and effort than developing the entire contents of the programme itself!

The next morning at just after eight, one of my hosts comes to the hotel to pick me up and transport me to the ministry where I am to make my next presentation. He apologises in advance that the traffic is bad and we will certainly be late for our 10 am meeting. Bad is not the right word. There are major roadworks taking place, thick queues of traffic coming from all directions and several cloudbursts of rain. We eventually arrive at the ministry at midday, only two hours late, and find a note to inform us that we should go to such and such a restaurant and meet up with the others who are eating there. Luckily, the restaurant is not very far away and so within fifteen minutes I am shaking hands with new colleagues as well as with the head of Agrhymet who coincidentally has also stopped off in Ghana. We, the latecomers, try to give our food orders to the waiter but he explains that the kitchen cannot cope with the influx of orders, would we mind waiting an hour. The head of Agryhmet solves the food problem by pointing out that the restaurant also sells meat kebabs, cooked on a BBQ, and there are about a dozen that look just about ready to eat.

The meeting in Accra finally takes place at 2 pm and I stand up to give my presentation to a very knowledgeable audience. All goes well until I get to a slide on the proposed use of remote sensing and suddenly I am stuck for a word in English. It sits there on the tip off my tongue but it just will not be said. I stammer for a few seconds and then admit, with lots of laughter shared with the audience, that I have made this presentation two times in the last couple of days; both times in French, and my brain just refuses to switch completely into English. I am saved by one of the participants who asks me to say the word in French and then he gives me the English translation. More teasing follows which lifts the level of humour of the entire meeting. As an aside, I have to say that I find the Ghanaians a most pleasant and welcoming people.

Off to Accra Airport and another Ghana Airways flight over to Abidjan in the Ivory Coast. The presentation goes well and the audience promise to think through the programme's propositions and come back with recommendations to be provided during our return trip to the country in a week or so for the sub-regional meeting.

Back at my hotel, near to the airport, I receive a call from Emilio. It is May 25 and he has just received a message from the Sierra Leone delegation informing him that there is an attempted *coup d'état* currently taking place in Freetown led by disgruntled members of the military. Freetown is currently a no-go area and considered extremely dangerous. My trip and meetings are cancelled. What to do now since I have a ticket that is to take me to Freetown and another that is supposed to take me from there to Dakar?

The simplest answer is to continue my trip but not go to Freetown itself. Let me explain. Freetown airport is not actually in Freetown but rather sits on the opposite bank of the Tagrin Bay. Visitors to Freetown that arrive, as I am doing, at the international airport then have to take a motor boat for fifteen kilometres or so across the sea to arrive at the capital.

I am able to bring forward my flight from Sierra Leone to Dakar by three days and so, in effect, arrive at the international airport at 11 am and fly on to Dakar on the 3 pm flight, the same day. That means holding my courage, with fingers crossed, at the airport in Sierra Leone for only a few hours. Easier said than done but I do arrive safely and on time in Dakar; back to my second (or is it third) home town! Cancelling my stop in Sierra Leone adds a couple of extra days to my stay in Dakar and so I make good use of my time by staying in an unpretentious hotel close to Rue Moussa Diop and using that as a base to visit many of our friends that we had left four years previously, including Alan, an octogenarian Brit.

Alan is famous for two things. The first, for which he is known as Mr Cockroach (or the old debugger), because he has a successful pest control business. This involves him phoning up clients and saying that he will arrive at the house in the afternoon in order to put poison in the sewers. He always expected to be received at our house, and indeed always was, with a home-baked cake and afternoon tea while his 'boys' got on with the work.

His second point of infamy is that he has set in place a tradition of holding champagne and canapés at mid-morning on Christmas day, thus destroying any will from his many friends to go home afterwards and cook the Christmas lunch!

I also take the opportunity to go back and visit my old project, now an 'Association of National Interest' that I had left with a lot of pride but a sad heart in 1993. I walk through the front door of the building, that I had discovered while drinking a sundowner with an American friend who lived on the opposite side of the street, and knock on the secretary's door and enter. I expect to find Aisha in her usual seat but instead am faced by an unknown young lady.

"May I help you, sir?" she asks.

I am a little taken aback not to find Aisha sitting there but, after all, personnel do change. "Is M. Camara in the building please?"

"Yes sir, may I give him your name please?"

"Please tell him that Malcolm is here."

She leaves her office, knocks on the door opposite and I hear her say in Wolof that there is a stranger called Malcolm asking for him. I then hear Camara burst out laughing and he gently pushes past the now bemused young lady and throws his arms around me in a long bear hug.

"Say hello to the father of the ecological centre" he says to the girl.

"Hello sir, sorry sir" she manages in an embarrassed voice.

"No trouble," I laugh, "Thank you."

"Malcolm, we are just about to have a meeting with a donor agency that is thinking of putting money into the association. Can you join the meeting? After all, you had so much to do with our evolution away from being a project. I am sure you can help us sell ourselves better." That small statement makes me feel happier about the centre and my time in Dakar than I had felt for many years.

The next leg of my trip takes me to Mauritania. While the country only sits on the northern bank of the Senegal river and is literally a few kilometres away from the town of Saint-Louis that I know so well; this is my first visit. The tragic events of 1989 have always left me reluctant to visit a country that could mutilate or kill a section of its community simply because of their country and ethnic origins; that is until now.

I am met at the airport by a hotel driver who takes me to a very plush hotel on the beach; it looks expensive and indeed is, very expensive. It also makes me feel totally anonymous, not what I look for in a hotel. But nothing to do now but spend the night, check out in the morning and find the time during the day to check into another, more suitable hotel.

After an initial and pleasant meeting with the local representative of the Agrhymet programme, himself an ethnic Senegalese, I ask if he can recommend me another hotel. He kindly drives me to a small, homely place run by a young Guinean originally from Conakry. This feels more like it, and at a third of the price too.

That evening, as I am sitting in the lounge reading a newspaper and thinking about dinner, he comes over and sits down next to me.

"Is there anything you need sir?"

"I could kill a cold beer" I reply.

He laughs and says "I think you know that it's forbidden to sell alcohol in Mauritania and so it is almost impossible to find any in Nouakchott. Of course, unless you know where to go!"

"Really, so tell me."

"Well, there is a restaurant, called the 'Saint-Louis', run by a Senegalese lady, a *méttise*. If you eat at her place and she feels that she can trust you, she might offer to sell you a beer."

"How do I find the restaurant?"

"Dead easy, it's over the road from the Saudi Arabian Embassy. Should I get you a taxi?"

Ten minutes later, the taxi drops me at the Saudi Embassy and I spot the sign for the restaurant above a closed gate on the opposite side of the road. On walking across a road with no traffic, I find the gate locked and there are only a few lights in the house cum restaurant. Nothing ventured, I ring the bell at the gate and, a few minutes later, the door is opened by a young lady.

"*Nan-ga-def,* can I eat in your restaurant tonight?" I ask.

"Oh, I did not expect to have any customers so I have not opened up. But please come in and I will prepare food for you." She re-locks the gate behind me and leads me into the front room of her house that she uses as her restaurant. "Would you like a beer?" she asks straight away and hands me a cold can of Heineken (the beer that reaches the parts – like Nouakchott – that other beers cannot reach!).

Half an hour later, I am handed a second can and served a delicious mafé with lots of stewed vegetables on a bed of rice; how did she know that is my favourite dish?

At the end of the evening I pay my very reasonable bill plus a grateful tip, hail a taxi and head back to the hotel.

I make my usual presentation the next morning and then catch the Air Senegal flight back to Dakar where I meet up with the rest of the team. Emilio decides that since I know Senegal the best (uproar and protest from Moussa, himself a Senegalese but from the far South; it should be known!), I am nominated to organise the evening meal and then the 'by-night' (the after-dinner night scene).

I agree and use a trick that I have used a few times in the past when living in Dakar. I state that I will take them to a Cape Verdean restaurant called 'Chez Loucha' where the food is copious. I tell Emilio and Moussa that if they can both finish their plates, I will cover the cost of the entire evening, their meals and drinks included. However, if either one leaves as much as a grain of rice on their plates, the evening will be on them.

"A no brainer," laughs Emilio, "I hope you have plenty of money."

We arrive at Loucha's without a reservation and push our way past the gaggle of *talibés* that hang around the door with their giant tomato sauce cans dangling on pieces of string. They know that they will be well fed by the leftovers from the tables and still have some left to take back to the other kids who remain at their crowded accommodation where they are housed and taught the Koran by their religious teachers, the Marabouts.

I enter first and am immediately recognised by Georges, one of the brothers who run the place with their mother and other members of the extended family.

"Heh, great. How are you, bro? Come this way I am just about to clear a table."

Given my reception, Moussa whispers "I told you not to trust him Emilio! He is too well known here"

"Too, too late my friends. *Bon appétit*!" I reply with a big smirk across my face.

Moussa orders, a *thieboudienne,* well he is Senegalese, if only from the south of the country. And I know that I have already won the competition because the rice, for one person, is not served on a plate but on a serving dish. The fish and vegetables also do not come on a plate but on a second serving dish. He will pop if he eats all that.

Emilio tries to be less greedy and goes for a *salade niçoise*, even Moussa thinks that is cheating. But am I worried? Not in the least because I know the size of the salads and he will have to leave even more than Moussa.

I go for a dish of octopus that the Cape Verdeans prepare just perfectly in a tomato and onion sauce.

Long story short, try as they will (and they do try very, very hard), my two agnostic colleagues finally have to admit defeat, much to my pleasure for getting a free evening, and to that of the *talibés* who will soon receive a lot of extra food in their tomato cans.

After finishing at Loucha's we go around the corner to the *Café Ponty* for some draught beers but before walking through the illustrious establishment's front door, I warn my colleagues that while the beer is excellent, as is the music – tonight there is a band – the place crawls with ladies-of-the-night. Simply show your wedding bands once we sit down and no one will disturb us. Finally, Moussa has to accept that I know Dakar, at least, better than him!

Four days later we are back in the Terminus Hotel in Niamey for the next part of our work. This involves bringing together all the ideas that each one of us has gleaned during our presentations and meetings across the fifteen member countries and developing them into the format of a European Union project document entitled 'Inventory and Monitoring of Natural Resources and the Environment for the Sahel and West Africa'. To speed up our work, we each develop our sections in French and bring them together into the project document. On completion, Emilio hands this over to me to do the translation to English once I return to France.

Our final activity in Niamey is to bring together the representatives of the fifteen countries – including a couple of junior ministers, that is the level of interest generated - and to present to them the penultimate structure of the future project. After constructive debate, we tweak our document as necessary, close the workshop and return home. We have been away for three months.

6 |

The Marvels of Madagascar

I arrive back in France and it is well into the summer. During my absence, the family has moved from Lyon to our summer 'pastures' in Cordon. After a couple of days relaxing at home, I begin to work on the translation of the project documents that I assume will take me about three weeks to complete. After all, there are over two hundred pages of text and tables to be translated.

After a couple of hours of intense concentration in the quiet of my attic office, I take a break for a coffee and sit with Véro out on our little walled terraced garden, appreciating the sunny morning of early September and the shade cast by the house. As we chat, Mélanie comes to join us.

"Can we chat a moment?" she asks, surprising us both because her middle name should have been 'chat', a trait she clearly inherited in her 'Eve Genes'.

"What's up, love?" we ask together.

"I've been thinking. What would you say if I told you that I would prefer to go to university in UK than stay here in France?"

Véro replies for both us by saying "you know we have no problem with you going in either country but tell us a bit more why you have decided that."

"Well, in France the only prerequisite to go to 'Fac' (university) is to pass the '*Bacc.*' (*Baccalaureate* equals A levels). There is no screening at entry, as in UK. So there must be a load of students who turn up without a hope of passing all the exams to get their degree. I don't want to be in that crowd. Also, and more importantly, I know what I want to do as my degree and I don't think there is as much choice here in France as in the UK. I have chatted with a couple of teachers at *Lycée* (high school) and they seem to agree."

"It sounds like you have thought it through pretty well. But you do realise that if you want entry to a good UK university, you will really need to take A levels rather than the *Bacc*, and get good grades too. That would mean moving to the UK," I reply.

"Would you send me to boarding school, then?" Mélanie asks with a smile (because we know she would be all for that).

I look at Véro and she reads my mind, as she so often does, and replies "nope, we would all move to England for the time necessary. It would be good for your brother too."

And just like that, the family comes up with a broad plan to change completely our lifestyle and country of residence.

Obviously we now need to put a lot of finer detail into that plan: where would we live, which schools would we target for the children, when should we make such a move?

The 'when' is perhaps the easiest to decide. Mélanie is now fifteen and recently passed her *Brevet* (like GCSEs but taken a year earlier in France) at the International School in Lyon and, based on that result and her overall work, she has been accepted into the *Lycée* section of her school and will start the first year of the three-year long *Bacc*.

in the autumn. David is now eleven and will join the school's *collège* section (that Mélanie has just left). And, for the record, despite his 'immaturity' and *lacunes* at age seven he has not had to redo any of his academic years. So we are fine for the next year in France, but would need to move to UK sometime after school closes in France next summer but before the UK autumn term begins in September.

The 'where' and the 'which' are linked but we have not yet decided which is the more important. Go for a great school and let that decide the area we must move to or decide first the place and then look for the best school in the area.

As is my admittedly rather weird way, I mull over difficult decisions while doing something totally different! In this case, I am painting the two rooms in our converted attic. As I paint, I am running different scenarios through my head that revolve around quality of schools, cost of housing, locality (especially for Véro and the children to fit back into UK society) and proximity to airports (for my work travel). As I carefully paint with pale blue around our beautiful oak beams, my mind juggles our dilemma and comes up with three main possibilities to talk through with Véro.

Number one, should we think about living somewhere in the south of England, near to Maidstone where my mum and dad live (especially as my dad is pretty sick at the moment with pancreatic cancer) or across the county line in southern Sussex? Problem: high cost of housing due to the London effect. Positives: close to routes to France and pretty close to the London airports of Gatwick and Heathrow. There are also many good schools available and lovely countryside that we all know well.

Number two, what about the beautiful south-west? Why not consider Dorset, Devon or perhaps even Cornwall? Problems: those are counties we know little about; houses are likely to be expensive due to the multitude of tourists' second homes while it would be a long drive for me to a suitable international airport. Positives: the beauty and relative tranquillity of those counties.

Number three: what about a return to our recent roots in good old Northampton Town? Problems: a little distant from Heathrow and Gatwick Airport (not so much in miles but in time needed to travel along the M1 and M25 motorways). Also, well to say it nicely, Northampton is not the most joyous town in the UK despite the beautiful countryside that surrounds it. Positives: we know the place very well, have many friends living in the county while the East Midlands, Birmingham and Luton Airports are also not too far away. House prices are still very reasonable and the ex-grammar school (Northampton School for Boys) has a talented headmaster and a growing academic reputation. It recently started to take girls into the sixth form.

A quick call to our great friends, the Coe, and the decision to go with number three has just gotten a little easier. However, Véro's wish, should we move there, is to live around the 'park' (as in Abington Park); a leftover desire from our previous days in the town in the mid-80s. But after she chats with Diane Coe, the number of named roads where we would look to live has now been whittled down to just three.

David seems ready to go. His only worry is whether he will be able to play football in the town. We believe he is actually quite looking forward to joining the English school system. He has always been a bit too much of a character to fit easily into the French system where square pegs have to fit into round holes, like it or not.

Talking about football, he currently belongs to a club in the little town of Corbelin, just on the other side of the river from Cordon. The trainer of his age group is 'Bilou' and the dad of one of his village friends. The philosophy of the club for the youngsters is simple: if you turn up regularly you will always get a game. The youngsters even have a faithful football reporter who follows their matches and does little write-ups in the local rag. He recently discovered, after talking to me on the touchline, that David is half-English. That also clarifies for him why the kids have nicknamed him 'l'*Anglais*'. Because David has no foreign accent when he speaks French, the journalist had until now thought that his nickname was because of his freckles and fair, almost ginger, complexion.

Since Dave has a growing reputation as a goal scorer and his team have been winning quite a number of under-eleven matches, the reporter has started to go to town with his match reports. Every few weeks we see headlines (on page 23 of course) of '*Sauvé par l'Anglais*' (saved by the English) or '*l'Anglais encore un coup de chapeau*' (another hat-trick).

All good fun and why French junior football can run rings around the oh so serious Brits ("*oh you want to play for the thirteenth team of our under nines? Come and have a trial and we will see if you are good enough!*" What rubbish such junior clubs spout in the UK).

Diane spreads the word among her friends that we are looking to move back to Northampton and would like a house on a few, very specific, streets around the park. One house in our price range comes up almost straight away. I ring the estate agent only to learn that it was sold within a few hours of going on the market. That is certainly going to be an issue for us. Nonetheless, we keep putting out feelers via friends and the internet and, in October, get an early morning call from Diane that her next door neighbour has, just this morning, seen a 'For Sale' sign being erected in Lime Avenue; one of our preferred roads.

I call the agents and get given a glossy rundown on the property. This sounds sufficiently interesting – even after discounting the usual estate agent jargon – that I set an appointment to visit the following day. I book an early morning flight into Stansted, hire a car and turn up at 39 Lime Avenue. A quick walk around the property shows me that, in fact, it is rather a bog standard 1930's three-bedroom semi-detached with bow windows and pebble-dashed walls. But, for me, it has two very attractive features: an enormous, well planted and pretty back garden and a space to the left of the house wide enough to park a car off-road. The pavement is dropped too, which means that the council officially recognises the driveway as a parking space. While having that space is a significant benefit, I can see clearly in my mind's eye that it is also sufficiently wide, should we so desire, to build a large extension. The house does need a little work to make it more attractive in our eyes but what house does not?

In conversation with the owner, an elderly, widowed lady who is selling this house in order to move to a rural village to be closer to her daughter, she tells me that the agents have already received an offer slightly below the board price. I offer to pay the full price with the proviso that the house is taken off the market straightaway. I explain to both the owner and the agent that we have nothing to sell, so there is no hideous chain behind us; a great plus in the UK. I also clarify how we propose to finance the purchase with 50% cash and a 50% loan. This convinces them, and the house is ours; well, once I can persuade a bank to lend me the other 50%.

A quick trip into Northampton town centre with the estate agent, and his office tells me that they have good links with the Coventry Building Society. I brought with me three or four annual French tax returns but these get barely a glance from the building society. The manager simply says "Dr, there is no issue for us to lend you the money you require because of your large deposit. Indeed, if you put 50% cash into any purchase with us, we would happily lend you three times more than you are actually requesting."

By early December, contracts are signed and the house is ours. We tentatively plan to move across to the UK in the summer next year.

In the meantime, we make a request to the Boy's School for Mélanie to gain entrance for the next academic year. Our house is in the school catchment area but this does not apply for girls trying to enter the sixth form.

We keep our finger's crossed because we learn there is a lot of competition for relatively few places. A couple of weeks before Christmas we are asked to attend for interview. I book us rooms for two nights in a B&B on the Billing road and we arrive at the school for the interview. I am nervous, Mélanie is most certainly not!

Both Mélanie and I are interviewed together with some questions being put to me and others to her. They show interest in my background and my work while with Mélanie they are clearly digging into her character; she has character in spades, so little to worry about there.

But the clincher is the final question she receives:

"Mélanie, while we are very keen on your academic performance and sporting achievements, we also look for what else you might bring to the school. Imagine you are asked to start a new activity in the school for the sixth formers. In a word, what would you propose?"

She looks them straight in the face and without hesitation says "canyoning."

There are several mystified faces looking back at her. Finally, one asks "is that a French word, Mélanie?"

I hold my breath that she does not choose to reply "oh durr, you Brits!" but instead she says "the word is English actually but we use it in France too."

A slightly embarrassed teacher then asks the obvious "can you explain, again in a few words, what you do in 'canyoning'?"

"In a few words? You walk to the top of a waterfall and jump into the water below."

Yep, that's right; there were indeed quite a few shocked faces looking back at this little slip of a girl for her bravery!

"Of course, you only jump when you know that the water at the bottom is deep enough, otherwise the fatality rate would be rather high!" And she burst out laughing along with the teachers who are trying desperately to retain straight faces while interviewing her.

No need to ask anything more in the interview, no need to discuss the decision further. The three teachers look at each other, still trying not to laugh, and the leader of the panel says "we look forward to you shaking up some of the sixth form machos, Mélanie!"

David will eventually go to the same school but not until he is thirteen. This means that we have to find a good school for a single year. Step up again dear Diane with the suggestion of a little private school in Northampton called Parkside, with very reasonable fees, and run by a strong disciplinarian; perfect to keep our cheeky boy in order.

While domestic duties are recently taking priority, I am still doing some consulting work to keep the bank account ticking over, thankfully most is based out of my home office. I do have a short trip to Essen that sees me take a flight from Lyon to Dusseldorf and then get on to the train for the remainder of the trip. This is a visit to the head offices of the company that I worked for in The Gambia. They have asked me to train their technical team in monitoring and evaluation. While the work only lasts a couple of days, it leads to several future requests from the staff to undertake pieces of work helping them to write sections of different contract proposals; fund-generating but, admittedly, rather boring!

In the evening, after delivering the first training session, George invites me to join him at the "Christmas Market" in Essen. We wander down the multitude of little cabins that have been erected on the main square, stopping at one store with a bar front to buy some mulled wine. As we drink our spiced and heated red wine, chatting about life in general, I feel a soft brush to my arm. On looking round, I see a young African lady with a pretty smile. A memory bell rings that links her to Dakar, but from where?

"*T'es Mark n'est-ce pas ?*" and indeed that is the name that Senegalese often call me, having difficulty in pronouncing my first name.

"*Oui, c'est moi. Excuses-moi mais ...*" and I hesitate to admit that I cannot place her.

She laughs pleasantly and replies "look over there at my boutique, do you remember me now?" She indicates a small jewellery store and I see lots of gold and silver trinkets; the penny drops. "*Et madame et Mélanie, comment vont-elles ?*"

"Still wearing your jewellery" I reply as she returns to serve a customer.

After a moment of listening to this conversation between a Brit and a Senegalese in his own city in Germany, George says "when we went together to The Gambia, I was a bit surprised at how many people we passed in the street knew who you were but now you come to Essen and people still know you. How do you do it?"

"Want another mulled wine George?"

We celebrate New Year *en famille*, welcoming in 1998. I try to be reasonable with the amount of good red wine and champagne that I consume for, in only a couple of days, I am off on my very first trip across the equator; to Madagascar to be precise. That trip is destined to open my eyes to the beauty, uniqueness and abject poverty, of this most lovely mini-continent.

I am going for two weeks, working for the same US company that had employed me in The Gambia and also gave me the one hundred day contract. My brief is to attend various meetings both at USAID and with staff working on other natural resources projects in Madagascar. USAID is soon to launch a Request for Proposals for an upcoming project called Landscape Development Interventions (or LDI for short) and the company hiring me asks that I represent them at a so-called 'bidders conference,' highlighting their skills and experiences, and collecting relevant information that will help in writing their contract proposal.

I take the morning flight with Air France from Paris. At around 3 pm we cross the equator, somewhere off the southern Somalia coast. And the only way I know that we have crossed it, is that the aircraft has left the flight map showing on the screens at the front of the cabin. I'm not sure what I had expected to happen as we crossed the line, but at least I had expected the pilot to say something!

We land at Ivato International Airport at around 9 pm. After clearing formalities and collecting my luggage, I take a yellow taxi and we drive in the still, cool air of evening the twenty-some kilometres into the capital Antananarivo; thank goodness always shortened to 'Tana'. Even at this time of night, I am enthralled with the countryside, barely visible in the moonlight, of farmland and forests dotted with little brick-built houses. Cute, charming, and unique. For I have finally arrived in the Ecologists' Paradise (all due respects to the Galapagos Islands). Let me explain.

Madagascar is a mini-continent. It has just about every vegetation type found in Africa, ranging from rainforests to deserts. It also has a unique fauna and flora. The most high-profile species are, of course, the lemurs, creatures found nowhere else on the planet. But while they are the most visible to the outside world (thanks to many children's books and films that portray the ring-tailed lemurs as special heroes), the uniqueness of all animal and plant groups is absolutely amazing. For example, of the one hundred and eighty or so species of amphibians on the island, 98% are found nowhere else in the world (they are said to be '*endemic*') while of the three hundred and thirty or so reptiles, over 90% are endemic. The percentage falls somewhat for more mobile species such as birds and insects but taking all species of plants and animals together, 80% are unique to the island. Few people realise that the entire mainland continent of Africa can boast only a single species of Baobab while Madagascar has over two hundred different species! It really is the museum of Africa, the landmass from which it split some one hundred and fifty million years ago, and a precious heritage that should be protected – far more than it actually is.

Sadly, on this trip, I am unable to travel outside the capital but I do manage to visit a small zoo that has many of the species of lemurs living in enclosures that are fenced around large ponds and many endemic species of amphibians and reptiles on display in cages and tanks.

I also discover the cute Hotel Colbert that sits neatly in the city centre with an amazing hilltop view across the town. But what makes the Colbert stand out particularly from the other hotels around is its amazing patisserie. What better jingle for the hotel than 'Breakfasting is a pleasure ... at the Colbert'.

Apart from discovering the city and lots of good places to visit and to eat, the trip also permits me to raise my professional profile. For that I will always be grateful to my employers in Washington. I attend the several days of conferences, presentations and visits along with members of the local USAID offices, different project staff as well as senior representatives of other US companies who also intend to bid on the project. As the official representative of my employers, I get a seat at the 'top' table and so am able to make a lot of important acquaintances that, unbeknown at this time, will bear fruit in the not too distant future.

Once back in France, I help the company prepare their proposal and they include me in their short-term consulting team to supervise all Monitoring and Evaluation inputs. Unfortunately, we lose out in the final round of selection to an excellent technical proposal and a very strong team fielded by a competitor company. I doubt many people are surprised that this company has won the contract because they are already running another similar and very effective project for USAID in Madagascar.

Before the summer arrives, I have a trip to Paris to write a full project proposal for the French arm of another US consulting firm. All I want to say about that trip is that they put me in an office for the entire two weeks and, not once, did anybody bother to speak to me. At the end of the two weeks, as I handed over the completed proposal, the managing director tried to renegotiate downwards my consulting fees that we had agreed before I had even left home to undertake the work. He even tried to back out of his earlier promise to reimburse my train fare and hotel room. Although they did pay up, suffice to say, they go on my blacklist of 'never again' companies!

In stark contrast, I then re-pack my suitcase and go off on a ten-day trip to the outskirts of Hamburg with a small German consulting outfit. I have never been treated with so much friendship and kindness as I receive during those ten days. On arrival at the company offices, I am taken to a nearby apartment, owned by the company, that is to be my accommodation.

On the first evening, I wander down a small avenue, heading towards some bright lights I can see in the distance. The lights prove to be what I am seeking: a restaurant/bar where I can order dinner.

The bar is large and split into two halves. It is also very busy but not overcrowded. In my half of the bar there appears to be a large group of friends, perhaps work colleagues, who are drinking and chatting animatedly and seemingly in good humour.

I go up to the bar and use a good percentage of my German vocabulary in saying "*ein bier bitta*."

As I await my glass to be filled with foaming lager, the gentleman next to me starts to tell his audience what I presume to be a joke. When he finishes and everyone roars with laughter he nudges me in a friendly way as if to suggest that I might wish to laugh too.

I have to admit "sorry but I do not speak much German."

"What? You are English?" and then at the top of his voice he shouts "everyone, everyone, listen: we have an English friend with us, so tonight, we only speak English. Does everyone agree?"

The crowd shouts back in unison "yes!"

He brings me into his group of friends and I pass the perfect evening. The next morning, I know that it must have been a good evening ... because I have a small niggle of a headache for my sins.

But that Hamburg friendship in the bar was not a one-off for the town. Every lunchtime, one or other member of the consultancy team comes to my office and insists that they will take me out for lunch. I can never find an excuse that they will accept. 'No you have to come.' Is always the reply.

What I am working on for the company is a technical proposal in French for a regional programme that will manage environmental information in the countries composing the Congo Basin. The programme is going to be financed by the European Union and the guidelines and descriptions they have distributed bear a remarkable resemblance to the project we had developed last year for West Africa! And, of course, that is why the German company has invited me in to do the heavy duty writing.

Time is tight to pull everything together so I work hard and am often the last person to leave the office. But this is typical of most consultants' work ethics.

As I finish writing sections of the proposal, I am passing them to the project lead and he is then handing them up the ladder to the company manager. On my last afternoon, I am asked to go to the manager's office. He has two piles of papers on his desk. The first, much thicker bundle is the almost complete proposal for the project and the second is my three-page CV.

"Everyone in the office is impressed with your work, so thank you. I am trying to fit a team to the work that you are describing in the proposal. I know exactly who I want to propose as the team leader, are you interested?"

Now that's a hard question. One year ago we would have jumped at the chance to go off as a family on another long-term assignment but now that we are all geared up for the move back to the UK, I really do not know how to reply.

He solves the problem for me by saying "but don't reply now. Chat with your wife. Also let me know what you would anticipate as salary and conditions; they would have to fit our budget, of course."

The next morning, my last in the office since I have a 5 pm flight back to Lyon, I arrive early in order to get everything finished. I am concentrating hard and so do not see the time pass but as I start to feel a little peckish, I check my clock and it is already 12.30. I am surprised that no one has come to push me out for lunch.

As I think this, there is a knock on my door and one of the technical ladies tells me that I have to come with her for lunch. However, this is not our usual lunch, because as I leave my office and follow her across to the conference room, I can hear corks start popping. These gorgeous people have laid on a champagne buffet to thank me for my work and to say goodbye. What a nice group of people.

Finally, it is time for us to cross the channel and start the next episode in our lives. The children, now 16 and 12, fly to Heathrow and stay for a week with my sister. This gives us some extra breathing space, and room in the car. We drive over in our *Citroën BX* (one of those cars with the pump-up suspension), loaded with as much luggage as I can fit in. We arrive in Lime Avenue just in time to meet the furniture removal company who had emptied our apartment in the *Point de Jour* and shipped the contents across to the UK. We spend the week unpacking and arranging furniture in our new home.

On the second day, we drive over to the local Morrison's super-market that sits handily near the market, just below my old work-place. We are obliged to do a big shop because we need absolutely everything. On the drive back towards Lime Avenue, I remark to Véro that it is lucky that we have our little driveway because I would hate to have to carry all those bags up the road. Only, on arrival, we no longer have our driveway because some chump has parked in front of it. Impossible to enter and I am obliged to park in the road next to Lime Avenue and indeed carry all those bags to the house.

As most people would be, I am clearly a bit annoyed that our driveway is being squatted and that I have to look for a space in the next road. However, I suspect that the owner of the car – a beaten up Volvo – does not know that we have just moved in. After all, the house has been empty for seven or eight months. So no need to make a big fuss. I write a simple and polite three-line note saying that we have now moved in and are using the driveway, and tuck it under one of the windscreen wipers. The following day I receive a response through the letterbox that runs into four A4 pages of twaddle about how property should be publically owned, how people should not be able to lay claim to sections of the public highway, how they had permission to block the driveway from the previous owner, and on and on. Not worth deigning a response, especially when I see the note writer is a tired and rather seedy 60s hippy that has certainly gone well past his sell-by-date.

In contrast, while washing some of the motorway grime off my car, a dapper-looking older gentleman stops to talk to me, trying out his very basic French. He has seen my car with its left-hand drive and French number plates and assumes that we must be French; which I suppose we are, well sort of anyway. It turns out he is the headmaster of another small private school in Northampton and lives further down our road in the house with a pair of (valuable) Staffordshire dogs on the window sill. On learning that I am a biologist and was once a teacher in another private school in the town, he offers me a job; that I must hastily decline. However, not until I have agreed to help-out and do some part-time and relief teaching for the school; strictly at times that fit around my future professional assignments. A chance encounter that will enable me to earn a little pocket money during my free time between missions.

But before worrying overmuch about work, I have a very serious problem to deal with: finding a football team for '*l'Anglais*'. As mentioned, in France it suffices to turn up regularly and game time is guaranteed. In Northampton, each team I ring either tells me that they are full or they tell me to make an appointment so that my son can be given a trial and, if good enough, he might be accepted into the club. What way is that to treat a football-mad twelve-year-old? And come on! Northampton can hardly crow about their football prowess when the top team in the county are the aptly named 'Cobblers'.

A frustrating afternoon on the phone passes with no success. What to do now? In exasperation I phone the local newspaper, The Chronicle and Echo, and ask to speak with their football 'lead-writer'. Surprisingly, I am put straight through to the journalist, explain the problem and am again surprised when he agrees totally with me. He tells me that he considers it criminal the way that kids' football is now trying to behave like a professional undertaking. He asks for twenty-four hours to see what he can come up with, before calling back and giving me the name and telephone number of a trainer, called Bob, who awaits my call.

David is asked to go for training on Wednesday evening and is likely to get a place on the bench for their Saturday match. Now that, in my mind, is how junior football should be run. The end of the story is that David's team wins through to the Final of the town's under-thirteens tournament, getting beaten in the last match played on a full size pitch at the Cobblers' Sixfields Stadium. Oh, and his nickname in Northampton is now "Frenchie"!

Now we are installed in Lime Avenue, I want to get on with making a success of my consulting business. The first thing I need to do is to get it registered and official as rapidly as possible. Looking into the Northampton telephone directory, I see that the local inland revenue office is in Sheep Street, a long but do-able walk from Lime Avenue. A quick call, rapidly answered (those were the days before 'your call is important to us, nonetheless, we will now put you on hold for the next two hours and play piped music') and an appointment given for later in the afternoon. Ten minutes before the appointed time, I walk into the Sheep Street office, am received with a smile from the receptionist and shown into a side office. An extremely polite gentleman stands up, shakes my hand and tells me that since he just had a little free time, he has already filled in all the forms for me. Would I therefore please check through the details and, if OK, sign. As the meeting with the tax official progresses, I ask about the levels of tax and national insurance I will need to pay.

His response is simple. "Until you earn over £700 per month, you will pay zero income tax while you will only start to pay national insurance when your earnings exceed about £370 per month".

That is very different from the French system where government charges on businesses have to be paid regardless of income or, indeed, lack of it. At the moment, the UK is a popular place for French entrepreneurs to register their businesses led by an association called *'France Libre d'Entreprendre'* that is regularly bringing trainloads of would be business leaders across the Channel to Ashford to set up their businesses' papers.

Thirty minutes later, I am officially registered as a freelance consultant and take my leave from the tax official with a firm handshake and his wishes of good luck with your new venture and don't hesitate to call me if you have any issues.

My little company 'Development Ecology' follows just behind, along with a webpage thanks to Richard Branson's Virgin Empire. The final cog in the organisation is the recommendation from a friend of an accountant who I wish to hire principally to look through my book-keeping and make my end-of-year tax declarations. I get a free one-hour appointment with the freelance lady accountant to kick off our professional relationship. After listening for fifteen minutes while I explain my business and my side of the requirements, she asks three main questions:

"First tell me who looks after your affairs while you are working abroad? You know, things like taking client telephone calls, going to buy office supplies, paying your office utility bills, getting you to and fro the different airports, things like that? Oh, and while I remember, you say that you do considerable English to French translations, is that work checked?"

"Well," I reply, "all those, including checking my translations, are my wife's responsibilities, of course."

"And do you pay her for all that work?" she asks in all seriousness.

"No, but she does have a free-run on my bank account," I say with an embarrassed laugh.

"But you do realise in the UK that husband and wife are now taxed separately so that if you give her a salary, it would be directly deductible from your business profits? And, even better, if we calculate the right threshold monthly payment, she will have neither tax nor national insurance to pay on her salary and you will not have to pay employer's national insurance contributions either."

That first bit of advice – coming in my free one-hour – allows me to save in the region of £7,000 per annum thereafter.

"And my second question is how long are your business trips?"

"Usually, a month or six weeks," I reply.

"OK, I am asking because after an absence of a certain length of time – I have to check exactly how long – your wife would be allowed a tax deductible ticket to come to visit you. Certainly if a mission lasts three months or more this would apply. I'll get back to you on that one. And my third question is where do you work in the house?"

"I have my office in an extension on the side of the kitchen," I explain.

"Is it your dedicated space or does your wife or the children use the space too?"

"No, no. It is uniquely my space. I will not let anyone else into my office," I stress.

"Good then", she replies, "you can bill a pro-rata amount to the business for all household utilities, insurances and council rates."

Well, that little hour saves me an incredible amount of money from future tax bills. And it was all for free!

The other thing I now do is to open a personal pension with the Equitable Life. For my age (shudder, but I am now 45), I can contribute up to twenty-five percent of my income and receive a full tax allowance on that amount. I decide there and then to ensure that I pay into the pension every penny I earn that is taxed at the top rate of 40% so that for every £60 I invest, the UK kindly tops it up to £100. Another brick added to our pension wall.

During the five years that we lived in France, I was never comfortable, never satisfied with the level of work I was able to generate as a freelance consultant. Yes, financially we were able to get by; but many months we were obliged to subsidise my income from savings we had built up during the six years working full-time in Senegal and then The Gambia, as well as from the share investments we had made. Now back in UK, it seems that a light switch has gone on.

First, in late October, the Washington company asks me to undertake a five-week mission to Dakar to work with the USAID office there to critique and analyse the results of three KAP (Knowledge, Attitude and Practice) surveys that USAID has undertaken in the last dozen years or so. On the basis of that first piece of work I then develop a methodology for a follow up survey that will allow results to be compared to the previous work. An interesting study and again, as in Madagascar, the chance to get to know the staff and so put my foot in the door of another USAID mission. Also, not to be sneezed at, a nice payday coming, as it does, immediately prior to Christmas.

But while 1998 is ending, the demand for my time is pleasantly growing. On returning home to Lime Avenue from Dakar, I receive a call from the same Washington company telling me that they have received a rather unusual request from USAID in Madagascar, interesting!

It seems that the company that won the LDI contract and recently mobilised their in-country team, now wishes to set up their

Monitoring and Evaluation system for the project and get their staff trained in using it. The M&E consultant whom they had nominated in their original proposal is no longer available, and the company is stuck for an experienced replacement. They had turned to the Madagascar office of USAID for suggestions and, in looking through relevant CVs in the proposals of failed bidders, came up with mine. Good fortune smiles.

However, in the world of consulting at this time, consultants are pushed to sign 'letters of exclusivity' to a single company before the company will include them in their bids. I had done this for LDI and such exclusivity means that my company, despite losing the bid, must wave their exclusivity before I can be approached by a competitor. This they are prepared to do but, in turn, they need my approval before they can give a definitive 'yes' to their waver; my approval is quickly given!

A perfect start to my 1999 work calendar, a six-week trip back to beautiful Madagascar to start as early in the New Year as possible. However, buses never come along alone. As I agree the mission to work on LDI, an old American friend called Chris Kopp, from Senegal days, calls me from Arkansas.

"Hey Malcolm, are you free to take an assignment early in the New Year?" he asks.

"I'm blocked until late-February on a mission with LDI in Madagascar but I'm free after that," I reply.

"Even better because we need you to start off the work in Madagascar and then go on to Mozambique, Uganda and Malawi. There will be a total of a month's work for us. Can you start our mission immediately you finish the LDI stuff?"

"Well, the timing fits so can you send me the terms of reference and, once I've looked through them, I'll get back to you?" I reply.

"I've just sent you an email with all the details. Thanks buddy, speak soon!"

Now I need to move quickly because once I leave the UK in two weeks' time, I will have trouble in getting visas. Luckily, I can get the Malgache visa on arrival while, as a Brit, I do not need a visa for entry to Uganda or Malawi (or Kenya where I will be transiting twice) but I do need one for Mozambique. Luckily, my old US company had always insisted that I use an official visa service company, based in Paris, and so with that contact, I only have to pay and then wait for a few days to receive my passport and new visa back in the post.

I arrive back in beautiful Tana and have opted this time to stay at the Hotel Ibis, just around the corner from the Colbert. The Ibis is perhaps not as luxurious as the Colbert but it is considerably less expensive; and, if I wish, I can still take my breakfast each morning in the Colbert's patisserie! Opposite the Ibis is a bar/restaurant/ pizzeria where the dish of the day is reasonably priced and varied. This becomes my usual evening hangout and, after the first two or three visits, the staff get to know me and treat me as one of their regulars. This results in a much more rapid service than the tourists and a corner table away from the hustle and bustle of the bar.

Next to the restaurant is a taxi rank. I quickly get 'adopted' by Pascal, a Malgache taxi driver who owns a very beaten up *deux chevaux* (a Citroen 2 CV). While my hotel is close to the top of a hill, the LDI office is even further up the next one, and the road to it is very steep. I appreciate Pascal's taxi getting me to work in the morning, and he is always at the taxi rank waiting for me at 8.30 am each day.

In order to develop a sound and do-able M&E system, the M&E consultant must become very familiar with all the documentation that describes the ambitions, activities and objectives of a project. I spend my first few days either wading through piles of documents or devoting considerable time with each discipline leader to learn as much as possible about their activities. I have the good fortune to be working with a gifted local counterpart who helps me enormously to cut corners in understanding LDI's operations.

The team leader is a pleasant and almost frighteningly intelligent Haitian gentleman. He always seems to be extraordinarily busy while at the same time available and approachable; a natural leader, and I can see why his team won the contract.

M&E is both a science and an art. It is built around a careful definition of what is or are the final objective(s) of the project. These might be, for example, to see project participants increase their annual incomes by 100% and so escape from an 'extreme poverty' definition. And, at the same time, to see an improvement in the natural resources managed by these same participants. (Participants were once erroneously called 'beneficiaries' but this suggests a passive, hands-out involvement, which is certainly not true if most projects are to succeed).

Taking this example a little further, a relatively simple way to increase incomes rapidly might be to chop down the forest and sell the timber, then plant crops on the denuded soil. However, that would clearly be disastrous for the natural resources and then, one has to ask the question 'are those increases in incomes sustainable?' Obviously, no sound project would consider going down that route. Our mythical project would therefore have to come up with a very different approach, perhaps by stimulating ecotourism or sustainably managing the forest's natural resources or something similar.

The next issue for the M&E consultant to consider, is how does one measure success in those two final objectives? Measuring income is doable but difficult, especially in such non-regulated economies where cash is king and informal exchange, favours, loans and debts are common; and record keeping non-existent. Also hard to measure are improvements in natural resources. Since measuring these two objectives is very difficult, how *does* one show that project activities are achieving their aims? The secret is to use *indicators* that, well, 'indicate' that desired changes are occurring. If, following the project's involvement, a village group starts to send girls over eleven to school while previously they did not, or families buy bicycles or hand carts, or a village committee decides to build a rice storage facility, could these 'indicate' that incomes are increasing? Similarly, to show improvements in natural resources, indicators such as increasing numbers of bird species in the forest or number of tree saplings growing per hectare might be considered a useful indication. Selecting suitable and robust indicators is where the 'art' side of M&E comes in, and requires much experience of what works and what does not.

The science side is how one can physically measure change and ensure the changes being seen are significantly better than at the start point, or baseline and, when possible, better than in control groups too. Here a knowledge of sampling of populations and then of statistics are essential ... and this harks back to my previous career in lecturing and research.

Once we are happy with the final objectives and their indicators, we then work backwards to determine intermediary steps between the final objectives and the starting point where basically no activities have yet begun.

For a simple example, imagine that the final objective is to see an agrarian population doubling its millet production in an arid environment. In order to achieve an increase in production, farmers might need to learn new techniques and to farm an improved, drought resistant millet variety. They might therefore reasonably need specialised training in cultivating this new variety. Thus a simple starting indicator might be 'the number of farmers receiving the training'. But then, once trained, the question has to be asked 'will they make use of the new practices or stay with their old methods?' After all, farmers across the world are incredibly conservative, and none more so than in developing economies. 'Percentage of farmers applying the new techniques' might therefore be a more suitable indicator that shows application of the training received.

Measuring production itself (remembering that our mythical project is looking to double production) is relatively easy in modern agriculture but a little more difficult in less advanced agrarian systems where kilograms or tons might not be typical units but rather baskets, boxes or cups. The M&E specialist always needs to be adaptable!

My counterpart and I complete our work for LDI within the original timeframe and together we make a presentation of the proposed system to relevant project staff as well as to interested members of USAID and other projects in the USAID natural resources portfolio in Madagascar.

My adrenaline level is high, as it always is for presentations and other times of stress. But this is how I prefer to be. My mind is sharper and concentrated; one never knows if difficult questions might be asked. But this audience is receptive, polite and, above all, interested in what we are proposing. The presentation, mostly in PowerPoint, is detailed and lasts for over an hour. Then we open up for questions which we answer with relative ease.

The meeting is drawing to a close, when I partially hear, partially lip-read an American from another project say to his colleague "you now, we could do with some of that."

As I leave the presentation space to mingle with the audience and chat further, the two members of the other project come across to me and say "can you find time to come and design our M&E system too?"

And from across the room, the team leader of my actual project calls out laughingly "hey you guys, he has to come back for us first."

Well, what a nice situation to find myself in. I get the heads of the two projects together and say "I am busy from now until late-March, so why do you two not get together to design a trip that will involve me working first for one and then the other. That way you can save on an expensive air ticket."

And that is what they do. I am expected back after Easter, first for LDI to take my work to the next level followed by an equal amount of time for another new project called Miray (Malgache for 'togetherness') to carry out similar work to that I have just presented.

My little consulting business 'Development Ecology' is really beginning to tick since our move to the UK!

Yesterday I was an 'Expert in Monitoring and Evaluation' for LDI and today I am an 'Expert in Ecological Monitoring' for an international group based in Little Rock, Arkansas. For the next week I am working alone in Madagascar and then moving on to Uganda, via Kenya, where I will meet up with another consultant before we travel together to continue the work in Malawi. I have just heard that our trip to Mozambique has been cancelled as the country is considered unsafe. Periodic civil wars seem to haunt that poor country since its independence from Portugal.

Our work on this new assignment is to determine the success of USAID Missions in the countries to be visited in following the guidelines of so-called 'Environmental Monitoring, Evaluation, and Mitigation Plans'. Basically, we need to determine whether the donor country offices have correctly developed these EMEMP (as they are called) and are they applying them, especially when things start to go wrong? A new and interesting area of work for me.

As I sit down to go through the relevant documents before meeting with the USAID personnel in charge of Madagascar's EMEMP, I receive a visit from the office messenger of LDI who has been trying to get my visa extended for an extra couple of weeks.

He hands me an official looking envelope and inside is a letter from the Ministry telling me that they are unable to affix a visa to my passport because it has no more completely empty pages. Why the small visa stamp cannot be affixed to one of the pages where only a fraction of the page is used, I do not know. It is just like that. And, the letter goes on to tell me that since my visa cannot be extended, in forty-eight hours I will become illegal and forbidden to leave the country!

Ouch, what to do? Since I have a further week or so in Madagascar for the EMEMP work, I consider that there *should* be enough time for the British Embassy to get me a new passport. I get a lift over to the embassy and am seen straight away by the receptionist.

But not good news "sorry sir but this embassy does not issue new passports, we have to send the papers back to London and that takes at least two weeks." Ouch again.

Just as I am wondering what to do next, I hear someone behind me say "right face, wrong country. What are you doing here?"

I turn round and find myself face-to-face with two old friends from Senegal days, husband and wife.

"And, more to the point, what are you doing here," I ask in reply.

"Bob is the new Ambassador; didn't you know?"

Well I did not but this is a gift from heaven. We move through to his office and I lay out my dilemma. He explains that it is true that new passports have to be obtained from London and there is a considerable delay but what he can do is to provide me with a

'Laissez-Passer' which will enable me officially to leave Madagascar. Since I have some passport photos with me, the laissez-passer will only take an hour to be produced.

That evening, back in my hotel room, I am cursing the now redundant Mozambique visa that is in the form of a sticky label attached to a whole page of my passport. If I had not gotten that visa, I would not have this dilemma. I flick open my passport and notice that the sticky label is actually not very sticky. Indeed, it is starting to peel off the page, so much so that if I was a less honest operator, I could hold the page up to the steam from my little travel kettle and the label would likely peel off easily ...

My EMEMP work over in Madagascar, I go to Ivato Airport and take the Kenya Airlines flight to Nairobi leaving Madagascar using the laissez-passer. In Nairobi, I hand over my passport and ask if the immigration service could put their entry stamp on a partially used page. The Kenyans being far less gourmand for passport space than the Malgache affix their entry stamp to a page that already has several stamps from other countries.

I travel in a bus to Nairobi along the airport road alongside which runs a game reserve. Just like that I spot a rhino browsing the desiccated grass like a contented cow! The bus drops me at the Inter-continental Hotel where I am to spend two nights before flying to Entebbe Airport and from there take a taxi to Kampala. Again the Ugandans generously reuse an old page in the passport.

I meet up with my new colleague and we spend four days visiting projects and interviewing project personnel and senior members of the donors in Kampala. Some of them are most certainly not happy to see us, and we soon discover why. One of their major projects is to provide support to growers of roses and off-season vegetables (like green beans) in a multitude of greenhouses built alongside Lake Victoria. We immediately notice that there is no provision to prevent herbicides and fertilisers from the greenhouses running into this most beautiful lake. A black mark on that activity and one that we describe in considerable detail in our report.

The next flight is to Lilongwe in Malawi via Nairobi. Even at this time, Kenya Airways possesses a good fleet of planes and its flights serve much of Eastern Africa. A taxi from Lilongwe airport takes us to a lovely bungalow hotel with individual rooms set in a tropical garden. Beautiful and a shame that I do not have more time to explore this country because Lake Malawi has an incredible number of rare endemic species; perhaps another time.

Our work here is to analyse the USAID mission's work – and respect of its EMEMP – of a 'Burley' tobacco support project. Although we dig hard and speak on-the-record as well as off- to staff and participants in the project, we can uncover nothing untoward. The project itself passes muster despite my loathing of everything tobacco!

On arrival in the country, and still feeling a little nervous about my passport, I take an appointment at the British High Commission in Lilongwe and ask if they could renew my passport during the five days I am in the town. The young man who is dealing with my issue flicks through my passport and notes that I have visited a lot of African countries in the past few years, I calculate over a dozen or so.

"But I don't see a stamp for my country of origin," he notes.

"You mean Nigeria?" I ask.

"Yes, but how did you know my origins are in that country?" he queries.

"I'll do even better, you originally came from Ibo country in the South, perhaps from Ife or even further East. The partial giveaway is your name but also your physiognomy."

"Oh my God. Do you know that part of the world?"

"Well yes," I reply, "I taught in the Department of Biology at the University of Calabar for four years. I left in 1983. There were plenty of Lagos stamps in my old passport!"

He laughs and says "my big sister was a student in Calabar at the same time. What a small world. But now you are here and you need us to express-renew your passport. Normally, we ask a minimum of two weeks, but let me see what I can do. Hold on a moment, I need to speak to the Consul."

I am given my new, ten-year passport the day before I am due to fly out of the country and return to France.

The children are soon on Easter holidays and so Véro asks her parents if they might fly out to Lyon and stay with them in Crémieu for two or three days while we drive a loaded BX down from Northampton.

We take the Chunnel to Calais and then are straight on to the almost empty motorway, direction Reims (pronounced 'Rance' with a 'rolled R' not 'Reems' with a 'soft R', as the Brits insist!). We are staying the night in the centre of Reims, the capital of champagne country, at the little Hotel du Nord. While the hotel is only able to scrape up a couple of stars, it is next to a public underground car-park that locks during the night and where we consider our laden car will be safe. More importantly, the hotel is only a couple of minutes' walk from the restaurant 'Chez-Flo'. Yes, we chose the town and the hotel because of a restaurant, what decadence the Marks clan has fallen into!

Chez-Flo is a seafood restaurant and is housed in a beautiful art-deco building. This evening, being warm and dry, we sit outside on the terrace while the waiter brings us a three-layered nested dish covered in oysters, mussels, whelks, shrimps, prawns and a dressed crab, all nestled into beds of crushed ice with seaweed for decoration.

To accompany the feast, we are served a dry white house wine that is the perfect companion to the seafood.

Despite it being only late-March, the restaurant and its terrace are full. As Véro and I pick and choose from the different layers of seafood, we chat, as we always chat, switching easily from English to French and back again.

After a few moments of hesitation, the elderly French occupants of the table next to us speak up. "We do not mean to be rude but we cannot help noticing how you two speak with such fluency in both French and English. Monsieur, your English is impeccable, and Madame, you hardly have an accent when you speak in French. How is that possible?"

We laugh out loud, and then excuse ourselves for laughing, as Véro explains "well that's easy because I *am* French and my husband *is* English."

"Oh goodness, we thought it was the other way around." And we all laugh together because indeed our proficiency in the other's language is pleasing ... but neither of us can ever really lose our accents; that should always be a giveaway. In contrast, both of our kids can switch backwards and forwards between French and English and no one can determine which is their maternal language (because in fact, it is both).

We leave Reims the following morning, direction Troyes and then towards Dijon (this more easterly route in France allows us to avoid the traffic jams around Paris) and we are soon heading down the motorway towards Macon and then Lyon. But, rather than going through the city and have to pass through the infamous *Tunnel de Fourvière* and its traffic jams, as we were once obliged to do, we now switch on to the '*Rocard Est*'. This road is a new addition to France's impressive motorway grid, and takes us towards Lyon's Satolas Airport and from there we switch on to the smaller roads to Crémieu.

The Easter holidays are graced by absolutely beautiful weather with brilliant sunshine. Indeed, it is so warm and clear during the daytime that I am able to dig the back garden of 'The Little House' (our annex) and plant the seed potatoes that will provide the crop for us to eat this coming summer. But when the sun sets, come the evening, the temperature drops sufficiently that I light our antique wood burning stove; still fuelling it with some of the old poplar floorboards that I had ripped up and sawn to length several years previously. We sit around the glow contentedly reading (Mélanie and Véro) or noisily playing draughts and chess (David and me).

This vacation is important to us two boys. In our small field, down the lane from our house, we had an old walnut tree that must have sprouted from a nut accidentally dropped by a thieving crow many years in the past. Our tree was long, thin and bent over at an angle as it tried to find a way to the light through the overtopping poplar trees. While the tree always produced bountiful nuts, we were never able to collect a single one that did not have a resident maggot. The tree had remained safe simply due to our lack of time to chop it down. Fully two years ago we received a knock on the door and a gentleman named 'M. Carrotte' (I promise that was his name!) pronounced himself a purchaser of trees. He offered us £50 for our walnut tree. Being a little suspicious, we took his card and said we would call him back. Basically, we forgot until last summer, when he came back to the door and upped his price to £100 plus a bottled of '*manicle*' (a rare white wine that is only grown on a few hectares of soil in our Bugey region). We shook hands on the deal and he handed over the £100, promising to cut the tree down in the winter.

When we arrive back to Cordon, the tree is gone. In fact, where the tree had been, is now a large hole. While the wood of walnut trees is highly prized in the furniture trade, the really valuable part of its wood is where the trunk morphs into the roots, and the wood-cutter had dug into the soil to get as much of this precious wood as possible. But the hole is not an issue because we want to replant with a grafted walnut tree and the hole saves considerable digging.

What I had not expected is that we have been left with the entire canopy. It sits in a single massive and tanged lump on a neighbouring piece of land. On the bright side, there is sufficient wood, branches and twigs to provide several years of fuel for our stove. On the dark side, the ruddy thing needs to be cut up.

As we sit around the stove after dinner sipping the *manicle*, and it really is a very good wine, I say to Véro that I will have to tackle that chore before we make our way back to the UK.

David is listening to the conversation and chips in "dad, I am thirteen now, and you always promised that you would teach me to use the chainsaw when I became a teenager."

And he is right, I did. With both our children we have always tried to teach them how to use home appliances safely and with us monitoring them. The kids had both learnt to use hammers, a drill and then a jig-saw by the time they were ten. But a chainsaw is a little more dangerous. The one I have is electric, not petrol, so not particularly powerful but still very dangerous, in fact lethal, in careless hands.

The following morning, David runs our sturdy extension lead from the house down to the canopy and I carry the chainsaw, oil and a spare chain. As we walk away from the house 'be careful' rings out from a nervous mum!

But nothing to worry about, David wants to learn and listens carefully to everything I tell him. We have agreed that only I will be sawing the thickest logs while his responsibility will be the smaller ones. Long story short, we work together all that day and all the next, still in beautiful early-year sunshine, and reduce the canopy to a pile of suitable sized logs and piles of kindling wood. Many wheelbarrow loads later, and all is stacked away to dry for two years on one side of our wood store. A job well done and a good father-son experience. While we are working hard, the ladies have gone on to the far side of the ruined chateau that overtops our little village and picked armfuls of tiny wild daffodils.

The history of the ruined chateau in Cordon is well known and was told to me one day by our Mayor. Previously I had imagined that it must have been destroyed in the Revolution, but I was wrong.

Notre Maire is very interested in the history of our commune where he has been part of the local council for decades. He explains that the Chateau de Cordon was actually destroyed by the "*Seigneur de Morestel* à cause d'*une histoire de cul.*" I will leave out the translation!

But what is interesting is that the local residents at the time the chateau was destroyed, recycled the stones, many beautifully carved and shaped, as well as some of the large timber beams and used them to build or to extend some of the older houses in the village, including our own. I am told that our '*fenêtre à meneaux*' certainly originated from the chateau as it is far too elegant to have been purchased by the peasant farmer who would have built our house sometime towards the end of the eighteenth century.

The little wild daffodils brighten our home for the next two weeks until it is time to turn off the electrics and the water, close the shutters, lock the doors, bid our village friends farewell and trek back to Northampton.

We always start the drive back to UK at around five in the morning. That way everyone can sleep, except me of course. For the next three or four hours I drive in pleasant silence on an almost empty motorway, passing around Lyon, going past Macon and reaching the motorway services just before Dijon. Breakfast time coincides with a slow waking of the sleeping trio. After eating, Véro takes the wheel while I snooze a little in the passenger seat.

We always break our trip somewhere in the North of France, trying to visit a different area each time. However, a couple of years ago we found a B&B close to Calais run by a farmer's wife and, by the children's popular request, we now make a habit of staying there.

I arrive back in Tana for my fourth, then to be followed by my fifth, mission in Madagascar. All that in little more than a year. On my first day back in the LDI office, I meet up with Pierre, a Frenchman who lives in Tana with his wife and works as a business development consultant for LDI among other projects. Pierre and I hit it off immediately and he invites me back to his home for Sunday lunch. That is when the teasing starts!

As his wife prepares lunch, she shoos us out of the kitchen and tells Pierre "go and show Malcolm your collection."

Pierre takes me to the attic of their home and, when he turns on the lights, I cannot believe my eyes. He has a veritable treasure trove hidden in the loft. Masses and masses of large lumps of rock sitting on thick cardboard cover almost the entire floor surface and shine in innumerable colours under the bright lights of the attic. Pierre is an inveterate collector of precious and semi-precious stones. And that is where the teasing starts for the name 'Pierre' means, of course, a stone or a rock! Just as Christ told his disciple Peter: 'Peter (Pierre), you are the rock on which I will build my church'.

After the teasing and the friendly rebuffs, I ask Pierre the obvious question "how will you get all these rocks back to France when you leave Tana?"

"In my container of course." I never did learn if he succeeded!

After a delightful and long lunch, as the French always seem able to provide, we relax and chat in the sitting room. Our chatting is disturbed by the ringing of the doorbell and, on opening, Pierre invites in a young Malgache guy.

"One of my rock suppliers" he says with a smile.

The young man draws an A5 envelope from his briefcase and pours the contents on to a sheet of newspaper.

"Garnets" confirms Pierre "they are nice sizes but I already have plenty of them in my collection, so no thanks."

"Pierre, please, I am short of money and only want five francs (50p) for the lot," the young man replies.

"I'll take them if you do not want them Pierre," I hear myself saying. And like that I become an enthusiastic rock collector but not in the same sense as Pierre but rather for adorning my ladies back in France with jewels!

The following weekend Pierre offers to take me to Andravoa-hangy Market, an artisanal market, mostly known for two things: beautiful hand-sewn tablecloths and napkins and ... semi- and precious stones. I purchase two tablecloth sets, one for Véro and the other for Mic, my mother-in-law, while for the kids I buy different solitaire games on palisander wood bases played with round semi-precious stones. Everything seems so cheap. I also look at some cut sapphires that could be made into rings but Pierre tells me that they are too expensive and better that I take you another time to a jewellery shop I know.

Although I am getting to know the town well, I have been a little disappointed not to have seen some of the countryside outside of the capital. All that changes.

As I am now setting up the data collection system for LDI, I need to visit the project's three sites near to regional capitals to ensure that my data collection suggestions are practicable in the field. The first site to visit is in the town of Moramanga, just over a hundred kilometres from Tana. A trip of a little over three hours in the project vehicle that takes us off the high plateau where Tana sits lording over Madagascar and down towards the eastern coast. The country-side on the drive down is beautiful and reminds me so much of the Alps or Highland Scotland with marshy vegetation composed of little ferns, mosses and insectivorous plants watered by a multitude of small streams and waterfalls. As we drive, I cannot help thinking that Véro would love the oldie-worldie feel of Tana and the beautiful countryside outside of the capital as much as me. And an idea begins to hatch as my mind wanders during the long drive.

My thoughts are as follows: I am here for the rest of April and almost the entire months of May and June. Véro's birthday is in May and mine in June, meaning that we will not be together for either of them. Our twenty-second wedding anniversary (how time flies) is on 2nd July. Why do I not arrange a surprise trip for Véro to Madagascar to share my pleasure in being in the country and to celebrate our wedding anniversary here? I still have four or five towns to visit during my work with LDI and *Miray*, providing me with ample opportunity to put some finer details on my surprise holiday for my lovely wife.

We arrive in Moramanga, a small town apparently named after the mangoes for which it is famous and pass along the main street where I spot one hotel, *La Veille Poste* (the old post office) that looks quaint and cosy, and then a few hundred metres down the road, a second hotel that resembles a block of cement. But we stop at neither, continuing through the town and back into the country-side. I ask the obvious question about where we will be staying and my national counterpart suggests mysteriously that I should wait and see.

I eventually spot a sign on the main road indicating a turning for the Andasibe Lemur Park: wildlife reserve, lodge and restaurant. My counterpart's smile tells me that I am going to enjoy this spot. We drive through a tropical forest composed purely of Malgache species, not a eucalyptus in sight, and pull into the reception area. The project has forward booked two bungalows for us plus a room for the driver. As we take our keys, I am told that I am going to adore the accommodation. And she is dead right. My bungalow is a beautiful Indonesian-style building, constructed on a slope and raised at the front with an enormous terrace looking over the forest.

We meet at the lodge restaurant at 7.30 pm for a simple but tasty meal of rice, Malgache sausages and '*brède mafana*' (a rather astringent vegetable) followed by sweet mango, all accompanied by a bottle of 'Three-Horses' beer. By 9 pm, my counterpart excuses herself for the night. Since we have our first meeting with the American head of the Moramanga office, and his team at 9.00 am, I suggest that we meet up for breakfast at 7.30 am. She laughs and says simply that I expect I will see you at about 5.30 in the morning!

And her prediction is spot on for in the Andasibe Lemur Park there is absolutely no need for a mechanical alarm clock; Mother Nature provides the perfect one: The Indri Lemur, the largest of the lemurs and the most musical. On this, my first morning in the reserve, the Indri choir starts to sing just before the sun begins to rise across the Eastern horizon. 'Johnny Africa', in his travel journal to the park, describes my alarm call as 'It is the voice that makes this lemur extra-special: while other lemurs grunt or swear, the indri sings. It is an eerie, wailing sound – a cross between whale song and a siren – and it carries for up to 3 km as troops call to each other across the forest.'

For me, this is a moment that I would not have missed; despite the admittedly very early morning concert. Another spot to be included in Véro's holiday itinerary.

On the drive back to Tana after a few pleasant days working with the local team, I remark that it is sad to see that her country has planted so much of the hilly land in Madagascar with eucalyptus forests. I receive a very rude retort, followed by a laugh.

"It wasn't us," she tells me, "it was you wretched French that chopped down the native forests and planted the eucalyptus so that the quick growing wood could be used to power your steam trains."

I hastily remind that I am English, but the colonial French did do untold damage with the introduction of the Australian eucalyptus. A nature walk under a eucalyptus canopy in Madagascar turns up only a handful of plant and animal species. The same walk in a native forest reveals several hundred. The stupidity or should I say cupidity of man?

Our next trip requires a plane flight from Tana Ivato to Mahjanga in the northwest of the country. We take what must be the oldest Boeing 777 in the world still flying. Although the plane boasts over three hundred seats, it can only drum up around twenty passengers for the trip. Take off occurs safely but the lack of doors on the overhead lockers means that it is far safer to keep our computer bags and carry-ons parked on nearby empty seats. After ninety minutes of flight we begin to circle over the Betsiboka River and I am astonished to see that the water is red, almost blood red. As if reading my mind, I am told that the colour is caused by laterite soil washed down by monsoon rains from the floor of illegally felled forests in the uplands. I realise that Madagascar is suffering a similar fate to the Amazon and Congo basins as well as that of Java in Indonesia. Greed is getting the better of good ecological sense.

Our final trip is by road from Tana to the area around the little central/southern town of Fianarantsao, a distance of around three hundred kilometres. I am doubly happy to be making this trip because the Fiana office is run by Mark, an old American friend from Senegal days. He is in Fiana with his wife, a sociologist, that I had also met a couple of times in Senegal.

Just after lunch on my second day of work in the office, it is proposed that we should go later that afternoon to meet representatives of the village communities that manage the world-famous Ranomafana National Park. This proves to be an incredible learning experience for me. I see at first-hand how conservation can be assured if the local populations are given an economic interest in its management. In this case, the locals are charged with policing the reserve to ensure that poaching and tree felling does not occur and, if it does, a few nights in the local police station is a useful deterrent. And in return they have been helped to set up tourist attractions like eco-lodges, restaurants, guided tours of the forest and so on. We are going to support the economic side by taking a night tour of the reserve and, once the couple of hours' walk is over, we will eat and share a few beers in one of the local-run restaurants.

Our guide speaks passable French and so we follow him along trails lit by the small head torches we have been given. These are mostly to stop us twisting an ankle on fallen trunks or partially buried stones rather than to find our way. We have total confidence in the guide and remember that the largest carnivores in the Malgache forests is the little Civet cat and the mongoose-like 'fossa' and there are no poisonous snakes or spiders to step on. So we have little to be worried about ... apart from the leeches. Yes, leeches. And just as we have all seen in films, they do silently bite and then puff up with the blood they suck from the skin capillaries; at least mine do. At a suitable moment, I show the guide that I have two leeches attached to my left forearm and another on my right shin. As all film buffs, I naively imagine that the guide would take the cigarette that he keeps in the corner of his mouth and touch it to the hind region of the leech (after all that is how it is done in the films). But not in the least, he simply scrapes his nail over my skin, taking the leeches with it. Oh well, I suppose we should not believe everything we see in films!

At a point in the forest that the guide knows well, we stop, turn off our lights and wait and listen in the pitch black. Very soon he indicates a pair of sparkling eyes and then another. These belong to the Golden Bamboo Lemur, a critically endangered species – but we are lucky because in this area we see and hear several of them, some carrying young. One of the French tourists in our group begins to snap off photos using a flash, and is soon corrected by the guide who explains that these lemurs, being nocturnal, have very light-sensitive retinas.

Our species of lemur is interesting, and a bit of an enigma, because it eats only young shoots of bamboo with an almost exclusive preference for the Giant Bamboo. And what is interesting is that its preferred bamboo contains concentrated doses of cyanide and the quantity of shoots eaten in a day by an adult golden lemur – about half a kilo – would prove lethal to almost any other species of mammal.

My amazing trip across the country is over and we have returned to Tana to complete my report and the training of the staff who will be responsible for data collection.

That evening at the hotel, still the Ibis, I call home to the UK and get Mélanie and David on the line while Véro has gone to have tea with Diane; perfect. I explain to the kids that I want to give their mum a surprise anniversary present comprising a trip to Madagascar, and they immediately love the idea and will take responsibility for the UK side of the planning. Mélanie is in charge of booking the flight on line with Air France while David's responsibility is to do his best to keep it all a secret. They will hand the tickets to their mum on her birthday.

Yesterday I was working for LDI and today I am starting my new assignment with Miray; a seamless transfer of my services. The Miray team is composed of three very well-known international NGOs. The lead is offered by PACT and the technical support comes from the World Wildlife Fund and Conservation International. What a star-studded ecological world I have proudly entered.

My work takes a similar path to that I have already undertaken with LDI and so progress is considerably faster; luckily for me because the three NGOs require me to develop the M&E system, define data collection methods and train the field team, all within the current trip. Very hard going but doable if I work through many evenings.

As a consultant, one has to forget eight-hour days while the thirty-five-hour week of the Hooray-Socialists back in France ... well, that is completed in the first three days of the week! But the work is interesting and enjoyable and I push on as rapidly as possible.

One evening, I receive a message from a Belgian friend. He works for Jorgen's company (of Barracuda fishing in The Gambia fame) and since he is in Tana for a few days' work he asks to meet up with me for dinner. He takes me to a *real* Chinese restaurant that is a short distance from Tana's main railway station. The restaurant is owned by an elderly Chinese couple that he knows very well. The couple apparently also own a rather seedy hotel down the hill from the Ibis. My friend loves that hotel and always stays there so I do not tell him my thoughts! But seedy is most certainly not the way to describe their restaurant. It is absolutely superb. The food is delicious, really varied, perfectly cooked and the service is impeccable – not surprising really since we are guests of the Chinese couple who sit across the table from us.

As the meal progresses through the fourth or fifth round of dishes, my friend asks "are you free to do some work for us this autumn?"

"Yes, at the moment. What do you have in mind?" I reply.

"We are bidding on an upcoming project in the Ministry of Forestry, funded by the World Bank. It's to develop a forestry information and communications system for Madagascar. Should be right up your alley. The Boss wants you to work with us. We also want you to help us develop our proposal. Can you do that too, in the next couple of weeks?" he asks.

"Obviously while I am working for my current project, I cannot really provide much time to you, unless you are happy if I just work on Sundays while I'm here?"

After my friend laughs and teases me about the perils of missing Sunday Mass, I explain that on USAID projects we cannot bill for Sundays even if they are worked; as they often are. So I can quite legitimately use my Sundays as I wish.

The German company does bid on the project, and we win the contract. I am now booked to come back yet again to Madagascar as the team leader for the work in the autumn. This year will have been pretty much dedicated to this lovely island.

Work for Miray is as interesting and as friendly as it has been with LDI. We also need to travel so that I can see the type of work they are doing and develop their M&E system based on the field reality. This time we are going to the very south of the island, a considerable distance and the roads are not brilliant. To save time, we take a flight from Tana to Fianarantsao and are picked up at the airport by a project vehicle for the long drive south.

After several hours on the road we enter a zone, rather reminiscent of the Sahel in West Africa with sparse trees and bushes in a parkland but considerably greener. I am told that this is the Isalo National Park. The vegetation has far fewer trees than I have seen further north replaced by wide rolling expanses of grassy plains. As we drive down a straight deserted road, I can see something flying through the air, seemingly coming out of several holes by the roadside.

"What is that I see flying through the air?" I ask.

"Dirt" is the one-word response from my counterpart.

I ask the driver to pull over so I can take a look. And indeed it is earth that is being shovelled up and out of a line of holes. At the bottom of each hole stands a Malgache complete with shovel.

"I don't understand, what are they doing?" I query.

"Looking for sapphires" comes the response. "If only small holes are dug, the government closes its eyes but will not allow heavy excavation equipment into the national parks."

"It's a shame we are not staying closer to here as I would love to buy a couple of uncut sapphires to give to my two ladies." I get teased no end about being greedy and having two ladies!

In the late afternoon we arrive at our destination for the night, the town of Ambovombe in the far south of the country and go to a hotel that the team knows well. My Malgache colleagues excuse themselves and go straight to their rooms for a delayed siesta while I go to the bar cum restaurant for a delayed cup of tea.

On entering the bar, I notice three obviously African, rather than Malgache, occupants and they look to me like the Peul of Senegal or thereabouts. Being a nosey character, I listen, and hear them speaking Wolof. I call out *nan-ga-def* (how are you?) and receive some astonished looks. They come over to my table, shake hands and laugh as I answer their question of 'do you speak Wolof' with *tutti-rek* (a little bit). These three young guys tell me that one is Senegalese, one Gambian and the third, a rather shy man, is from Guinea-Conakry. They are also – surprisingly – sapphire traders, buying from the Malgache artisanal miners and selling on to large-scale purchasers, most apparently hailing from Thailand (now my readers will know where the stones sold around Bangkok actually come from!).

I go 'fishing' and mention that I am hoping to buy a couple of sapphires for my wife and daughter but none offers any possibilities, a shame.

The next morning, I take breakfast early before my Malgache colleagues have come to the restaurant. At a table across the room from me sits the Gambian. It looks like his two colleagues are not early birds either. Soon after I am served my breakfast, I spot a very short man – the Malgache are generally not very tall – but this chap is smaller than usual. He walks over to the Gambian and hands him a folded envelope. The Gambian tips the contents on to the table cloth and pushes around the stones, for they are uncut sapphires. I hear him tell the miner that the stones are rubbish, mostly dust, and only worth $20. The miner tries to argue but he cannot budge the Gambian. Finally, he holds out his hand and accepts the proffered $20 bill.

"*Toubab, kai*" the Gambian instructs me to come over to his table and look at his purchases.

I can now see that there are four uncut sapphires, all pink and each about the size of the top of my little finger. There are also a number of very small stones that are little larger than fat grains of sand.

I pick up the four larger stones and hold them up to the light (I have seen people do this to check on potential fissures or impurities in the stones) and place one to the side.

"Here's $5" I say to my new friend offering him a brand new US banknote.

"*Dedit,*" he declines, "it's worth a lot more than that."

"What," I feign shock, "you just told the miner that his stones were rubbish and now you tell me that the stone I have chosen is valuable. Am I correct? Because if so, either you did not tell the miner the truth or you are trying to cheat me!" we burst out laughing together.

"Take it my friend," he replies "you are too clever for me this early in the morning! It will make a nice ring for your wife."

Later in the morning as we are checking out of the hotel, the Senegalese trader spots me and comes over to say goodbye.

"I hear you bought a nice stone from my Gambian friend" he says

"Yes, I had hoped to get another for my daughter. Perhaps I will get one in Tana."

"Show me the stone." He takes it and holds it up to the light and purrs with satisfaction "and how much did you pay?"

I tell him, he laughs and takes from his pocket a small cloth sac closed with a drawstring. He tips out four blue sapphires into his hand and makes me a challenge:

"If you can tell me which is the best of these four stones, I will give it to you, *gratis*. If, on the other hand, you cannot pick the best one, you pay me $5 for the one you choose. Is it a deal?"

"Sure" I say holding the four stones up to the light before saying "I think this one is the best."

"*Cadeau mon ami*" he replies, shaking my right hand in farewell and leaving the sapphire gift in my left.

So I have the two stones I was hoping to find. A rare pink sapphire for Véro and a beautiful deep blue for Mélanie.

Back in Tana, Pierre gives me a lesson in sapphires. As he tells me, most people believe that sapphires are blue and are surprised to know that they exist in a wide range of colours. The base of all sapphires is the compound 'corundum' while the different colour possibilities are caused by small amounts of other elements as 'impurities' within the corundum.

On the first occasion possible, Pierre takes me to his favourite jewellery shop, run by a pleasant, middle-aged Malgache lady. I show her my two uncut sapphires and, after placing them on a light table, she declares them 'very nice'. She tells me that her stone-cutter will cut them to the best shapes and then, when my wife is in Tana, she will help her to choose the ring settings. I also hand over the envelope full of uncut garnets and tell her that I would like her stone-cutter to cut me a collection of all the different shapes possible – about a dozen – and then she can keep the rest of the packet; probably another fifty stones. After drinking a strong coffee with her, we take our leave but not before I fix a time and date to come back with Véro. I'm getting quite excited!

My work with *Miray* is coming to an end, everything is complete. At the End of Mission presentation, the LDI boss, who is also there, tells me that data collection using the system I designed is going well on his project and should be completed in a week or so. The data will be entered into a database in Access software and, as the next part of my help to the project, would I accept a further contract to analyse all the data, region by region, and build data tables for them to use? He explains that LDI is thinking of writing up those data in-house but there is the strong likelihood that they will come back to me to do that work too. He also adds that the data analyses and all related statistical analyses can be done from home, and I am allowed four weeks to complete the work that can be spread over a couple of months, to suit my availability. Great!

During the last couple of days of the Miray work, I have been feeling pretty grotty. I believe that the thinner air in the altitude of Tana must contain high levels of micro-particles from the poorly maintained and very old diesel vehicles that belch black smoke as they make their way around the capital and up and down its many hills. I would not be surprised if I have some kind of allergic bronchitis from the pollution just as I had caught a similar illness several years ago in Senegal when working in thick, damp, rotting grass around the town of Tambacounda. At that time, my doctor prescribed antibiotics and so now, I make my way to a reputable pharmacy near to my hotel for help. I start to speak with the pharmacist but break into an uncontrollable cough before I can finish my sentence. That little episode is enough for the pharmacist to make a diagnosis of a chest infection and hand me a pack of antibiotics and the firm instructions to take three per day until finished.

Véro is arriving at the airport tomorrow evening and I have pretty much finished my planning for her trip. We will spend the first three days in Tana so that she can catch up after the long flight (sitting still for twelve hours is shattering, believe me) and I can show her around Tana ... and hope that the antibiotics work their magic on me. I plan to take her the following day to the jewellery shop, without giving away any of my secrets, and the day after, which is Saturday, to the market in Andravoahangy. On Sunday we take the plane to Nossi Be (or 'Big Island' in Malgache), a holiday paradise according to both my Malgache and international colleagues. We will stay there for four nights, return to Tana for two nights and then take off for a six-day break to hear the Lemurs in Moramanga (of course!) and then continue to the coast before turning North along the coastal road. At the end of that trip, we come back to Tana for the final couple of days before returning home to the kids in Northampton.

On one of my morning runs to the office, I discuss the planned holiday with Pascal, the taxi driver, and ask him if he can recommend someone who can drive us for the Moramanga section of the vacation.

"Me of course," he replies.

"But Pascal, your *deux-dosh* (French slang for his 2 CV) is too small to take us on that trip. My wife's suitcase alone is as big as your car. Trust me, she does not travel light!"

"I have just bought another car that I use for longer trips. It's new and comes from *La Réunion* and passed its *contrôle technique* before I bought it."

I am a little suspicious because a new car would be very expensive and, if new, would not need to pass a *contrôle technique* (or MOT) until four years old. So something is not quite right. But before I can dig deeper, Pascal proclaims that he will bring the car for work tomorrow and I can check it out.

The following morning, true to his word, I find Pascal polishing his car at the taxi rank. It is actually a Peugeot-305 estate car, just like the one I used to own in Senegal, a real workhorse, and probably twelve to fifteen years old. Clearly it is not 'new' but I think Pascal meant 'new for him' so I am not going to press further. Anyway, the car looks suitable for the trip I have in mind although I have not thought the trip further than visiting the Indri Lemurs. After that we can play it by ear.

"Pascal, how much will the trip cost me" I ask.

"Ten pounds per day for the car and me but you will buy petrol, OK?"

Well there is no way that I can argue with such a price. In fact, I do not think it is enough and so I ask the question "where will you sleep Pascal?"

"In the car, sir."

I cannot have that. For a start it would be too dangerous to have a driver that does not sleep properly, also cars tend not to smell very nice if people sleep in them regularly then, more to the point, I am not such a mean-arse as to begrudge my faithful driver of so many months a bed for the night.

"I refuse to pay your price Pascal," his face falls, "I will only hire you if you accept ..." and I watch his face drop even further "... fifteen pounds per day" and his face lights up "and you agree to use some of the extra money to pay for a bed each night and you let me buy your food." Deal done.

Pascal takes me to the airport to collect Véro using the 305. Luckily she is on time and passes rapidly through passport control and customs and so we are soon taking, for me, the now familiar road from Ivato to the Ibis Hotel. Just as I had been on my first trip to Madagascar, Véro expresses the loveliness of the little brick-built Malgache houses as they appear in the moonlight or are lit by our car's headlights.

The following morning, we walk from the Ibis to the neighbouring Colbert and eat our breakfast on the terrace of their patisserie.

"The perfect start to an unexpected holiday," I am told.

For much of the year Tana has a quite perfect climate and this morning is no different with a temperature in the low 20s and not a cloud in the sky. After all, we are late-June and so into the winter months here in the southern hemisphere.

After a copious breakfast of fresh coffee and a few too many cakes and croissants, we make our way back to the Ibis, a walk of only a few hundred metres.

"*Madame Ibis, bonjour.* Do you have any change you can give me please?" speaks up a little raggedy girl of about eight years old.

"Now who are you?" asks Véro in her motherly voice.

"My name is Céline and I live over there with my mum and my little brother." Céline points out a cardboard structure that sits on the pavement and hugs the wall of a public building. "I am trying to collect a little money so that my mum can buy some food for us. Can you give me some please *Madame Ibis*?"

And just like that, Véro has a new nickname that stays with her throughout our time in Tana. I hand over the small change that I had received from the Colbert and also the bag of leftover croissants and cakes that we had not been able to finish at breakfast, telling Céline that I had bought them especially for her and her little brother.

Pascal is waiting for us patiently and, follows my directions as he drives us to the jewellery shop, and our appointment with the lady-owner. Véro's eyes pop, as mine had done on my first visit, to see all the jewellery, individual gemstones and lumps of rock containing precious and semi-precious stones in this Aladdin's Cave. She is not quite a child in a sweet shop but I am sure that her reaction can be imagined.

My wife has never been a spendthrift and neither has she ever anticipated that I should gift her very expensive items. Neither of us have ever had that sort of relationship with money. We know what we have and we make ends meet very well. Nonetheless, the shop is tempting for both of us.

We start off looking at some gold earrings with large cut garnets. While garnets are only considered semi-precious, they really are beautiful deep red stones. The price of the earrings is very reasonable and I propose that it would be nice to have a matching pendant made with a larger garnet. The lady jeweller tells me quietly that a larger stone will cost rather more than the ear rings because larger garnets are considerably rarer and so more expensive. Because she wants to avoid embarrassing me in front of Véro, she discretely writes a figure on a piece of paper and hands it over to me the equivalent of £20. Perfect, add it to the list.

Véro then picks up other items that attract her eye, mostly to give as gifts, and then she espies a beautiful orange granite sphere, about the size of a small grapefruit, saying that this would make a lovely pommel for the stairs in Cordon. Add it to the list.

We move on to a locked presentation cabinet where madam keeps her display of cut sapphires blinking in an array of colours in the overhead lights. Véro can see the prices of individual stones and, since they are quite expensive, starting at around £120 each, she tells me how pretty they are but does not push the topic any further.

Madam-the-jeweller then walks over to us holding a small display box made of rice straw with a glass top. "What do you think of these Véronique?" she asks.

"Oh my goodness, they are so beautiful. I particularly love the pink stone but the deep blue one is also beautiful and of such a lovely shape, like a teardrop."

"Would you like them then?" madam asks.

"Of course I would but I am sure that they will be too expensive for me."

Madam laughs and simply says "here, take them, they are yours."

"What do you mean?" and she looks at me and then back to the jeweller.

"They are yours," she repeats with a big smile, "your husband brought the stones for me to cut a week or so ago and here they are. The pink sapphire is for your wedding anniversary and the blue one for your daughter. Now let's work on choosing the settings."

"Darling, but how? Where did you get the sapphires, they are lovely? Ohhh thank you!" And I receive a hug and a big kiss.

Our lady jeweller then goes off to make coffee – I never once visited that shop without being served a strong coffee – and comes back with three cups and several jewellery catalogues from famous Parisian jewellers like Cartier. The ladies flick through the catalogues and every so often, madam says that she could use the sapphire for a ring like this or like that. Finally, the choice of settings for the two sapphires is made. The rings will be in gold while the diamonds encircling the sapphires will be substituted with zircons. When we collect the rings, after our Nossi Be trip, the rings are very faithful copies of the catalogue photos.

The story behind that pink sapphire ring is to be told many, many times in future years, showing French friends and family that even an Englishman can sometimes be quite a romantic!

That evening we decide to eat at the Ibis because the 'dish of the day' is lobster-a-go-go, accompanied by a quarter bottle of Malgache Rum each. Since I still feel a little grotty from my chest infection, I forgo the rum while half of my lobster is eaten by the hungry lady beside me.

The next day is our trip to Andravoahangy Market, particularly the area dedicated to embroidered tablecloths and serviettes. When we arrive at the entrance to the embroidery section; the section must be about one hundred metres long with little boutiques and open-air tables on both sides, and all selling embroidery. I advise Véro that before we select anything to buy, we should walk up and then back and note which stalls have embroideries that we particularly like, from which we can make a final selection. She agrees.

We stop at the first stall and I am immediately told "Oh look at this one, it is so lovely and so well embroidered, I know this will be on my list to buy. So I will pay for it straight away!"

"I thought we had agreed to walk down and back and make selections as we go."

"Oh, no. I know that I will want this one so I will buy it straight away." She feebly tries to bargain, and I already have a parcel to carry.

We arrive at the next stall and, of course, everyone can guess: this also has an embroidered set that would be on our list, and is every bit as nice as the one we have just purchased. Why wait, why not purchase now?

"If you had to choose between this table cloth and the one you have already purchased, which one would you choose?" I ask.

"Oh this one is even nicer than the first one," She replies.

"Can you see why I said we should walk both sides before selecting which ones to buy?"

"Woops, sorry" says my lady as we finally walk the line before selecting more to purchase!

In the afternoon, we decide to explore on foot the neighbouring hillside where the LDI office is located. While walking up a side street, above the office, we see a little catholic church and decide to look inside and then walk around the graveyard; gravestones can often be quite revealing. In this one, the gravestones are certainly revealing but in a way that makes us both extremely sad. We come across a section of the graveyard dedicated to missionaries and the stone that really saddens us is to see the inscription that gives the names and ages of the interred. They range from an obvious husband and wife in their mid-thirties to three small children, including an infant of a few months. The inscription tells us that the family were massacred while serving God, and the date? The very late 1890s; little more than a hundred years ago.

We take our flight to Nossi Be, flying across the north-western portion of Madagascar and then over a beautiful deep blue sea before arriving at the island's airport in the early afternoon. The plane is tiny, as is the airport. We descend the stairs on to the tarmac and are immediately hit by a strong fragrance that Véro tells me is the perfume of 'ylang ylang' – a new fragrance and a new word for me. And she is right.

Inside the airport terminal are large displays advertising the fragrance. I pick up a brochure and note that ylang ylang is an essential oil distilled from the flowers of the ylang ylang tree (*Cananga odorata*) and the oil is good for just about everything, from bringing comfort to body and mind to healing wounds, to inducing a 'sensual mood'. Madagascar's answer to snake oil, I propose. Just over the terminal fence I can make out an orchard of 'tortured' trees, these are ylang ylang and the source of the perfumed air.

The hotel has sent a taxi to collect us, a nice gesture, and the driver hands over his card bearing a telephone number and tells us that he is a freelance driver and available to transport us whenever and wherever we wish. We book him for the following day, saying we would like to do a tour of the island and visit local beauty spots.

Our hotel opens on to the beach and is half empty; tourist season has not yet gotten completely underway. We spend the late afternoon relaxing on the beach and then at around 6 pm as the sun begins to slide into the Mozambique Channel, I suggest a walk in the moonlight along the strandline. After around half-a-kilometre, we can see the lights of a small beach bar; perfect for a sundowner before we go back to the hotel and prepare for dinner in its restaurant.

Véro asks for a glass of 'punch' that is made with Malgache rum while I take a bottle of Three-horses beer. I explain to her that my friends in Tana tell me that the beer gets its name from the number of horses required to fill a bottle. And that we have nicknamed it 'headache in a bottle' (because I find it must be drunk in strict moderation).

Without me noticing, while I recite my little anecdote about the local beer, Véro has already finished her half-pint glass of punch and signalled the waiter to bring another. She is not a heavy drinker, by any means, but one thing she has a penchant for is rum. When ordering her favourite dessert of rum-baba, she invariably tells the waiter '... and go heavy on the rum!'

My beer finished and her second punch dispatched with some vigour, I suggest we should begin to wander back to the hotel and get ready for dinner. But all I get from my nearest and dearest is a smile ... and I know what that means. The punch was strong and (sorry I have to stop the story here because I promised I would not write that I was obliged to give her a piggyback to the hotel, put her into bed and go off to the restaurant on my own; so I had better not). Our evening on the romantic Indian Ocean island of Nossi Be is at an end!

The next day we are taken by the taxi driver who had collected us at the airport to visit the island's beauty spots; there are so many of them. But we particularly enjoy our trip to the almost circular lakes that lie to the centre of the island followed by a long walk down the north-western coast. That is, until we come upon a large, fenced area proudly proclaiming '*Prochain Site du Club Med*'! is this paradise about to be lost to a holiday company and hundreds of tourists? 'No' according to the lady-owner of the little beach restaurant where we stop five minutes later for the dish of the day: Lobster and Chips!

"I cannot wait for the holiday resort to open. Imagine what it will do for my restaurant trade" she explains gleefully to us.

Sadly, I can imagine that all the lobsters will be sold directly to the holiday resort and the poor lady may, in a year or so, find that she faces enormous competition for the tourists from other restaurants that will very quickly spring up. While we both love eating in restaurants that serve local food (even if services like toilets may be a little basic), we have, it must be remembered, spent two decades living in Africa. The average Parisians coming to Madagascar for their very first trip to Africa may well pay close attention to all the (rather foolish and over the top) health warnings and give *gargottes* like this, a wide berth. We wish the owner good luck and begin our trip back to the hotel.

Late in the afternoon, we go down on to the beach in front of the hotel for a quick stroll. We are approached by a young man who asks if we are interested in going to a 'desert island' the next day, lunch is provided in the price of £15 per head. That sounds a very attractive proposition to both of us although experience has made us a little reticent to believe everything that beach touts say. I ask where the boat is that will take us to the island and the young man points out a rather large and modern motorboat with twin outboards bobbing in the shallow water. To seal the deal, he tells us that we only need to leave our names and that of our hotel for the boat reservation. We can pay tomorrow just before we board. The trip is on!

Straight after breakfast we pick up the bag with our beachwear and head off to the boat. There are about dozen other tourists waiting, most are Europeans but there are also a few Malgache tourists too. As we wait, a very stout lady – on this occasion I cannot say of 'traditional build' because Malgache ladies are traditionally small and willowy – waddles down the beach balancing a most enormous woven bag on her head.

"Here comes lunch," Véro whispers to me.

We all climb into the boat with the tourists showing their lack of manners by pushing and shoving to try to claim the seats nearest to the sides and front of the boat. We happily take more central seats as the back because we know that when the boat gets up to top speed, the passengers at the sides and front are going to get drenched in cold salt water. We may be in the tropics but being soaked for an hour when a speedboat is doing thirty knots is, at least, uncomfortable if not downright chilly.

We go at top speed across the beautiful open sea for around an hour, perhaps more, until we spot a small dot of an island in the distance. None of the tourists seems to know exactly where we are headed but, according to the map I brought, I believe the dot to be Nosy Tanikely; a nature reserve and an important turtle nesting site.

We arrive on what looks like everyone's idea of a desert island, including mine. We anchor just off the beach, being helped down the boat ladder into a few centimetres of warm clear water. The beach has no footprints, no sign of any other human existence. A real paradise of golden sand sprinkled with a few broken pieces of bleached coral and with a band of palm trees in the distance.

We watch as our cook makes her way slowly and carefully down the ladder. She is followed by the boatmen who carry her enormous woven bag, a small, round charcoal stove of the type that development projects are touting all over Africa, and a sack of charcoal. She sets up her 'kitchen' to our left and soon has the stove smoking and then burning brightly as she fans the embers. As the morning arrives towards its end, delicious odours waft towards us. From her simple bag, she is putting together a feast for almost twenty people.

While the tourists sun themselves on the sand, waiting for lunch to be served, we decide to explore the little island. I notice a small path at the top of the beach which seems to lead into the palm trees and so we follow it into the grove of trees and keep walking. At a distance of about one hundred metres, I spot what looks suspiciously like a small landing strip with a group of round-roofed buildings composed entirely of corrugated sheeting, and all is surrounded by a high fence topped with razor wire. What on earth is a landing strip doing in the middle of this nature sanctuary for turtles? We do not get to spy any further because two rather burly Malgache walk up to the other side of the fence holding machetes and tell us in very poor French '*privé monsieur*'. We do not push our luck.

A few days later, when back in Tana, I speak to a senior member of the WWF who pushes the information further up the NGO line as well as into the Malgache government. It seems we stumbled on an illegal activity but I never did learn if that activity was related to drug running, smuggling or something quite different but equally nefarious.

We are now ready for the last part of our vacation, the trip to Moramanga and beyond. Pascal has polished his 'new' taxi so hard that the metal underneath almost shows through the paint on top. Before setting off on the trip, where I know that I must pay for everything in cash, I go to the bank and change Pounds into Malgache Francs. The exchange rate today is over 23,000 MF to a pound sterling. I calculate that I need to change around £400 in order to pay both Pascal and all the expenses of the trip. For that sum, I receive in exchange the grand amount of over nine million Malgache francs. Luckily I brought my briefcase with me to carry it in; shades of the Bissauan Pesos!

I go back to our room at the Ibis where Véro is waiting and hand her my briefcase. As she takes it with a quizzical look on her face, I say "open it love," she complies, "and now you know how it feels to be a multi-millionairess!" The briefcase is stuffed full of banknotes, nine million two hundred thousand Malgache francs to be precise.

Our trip starts with the drive off the Tana plateau and we descend rapidly to lower altitudes. We pass the mountain scenes that I so loved, when I first saw them, of mosses and ferns soaked by a myriad of streams and splashed by little cascades. Just as I had imagined only a few months back, Véro is as enchanted by the scene as I had been.

We arrive at the lemur camp and are handed the keys, coincidentally to the same bungalow where I had previously stayed and, the next morning, follow the same enchanting routine with a very loud 5.30 am alarm call by the Indri Lemur Choral. We are booked to stay in the reserve for three nights which gives us time to walk and explore in the forests and then to visit the town of Moramanga before packing up and driving eastwards towards the ocean. During the trip to Moramanga we visit a local market. The markets of Tana have nothing on this one. It is a local market for local people. We are the only foreigners to be seen and so a bit of a curiosity when we stop to look at items.

Today there is a fair for the children and the highlight is a small merry-go-round that seats about a dozen kids. It is not electric or even steam-driven but turns thanks to a lean gentleman who sits on a contraption rather like a bicycle without wheels, and he pedals for all he is worth! This is a sight not to be missed.

Local items made of recycled material always catch our eyes and show just what can be done with used items that we, the affluent West, consider as trash. Véro spots a lady selling an array of night-lights made from old, cut-down tin cans – we can still see the labels for sardines, tomatoes, shoe polish and kidney beans – with the small pieces of candle they each contain covered by the glass of an old light bulb. Ingenious and they work, because we shipped half-a-dozen back to Cordon for testing!

Our first destination from Moramanga is the coastal town of Toamasina where we propose to take a late lunch in a roadside restaurant. As we drive towards the coast, a deviation sign sends us into a parking area where there are several police vehicles and an ambulance. Just before leaving Tana, I had heard that there was a serious outbreak of cholera on the island; brought in, so the local newspapers report, by illegal refugees from the Comoros Islands. In an attempt to control the spread of the disease, all people travelling around Madagascar are being pulled over into areas like this and told to swallow what I can only describe as horse antibiotics, a single enormous pill. Pascal drops us to join the short queue of people, and states that the medicine is only for foreigners, not for him; despite the fact that everyone else in the queue is Malgache. He drives his car on a further fifty metres and parks.

Our turn arrives and we are each handed our pill, given a certifi-cate and offered a beaker of water.

"Is this bottled water?" I ask.

The nurse replies "no sir, it is well water."

"Oh, you know that us foreigners have fragile stomachs, may we go to our car to get our bottled water?" Véro chips in.

"Of course you can dear," she answers, "and tell your driver to come straight over for his pill. He is not going to escape the treatment."

From the safe distance of our car, we both make a show for the nurse of pretending to put the pills in our mouths and take swigs from the bottle. We then pocket the pills. Meanwhile, poor Pascal cannot use the excuse of being a foreigner with a fragile stomach and is obliged to swallow the pill under the very watchful eyes of the nurse.

We arrive in the little coastal town of Toamasina and take a sharp left that leads us along the coast road. In front of us is the magnificent deep blue Indian Ocean and a beach that takes our breath away. Miles upon miles of clean sand with not a single sunbather or swimmer in view.

"Where are the tourists?" Véro asks Pascal, indicating the beautiful ocean ahead.

"Any that ventured in there are surely being digested by the sharks!" he replies straight-faced, "this is known locally as 'Shark Beach', madam".

So that is the reason for the lack of activity on this beautiful shore! One hundred metres further along the road, we come across a splendid-looking but clearly decaying hotel with a restaurant on a raised terrace. We decide to stop for lunch and invite Pascal to eat with us. However, he mumbles about the pill and an upset stomach and prefers to go to a more modest place for his food. He asks if we do not have the same stomach issue after taking the antibiotics. I show him our two pills that are still in my pocket.

"You foreigners are really sneaky!" he grumbles with a smile.

We walk up the broad stone stairway that leads to the terrace restaurant having to watch out for the packed ranks of seated beggars that are sharing the stairs with us. Each puts out a hand in anticipation of alms but no one speaks to us or tries to stop us.

We are met at the top of the stairs by the Maitre d', a most elderly gentleman resplendent in shiny black shoes, black trousers, pressed white shirt and a black bowtie.

He makes a little bow to Véro and asks "would madam and monsieur partake of luncheon?"

"If we may," replies Véro, being a little taken aback by such a gentlemanly reception.

The restaurant terrace is empty, apart from us, and so we ask for the table that gives both of us a view over the slightly abandoned gardens of what must once have been a really beautiful hotel.

We are handed the menu and I note that the '*menu du jour*' starts with a *salade lyonnaise*, follows with cold tongue in a mayonnaise and gherkin sauce and finishes with a slice of apple pie and ice cream (vanilla of course, after all this is Madagascar). The salads arrive and the quantity on a single plate would easily have fed us both. I have to confess that this is my favourite salad and the restaurant does not let us down. The bacon pieces and croutons are crispy and served on a bed of frizzy lettuce (the first I have seen in Madagascar) all overtopped with a poached egg cooked just right, not too hard not too runny. I express my satisfaction to the Maitre d' and he promises to congratulate the chef.

Next up is the main dish of the tongue. Tongue is hard to cook as it can be tough but these must have been simmered in a pressure cooker because they are delicious and soft. The mayonnaise sauce is obviously homemade and full of gherkin pieces, not a Coleman's in sight.

As we are enjoying this tasty dish, the Maitre d' comes over and says to Véro, "madam, would you please excuse my interruption but I must ask you to move table."

"I'm sorry but I do not understand, why do we need to move?" she queries.

"Oh, you see the sun has started to move around the building? In five minutes it will begin to shine on your arm and I would not wish for madam to get sunburnt while enjoying luncheon."

I wonder how to reply to that without laughing? Véro beats me to it.

"Oh, you are such a gallant gentleman," she responds bringing a delicious smile to his old lined face, "there exist so few real gentlemen today, so thank you. But I will be fine, please do not worry."

"If madam is sure," he replies with a bow.

Our meal ends with a local coffee served at the same time as the dessert. I pay the bill (the equivalent of £5 each) saying that we will soon have to leave the town, moving north along the coast. But before taking our leave, I ask if we might see around the hotel. It strikes me as being furnished from the Art Nouveau period and we can see what looks like beautiful period furniture and large decorated vases through the windows of the terrace. The Maitre d' himself gives us a personal tour and even opens a door to a bedroom to show us the very faded luxury that the hotel still tries to offer.

"Let's book to stay here for the night on the way back to Tana," I suggest and Véro concurs. We do stay there at the end of our road trip and, while the hotel and the few staff retained to manage its sad decline are gentle, lovely people, the mattress must also have dated from the *Belle Epoch* as it offers a deep trench in the middle into which we both roll throughout a pretty sleepless night! Once more, Paradise has been Lost.

After leaving Toamasina, we continue to hug the coast as far as possible looking for a place to spend the night. We are very relaxed about lodgings because Pascal has already told us that if we find nothing suitable on the road, there is a comfortable tourist place in the village of Ambodimanga run by a young French woman to which he often brings tourists.

The following morning our trek continues to the North with our destination being the village of Mahambo. The French lady of our hotel in Ambodimanga has told us of a quaint beach hotel that is well worth a visit. We arrive in the village by mid-afternoon, and Pascal follows the signs for the hotel and, once we turn off the road on to a track, those to the reception. We jump out of the car and are met by a middle-aged Malgache lady who introduces herself as the manageress. We follow her along a small pathway lined by pretty Malgache periwinkles. This is an interesting pink-flowered plant, frequent in many European gardens, with the scientific name of *Vinca rosea*. Interestingly, it is the source of *'vincristine'*, a powerful drug used against certain types of Leukaemia.

We are shown to a bungalow that has a broad terrace opening straight onto the beach. The only sound to be heard is that of the ocean gently lapping the shore of our small bay.

As the manageress takes her leave, she turns and says "I am so sorry not to be able to provide you with a meal this evening but in reality we are closed! I saw that you are a lovely couple so have opened a bungalow for you. The maid will come in a few moments and make your bed." Malgache kindness, a way of life.

We arrange with Pascal that he will collect us at 7 pm and take us to a restaurant he knows in the village. Since it is the only one, I ask him to eat with us and help with the translation. I doubt anyone will speak French.

At 6.45 we wander across to the reception and tell madam where we will be eating. She replies with "would you like an aperitif before you go, I have cold beer."

Cold beer it is then. She goes to the antiquated fridge humming in the corner and takes out three bottles of Three-horses beer, placing them lying down on a tray and adds three straight glasses. We sit at a table in the reception and she joins us for her aperitif too. Cheers!

The restaurant food is pretty good if a little spicy for Véro but tasty, filling and incredibly cheap. Back to the hotel and we say goodnight to Pascal. As we pass through the reception, Véro sorts through her handbag muttering that she is sure there is a torch hidden in there somewhere! But no need. The lovely manageress has placed at least fifty artisanal nightlights along both sides of the path guiding us with their little pixie lights flickering in the tiny breeze of evening all the way from the reception to our bungalow.

We awake gently at 8.30, the next morning to hear hushed voices coming from outside our bungalow. I look through the window and see that the manageress has set up breakfast for us on the beach under a trellis of palm fronds. What a perfect start to the morning, what a welcome and service we have enjoyed throughout our trip along the coast but all holidays come to an end and we have to start making our way back to Tana.

There are only three more days to go before we take our flight home to France. Véro had asked me before we started the trip to Moramanga and Toamasina if we could look for another hotel for our last few nights. The Ibis is great for a working consultant but not really for tourists like us. It lacks local colour and it seems a bit sterile belonging, as it does, to a large hotel chain.

It was my friend Pierre who had first taken me to a French restaurant called *La Boussole* (the Compass) and while chatting to the French owner about guesthouses, he told that he owned one quite close to his restaurant. We are booked to stay our last few nights there, and what a beautiful place it is. Our bedroom (really the wrong word, apartment would be more precise) is, in reality, the whole attic of the large house. The room is fully sixty metres square and has the most beautiful parquet of palisander wood, polished to a shine, that gleams as light plays across the surface. Véro, being impressed by that sort of thing, seeks out the housekeeper and asks how she manages to get the floor to look so beautiful.

"Come back with me to your room dear, and we will show you," declares the lady calling out to one of the young maids.

A few moments later the little housemaid knocks on our door. She is carrying a contraption made of coconut husks (the hairy stuff that grows around the shell) with two sets of leather straps. She attaches the contraptions to the underside of her bare feet and tightens the straps. Then she literally skates across the floor. *Et voila*, how to have the perfect shining floorboards!

All beautiful things eventually come to an end and Pascal drives us out to Ivato in his *'deux-dosh'* proudly proclaiming that madam's suitcase does fit in. We catch the late evening flight to Paris, bidding farewell to Madagascar. This is the last time that Véro will see the beautiful island, I will be back in a few months for my mission with the German company. We are given seats at the very back of the crowded plane. They are against the toilet wall and so will not fold backwards to allow us to sleep in a slightly more comfort position. To make matters worse, (and 'damn' that airline) these seats are normally reserved for smokers, which we most certainly are not. Despite offering my Frequent Flyers card to the hostess at check in and asking for a seat in no-smoking, she is not interested at all in the requests of her passengers. How to ruin the end of a perfect vacation!

But dear me and damn them again, this well known airline has yet another trick up its sleeve, reserved just for me. Breakfast is served in the early morning and the hostess is asking passengers in the seats in front of us 'would you like Croissant or Omelette'. Our turn comes last, being right at the back. Véro asks for croissant and I ask for an omelette. Two tin foil containers with different coloured labels on the cardboard lids are handing over to us. Véro's contains the advertised croissant with little catering packs of jam and butter. Mine contains (*mais non*, not an omelette) a cold ratatouille! I swear on my life.

"Excuse me Miss but I believe there has been a mistake because you have given me a ratatouille instead of an omelette," I say this calmly and politely.

"Yes, that's right," she says in her 'I could not give a damn' voice, "the omelettes are finished."

"Might I have a croissant instead then please?" I ask respectfully.

"They are finished too. This is all that we have left, and it's from last night's meal. It's that or nothing!" she replies.

That response rather gets my goat a little aroused and so I reply "but ratatouille is not usually served at breakfast, I'm sure you agree. I'm equally sure that if you look in Business or First Class you can find something more appetizing, like a croissant." I suggest.

"Sir, if you want business class food then you must buy a business class ticket," she spits out.

That was it, that last comment has really succeeded in getting my goat completely out of his stable!

"Shall I tell you something miss?" I ask, and continue without waiting for her response, "I paid the same price for my ticket as all the other passengers in economy. Nonetheless, you find it fit to serve me a breakfast that comes from last night's leftover meal because your company did not calculate the number of meals correctly. I call that at least clumsy if not downright insulting. Please ask the purser to come to speak with me."

She goes off in a huff, muttering to herself. Ten minutes later a balding, middle-aged gentleman comes to my side and asks if I am the person causing so much trouble over breakfast. I do not need to defend myself, nor indeed to say a single word because passengers on both sides of the aisle had overheard my exchange with the hostess and several jump to my defence. A few moments later I am brought a breakfast tray from business class.

When we arrive back in Lime Avenue the kids are close to finishing their respective summer terms. Hard to believe that we have been back in UK for a whole academic year. In that time, my little girl has grown into a lovely young woman of seventeen while my cheeky little boy has grown, well, into an even cheekier young adolescent of thirteen. David's term at Parkside finishes at least a week before Mélanie's at the Boys' School so Véro has the good idea of flying to France with David while Mélanie and I will drive over in the Citroen BX the following week. This gives Véro a few days to spend with her parents before heading over to Cordon to open up the house after its winter slumbers while I can use the week of calm to catch up on six months' of accounts and then begin to work on the absolutely enormous databases that have just arrived from LDI.

The next three months of work are all for Madagascar with a return trip for the German company to develop the information system for the Forestry Department sandwiched between the analysis of the enormous LDI databases. But finally, in early October, both activities are complete, and I realise that I have no more work currently in my diary. This is the first time that I have nothing on the horizon since we returned to the UK although this time I am less worried because my work year to date has been absolutely brilliant with almost every day, with the exception of Sundays, billed as work.

7 |

Africa's Loveliest Nation

As I am once more washing the Northampton grime off the BX, the Headmaster with the Staffordshire Dogs on his windowsill, as has become his nice habit, stops to chat. He asks if there is any chance that I could help him because one of his biology teachers has left suddenly and he has few options available to teach the A-level Biology class. That is quite a coincidence since I am currently free, and want to keep my bank account ticking over, even given the school's rather ungenerous hourly rate. But again, I insist, that the proviso still stands that my consulting work will always take priority. I turn up to the school the next day and teach a total of five hours, and wham back into the swing of teaching!

But a prolonged return to the classroom is not to be. I get home in the late afternoon from the school and receive an email message from my old PhD supervisor now living and working in Maryland, USA. It seems that a UK consulting firm is trying to track me down. The firm was apparently one of the many recipients in early 1995 of my CV that I had broadcast far and wide in a desperate search for consulting work. However, when we moved from France to the UK in 1998, I stopped my professional telephone line in Cordon and so

I could no longer be contacted on that number. By a piece of luck, and in 1995 not knowing what the future might hold, I included in my CV the contact details of a couple of referees, including my old supervisor. He provides me with the name of the company based in Ripon, Yorkshire plus their telephone number.

I phone, despite it now being almost 6 pm, and my call is taken by the receptionist and I am passed straight through to the managing director. We chat for a few moments about my work since 1995 (the date of the CV). He goes on to ask if I can travel to Ripon tomorrow and immediately on to Botswana! While I am excited about this new possibility, I cannot let the headmaster down at such very short notice. I manage to negotiate that I will travel to Ripon the day after tomorrow instead! I do not realise at this moment but a new and lovely chapter in my life is about to open.

Northampton Town might be near to the centre of the UK but it is a backwater in terms of rail linkages. My trip to York requires two changes but eventually I arrive, complete with suitcase and computer bag and am met by a minicab that works extensively for this new company. A half-hour drive across the beautiful Yorkshire countryside and we arrive in the quaint little market town of Ripon. Old Ripon surrounds the market square and can boast two pubs that I will soon get to know well (thanks to one of my new colleagues, I hasten to add!). The office is located on one corner of the square and occupies an old coaching inn, a most beautiful fifteenth century building with exposed beams, plaster walls, wonky, narrow stairs and an odour of history, lovely.

I arrive in time to be taken out for lunch by the MD and a young colleague with an enormous smile and not much hair. By one of those odd twists of fate, my career for the next twenty years is destined to be intertwined with these two lovely characters.

As we are eating, I am given a little more information on the proposed Botswana work. The company wants me to travel to the country for a week to scope out the upcoming second phase of a project in Gaborone and then come back to Ripon for the second week to lead the small team in preparing the company's contract proposal.

At 3 pm I am back in the minicab and on my way to Leeds and Bradford Airport, having been handed three envelopes. The first contains, my air tickets: Leeds-Heathrow-Johannesburg-Gaborone return. The second, a bundle of UK banknotes to pay for my food and hotel; my per diem. I have been pre-booked at the Cresta President Hotel, in the centre of Gaborone town; conveniently within walking distance of the ministry, the project offices and the UK donors. The final envelope is the most interesting as it contains the ToR, developed by the Botswana office of the UK government's Department for International Development (DFID). The ToR describes the upcoming project that I am now to investigate. I put all the envelopes back in my briefcase thinking that the long overnight flight will provide the ideal opportunity to read and digest carefully all the information contained in the ToR.

In the massive airport that is Heathrow, I find my way to the terminal that houses British Airways flights to South Africa and check in my suitcase. The BA frequent flyers card that I hand over with my tickets ensures that I receive an aisle seat and, thank you BA, there is no need to request a non-smokers seat since the airline has not allowed that habit on board their flights since early 1998.

While in the departure lounge awaiting boarding for the overnight flight, my name is called by the BA lady who will shortly ask economy passengers to board. I move to her desk, receive a big smile and a request for my boarding card. This she rips in two and hands me a new one.

"You may board now, Dr Marks," she says.

I look at my new seat number and see that I have been up-graded to Business, thank you BA. My reward, I assume, for having a frequent flyers card.

Once everyone is seated, we have been handed our complimentary glasses of champagne and the plane has soared into the night sky, I remove the ToR from its envelope, take out a pen, put on my new spectacles (oh, yes, the Itinerant Ecologist is getting old too!) and start to read.

The gentleman next to me suddenly speaks up "I can see that you are reading some good news."

"Well actually, yes," I reply, "but how did you know?"

"Because I saw a smile begin on your face and it has developed rapidly into a very wide grin!"

I laugh because he is spot on although I did not realise that my pleasure was playing out so evidently on my face. What had brought about the noticeable grin was the first couple of paragraphs of the ToR that informs me that the company winning the contract is to be responsible for developing a mini ecology centre within the Ministry of Agriculture and must get it ready for some form of privatisation. Why the pleasure? Because that is exactly what I had undertaken five or six years previously in Senegal at the ecology centre, based in Dakar. Would any of the other five companies still in the competition for the Botswana contract have such in depth first-hand experience? No way, I am convinced of that!

We arrive early in the morning in Johannesburg after the twelve-hour flight and I am guided by a kindly South African lady through the arrivals hall, past passport control and into a small side terminal where local flights serve nearby international airports like Windhoek (Namibia), Tana (Madagascar), Lilongwe (Malawi) and, of course Gaborone (Botswana). Our aeroplane is a small turboprop and, during the short one-hour hop, flies at a relatively low altitude allowing passengers to get a great view of the South African and then the Botswana countryside spread out below. During our flight, we pass over several enormous open cast mines but I have no idea if they are looking for diamonds, vanadium, iron ore or something equally rewarding. When we are not flying over the mines, we are traversing open 'veldt'. The vegetation of these parkland-like areas is dominated mostly by Acacia-like vegetation; after all, the Kalahari Desert is not too far away.

Just before landing in Gaborone, we fly low over a large lake and I can see yachts dotted over the surface. This is an artificial lake that was created by the damming of the Ngotwane River and it provides the backdrop for one of the most popular 'The No 1 Ladies' Detective Agency' books written by Alexander McCall Smith a year or so ago. In that novel, the 'traditionally built' heroine, named Precious Ramotswe, tracks down and shoots a crocodile that had eaten a client's wayward husband. And, yes, there really are crocodiles in the lake that we are flying over!

I arrive at Sir Seretse Khama Airport, pass quickly through the formalities and, outside the terminal, spot the Cresta courtesy bus waiting in the carpark. I am soon travelling down the A1 and, within fifteen minutes, standing in the reception of the President hotel. My first impression, or rather impressions, is how welcoming, friendly and relaxed are the Batswana people.

The ToR that I had read in detail during the flight states that it is anticipated that the company that wins the bid will make use of three independent British consultants that have set up businesses in the capital. Although I feel this to be a little irregular, after all bidding companies usually have their own local and international specialists on hand. Nonetheless, in the consulting world, we usually accept that 'What the client wants, the client gets'.

Included with the ToR are several telephone numbers including those of the national director of the project, the outgoing project team leader (who happens to be from Namibia), the local DFID office with relevant names, and those of the British consultants. I sit down on my bed and call one after the other, setting up meetings over the next few days. I feel it is preferable to start the series of meetings with the three local consultants for while they will likely have little say and no vote in selecting the company that will eventually be awarded the contract, they should have lots of local knowledge to share. I feel I may be able to extract useful information from them before I meet up with the DFID and Botswana government representatives who do carry the selection votes.

By chance, my call finds all three of the British consultants together having an end of afternoon drink and, by an even greater coincidence, they happen to be in the bar of my hotel. Rather than fix appointments, they simply tell me to come down to the bar and we can chat there. They are the only people in the room and occupy a table close to the bar. I can see that all are drinking lager and the logo on their pint glasses says 'Castel'. We shake hands and I notice that they are all around my age. A good start. Immediately, a waitress comes over to take my order and so I request a new round for everyone. That little gesture is appreciated, even before we begin talking in detail. For the first fifteen minutes or so we chat about everything except the upcoming contract; let's get to know each other a little before we start talking about the more serious stuff.

Our pints are finished quickly and someone orders another round. The consultants, now being into at least their third pints, are beginning to enter that warm, friendly, verbose phase that often occurs as sufficient alcohol hits the bloodstream. Being tired after my overnight flight, I will not be too far behind them.

I am told in all seriousness, even if in a slightly slurred voice, by one of the consultants "we have to say that you are the friendliest of the company representatives that have come to Botswana to scout out the project. Some of the others didn't even bother to meet with us. But obviously being a nice guy will not be enough to win the contract. Just before you arrived we were ranking the six companies who are after the contract and yours is in our list in sixth place, sorry."

Am I worried about their unofficial ranking? Not in the slightest!

"What do you know about me?" I ask, "and even more important, what do you know about the company I represent?"

"Absolutely nothing. You seem to be a small, anonymous company and that is the reason that we placed you last."

"Then I promise you will be surprised but I will say nothing more, except 'cheers'," I reply as I pick up the new pint of Castel lager.

"And, by the way, good luck with the director at the ministry," they add, making me feel as if I am receiving a warning while their exchanged smiles only add to that feeling. "But let's meet back here on Saturday afternoon because England are playing South Africa in the Rugby World Cup. It will be quite a game and the place will be packed with noisy Boers! England will need some support."

The next morning, I travel to DFID and have a short and not very informative meeting with the project lead and his assistant, a young Batswana lady. As always in such meetings while a contract is in the bidding stages and is therefore still to be awarded, the level of information provided is about equal to that contained in the ToR; so it is more a question of being seen to be interested than to obtain any additional detailed information.

In contrast, my meeting with the outgoing team leader is friendly and highly informative. He is leaving the project in a couple of months at the end of this first phase and is not available to us or any other company for the second one.

My final important meeting is with the project director. In contrast to what the consultants had intimated, I immediately take a shine to him. While the vast majority of Batswana are very polite and friendly and rarely raise their voices, I can tell immediately that he is a bit of a firebrand and likes to criticise; a real character. He tells me straight off that he is getting bored by all the companies that trek through his office to try to get his support for the contract. My response is not defensive. Rather I tell him that I am prepared to bet him a big steak at the 'Bull and Bush' restaurant (a tip I received during the afternoon drinking with the three local British consultants) that the other companies have all told him the same thing about how good they are and how the second phase will be even better than the first; but that none provided him with any real details.

He nods and smiles and tells me that I am spot on. He goes on to say that he will therefore collect me from my hotel at 7 pm this evening so that I can take him for the promised steak!

And we do go for that steak and as we discuss what my company might bring to the table (apart from the largest steak in the restaurant that already sits on his plate) I ask him "has anyone tried to explain to you how they would go about developing the ecology centre?" he shakes his head, "and have you heard anything about how they propose to privatise it and on what model?" Again a big shake of the head as he chews an enormous chunk of prime Botswana beef.

I explain to him about my work in Senegal and how we developed the ecology centre in Dakar. Also the problems we encountered along the way and how we solved them, the move to signing contracts with private companies, NGOs and donor agencies for paid work, and how we struggled but eventually succeeded in developing a legal framework that the government was able to accept and support.

All my points are met with enthusiasm and further questions including the key one "after more than six years, is the centre still operating?"

"Yes, indeed it is still functioning well and generating sufficient funds to cover running costs. And, furthermore, the staff enjoy good salaries and plus they have a profit-sharing scheme."

But the clincher, the real clincher, not only to round off a successful evening but for his future support for my company is when I tell him the approximate salaries of the top team in Senegal. He is so excited I almost think he is going to pick up the tab for our meal!

My week in Botswana ends and it seems to have been a relatively successful one. I fly back to Leeds and Bradford Airport, arriving in the late afternoon and am driven by the same minicab to the pub next door to the office. I should hasten to add that the pub also has a few rooms and I am going to stay there! After a sound night's sleep, I am back early in the office to provide some feedback on my trip. My two new colleagues seem pleased with what they hear and suggest we make a start on the proposal while the details are still fresh in my mind. But, before getting down to the hard slog of writing, I make a suggestion about altering slightly the usual way that companies put together the layout of contract proposals. I suggest that I develop an additional section on 'likely problems' and 'potential solutions'. From what the Botswana national director has told me, none of the other five companies will have the experience and knowledge to develop such a section, and so it should catch the eye of the contract selection committee. This extra information I propose to write is fully based on personal experience from my days in Senegal.

When the proposal itself is finished, we need to select an international team of two to work with, mentor, guide and build the capacity of the fifteen or so local ministry staff assigned to the project. Given that my children are at critical periods in their education, especially Mélanie will take her A-levels at the end of the current academic year, I say straight off that I cannot be put in the proposal for a long-term position based in Botswana. The solution therefore, to involve me as much as possible, is to add me into the proposed team as the project's technical director and institutional building specialist. In addition, I go in as responsible for setting up the M&E side of the project too.

The company finds an apparently experienced Aussie to assume the team leader role and a young Brit for the second, more junior position. Long story short, in early 2000 we win the contract edging out the incumbent and several other companies that are much better known than us. Experience has been rewarded and I have too. My initial budget line for the two years of the project shows 90 days anticipated work in Botswana plus 45 days to support the project from the UK. A solid amount of work in the bag for the next two years, but little did I know ...!

I arrive back in Northampton after the Botswana and Ripon trips and find that work is beginning to pile up in my lap; of course that is how I like it to be. No more worries, for a while anyway, about earning enough to pay the bills. This financial year, ending in April, looks like being a bumper one.

The period from November through to Christmas and then from New Year to the end of January 2000 is spent in Northampton where I am totally taken up with writing reports covering the base-line data from the three different eco-regions where LDI is working in Madagascar. There is so much data and so much to say about them that I finally manage to produce three large volumes, one for each of their ecoregion.

It is said that the 'Devil never rests', and I know well how he must feel for this consultant does not either. I get a call from the German company, to help write a proposal for another forestry project in Madagascar.

Next on the phone is my dear buddy Chris, calling from Arkansas. After the usual niceties for the New Year, he says. "You would make a great team leader for our new project in Guinea-Conakry called the Enlarged Natural Resources Management Project. Are you interested?"

"I might be but that depends on when and where. We have to stay in UK for the next few months until Mélanie finishes her A-levels, after that she is flying the nest and off to university. David is a little less of a concern at his age, providing there is good schooling available."

"That'll be difficult then because while the project is currently based in Conakry where there is a good American school, over the next year or so all staff, including the team leader, will need to move to Labé, up in the north in the Fouta Djallon. You know it's one of the most beautiful regions in Africa."

"Sorry, Chris but I can't do that to the family and I am pretty busy with other work too."

"But you will have time to do a few missions for us over the next couple of years?"

"Of course I will. In M&E I expect?"

"Yes, exactly. Can you be off for us in March through to around Easter?" Chris queries.

Since that timing fits between my first two programmed trips to Botswana, I accept.

Next up is my first official trip to Botswana for our new project. The international team have mobilised rapidly and I am to undertake a short supervisory mission, wearing my Technical Director's hat and during which I will develop a work plan covering the two years of the project. It is also an opportunity to get to know the national team, composed of around fifteen civil servants seconded to the project by the Ministry of Agriculture, the two international team members, as well as the relevant personnel in DFID. Of course, I will also take the director out for another mega-steak at the 'Bull and Bush'!

During this trip I have decided to move from the Cresta President Hotel to its sister hotel called the Cresta Lodge. Although a little further away from the centre of town, the surroundings are much prettier with far less concrete. I will also have the occasional use of a project vehicle which is a bonus because I discovered another great restaurant called Mike's Kitchen in Kololi after exploring the area where McCall Smith based his Precious Ramotswe detective stories (most people will now have guessed that I am The No 1 Ladies Detective Agency's No 1 fan!).

I receive a friendly email from our new team leader insisting that he will pick me up on arrival at Gaborone Airport and take me over to my hotel, a nice gesture. I arrive, rather shattered in Botswana at about 3 pm. After all, the door-to-door trip from Northampton to Gaborone takes more than twenty-four-hours. What does not help is that I always sleep badly on flights; especially squashed in economy as I am on this trip, courtesy of Virgin Atlantic.

The small plane from J'burg to Gaborone has only around thirty passengers and there are only a couple of obviously non-Batswana, so it should be easy enough for the team leader to spot me. Once through passport control and then customs, I pass through the exit door and stop just outside and wait. I look exactly what I am: a very obvious new arrival with suitcase and computer bag; a consultant in all his splendour!

No one comes up to me, no one tries a tentative smile to see the reaction, I am just left standing there and waiting. Now, this throws up an issue: Botswana is not like the other African countries

I have visited. It is a very modern and thriving country and economy (mostly thanks to diamonds) and does not go in for broken-down yellow taxis as in many other countries on the African continent. Transport from the airport is either private or by hotel bus. And, just across the way, stands the Cresta bus and, if I do not jump on it soon, I will be stranded at the airport. I notice a little, chubby guy wearing a French beret and wrapped up in an overcoat despite the warmth of the afternoon. He certainly does not look like any Aussie I have ever seen. Nonetheless, I raise my hand and wave at him and add a smile but he turns his head and ignores me; so I am sure that he cannot be our new team leader. The bus starts its engine as two passengers board and so, a quick decision, I hop on and we leave direction the two Cresta hotels.

Several hours later, as I am dozing in my room, the phone rings and I am told by the receptionist that there is a gentleman to meet me. A quick walk to the reception and there stands my little chubby guy with the Frenchman beret and overcoat; so some Aussies do look like that after all.

"I came to the airport but did not find you there," he tells me.

"Yes, I saw you as I waited just outside arrivals. I even waved to you but since you made no response, I thought it better to hop on to the Cresta bus. But anyway, I arrived safely and we can talk more tomorrow."

The following morning, he stops at the hotel to pick me up and we drive four or five kilometres northwards on the Old Lobatse Road before turning left just before the Railway Station. We enter the Agriculture Ministry carpark and I cannot help noticing all the new white Toyotas that it contains; courtesy of generous government car loans to its civil servants.

We walk together to our section of the ministry building and, knowing my way from my previous visit, I start to walk up the stairs.

In contrast, my new colleague ignores me and walks straight to the lift, awaiting its arrival. Strange because our offices are only on the first floor!

Once I have been introduced to all the team members, many having offices on the same floor as us but a few on the floor above, I begin sharing the team leader's office and start to develop this new project's two-year work-plan.

For the first day or so, I concentrate hard on my own work and do not take much notice of what the team leader is doing on his computer. Every so often, when I turn round to speak to him or to ask a work-related question, I vaguely see that he is looking at something on the internet but nothing that overly disturbs me. As I develop the work-plan for the different sections of the project, I go from office to office to speak with my new national colleagues getting their inputs and feedback. But, on day three, I suddenly twig something rather odd: in all that time, not once has the team leader left his office to visit a colleague nor has any member of the team come to talk to him. That seems very strange given that we are at the start of a new project, albeit the second phase.

Finally, my curiosity gets the better of me and I have to ask him, "since we are now setting up the project, why is it that no members of your staff have come to speak to you, why have you not gone to speak to them, and why have there been no team meetings?"

He lets out a loud guffaw and, I will remember to the day I die, responds sarcastically "clearly you have no experience of this type of work. Listen carefully, my job title is 'Chief Technical Adviser', do note the last word: 'Adviser'. If no one comes to me for help, that means that no one needs advice, there can be no issues to be settled and thus I can continue doing my work in the knowledge that the project is running smoothly and happily."

That he has not bothered to look at my CV and noted my experience in similar situations is of little worry to me but that he has such a foolish understanding of his own job description is of very great concern. My concern deepens when the three British consultants who are to work with us come in individually to help me fill the gaps in their work planning. Each tells me that they have considerable doubts about the quality of the team leader. I try to dampen things down by saying that they should give him a little time, that he is new in the job and is just settling in. But their statements do rather confirm my own observations and worries and so I speak at length with the team leader to try to get him moving with project work and interacting with the other members of staff. After all, my own interactions with them have shown me that they all seem nice people and keen to learn. The final straw is during my last week in Botswana when I go to the DFID office to present my work-plan. When our discussions are over and the DFID staff have made a few comments and suggested additions to the plan, the DFID lead takes me to one side and tells me very clearly of their total dissatisfaction with our new team leader. He has to go. Ouch, but admittedly no longer a great surprise to me.

A quick call to the company MD in the UK who is understandably staggered by what I have to report to him. He jumps on the next flight and the day after we are sitting together across the desk from our Aussie team leader. As company MD, I let him lead with the issues while I counter any attempt to argue from the team leader. Within fifteen minutes he is given two months' notice to leave the project. The government weighs in with a request that he leaves the country within the two months. This is the most rapid firing I have seen in my entire career!

The company asks me to do some extra work to cover the project, especially from UK, while they search for and recruit a replacement.

Luckily, within the two months' notice period, they come up with a British candidate acceptable to DFID. He mobilises soon afterwards. Since this is a Rangeland Resources and Monitoring project, the company has gone for a livestock specialist who can get support from me for the monitoring-specific and institutional building aspects. All sounds quite logical and, from a distance, the project seems to have started to move forward.

My next trip occurs only a week or so after the new team leader begins to work for us. On this trip, my primary job is to provide a training programme on M&E and then, when the staff have reached a certain level of comfort with the topic, work with them to develop the M&E plan including indicators and targets for the project to monitor. My training workshop starts at 9.30 in the morning after I have flown in from the UK the previous day. It is attended by all project staff plus a few additional ministry personnel who have asked to follow the training. Before setting off for Botswana, I had spent some of my UK-based days to develop the training programme, borrowing aspects from other such courses I have given in the past and adding extra details specific to the project itself. Thus I know that most of my PowerPoint slides and their contents have already been tested on a number of previous occasions. The team seems to follow the training programme with interest and they are not afraid to ask questions or for clarification as needed. I note the new team leader is also present, a good sign, and taking notes as I go through my presentation. At the end of the workshop and presentation, just before lunch, we wind up by taking last questions and then the team walks out, thanking me for an interesting presentation as they go off to eat.

The new team leader is the last person to remain in the room and he comes across and says "I enjoyed the presentation and it was clear and easy to understand. But I did make notes about your presentation and will be sending a full report to the company."

I reply with "I'm not sure that I quite understand what you mean. Do you have specific criticisms or suggested improvements? Did I make errors in what I presented? Are there areas that I missed out? I would be happy to hear from you and equally happy to learn from you."

"No problems with anything you presented and you were very well prepared and familiar with the subject matter. But as your boss, I will be making a report back to head office on every consultant input we receive," he replies.

"That's an idea," I state, "but tell me to whom will you be sending your reports?"

"Well, to my new boss, the Technical Director, of course, who else?"

I hand him my company business card and a very embarrassed team leader reads that he is actually speaking to the technical director in person!

The project seems to be moving along slowly but surely although I am beginning to get a little uncomfortable with the lack of speed in starting to develop the maps of rangeland resources – one of our key deliverables. Such maps are now being developed quite routinely by using images produced by the NOAA satellites, with the satellite data being corrected and improved by botanical field testing, just as we had started to do in Senegal more than a decade ago. The maps we are expected to develop are to be at a far smaller scale than the highly detailed maps developed in The Gambia so we do not need to use aerial photos. Since my time in Banjul, now six years ago, software and computer technology has rapidly moved on while the clicking and clunking of the computers driven by 386 microprocessors have been left far behind!

My next visit to Botswana is, on the surface, to continue the M&E work. However, since we are receiving criticism from the donors about the lack of progress on the maps and from the ministry about lack of application from our international team, I am also going back with a brief to check-out the team and shake them up, if necessary.

I arrive in the office in the ministry one morning and spend the day working with and talking to each activity leader. The Batswana do not like to criticise other people but I can hear that there are issues from what they are not telling me. There seems little enthusiasm and few have much in the way of detailed ideas for their work going forward. I am talking with one technician towards the end of the afternoon when there is a knock at his door and another local colleague enters.

"Malcolm, you should go to the director's office. He is really shouting at the team leader, it sounds bad."

I know that the director had taken an instant dislike to our new team leader but I had hoped that time would make him more positive, I guess not. I jog along to his door and I can clearly hear the one-sided shouting. I enter without knocking and the scene that greets me also appals me. The national director is standing over the team leader screaming at him, fit to burst a major blood vessel while, sadly, the team leader does not have the courage to stand up to him. He is cowering, cringing in his chair with his hands over his head as though for protection.

I tell the team leader to leave and then face off with the director. "How dare you talk to anyone like that, not least the team leader," I say standing face to face with him.

"He is useless, has no ideas and even less courage. He's a wimp," laughs the director. "You wouldn't let me talk to you like that, that's why I like you. Why does he?"

"You can't judge people purely on their courage, you have to see what he brings to the team and what efforts he is making. I see that he is always the first to arrive in the morning and often the last to leave in the evening. No one can fault the energy he puts into his work."

He looks at me and nods and says "I agree that he puts a lot of hours into his work and effort into his tasks but you must balance that by asking yourself 'is he doing the work he is supposed to be doing', you really must."

While I do not like the loss of temper and verbal abuse that has just been dished out, I do ask myself whether the director does not have a point. To verify this, I monitor the team leader's work closely over the next couple of days. After forty-eight hours, I have to concur. Yes, the team leader is putting in a real effort but he is directing that effort at doing other people's work for them and not in managing the team and consultant inputs as he should. His current 'efforts' are all directed at learning how to interpret satellite imagery (and I can assure you, that is not an easy skill to master), to the exclusion of all else, rather than bringing in recognised specialists in their field. I will have to try to reorient his activities towards managing the team and consultants rather than being uniquely hands-on in single areas.

But I am never able to bring about that change of direction. That same evening, while I am eating dinner in the Cresta Lodge restaurant, I get a phone call from a visiting high-level DFID official who informs me that he saw our team leader at the airport. He has left the country without a word to anyone.

His departure also means that I must prolong my stay in Gaborone and try to steer a captainless boat away from the looming rocks.

It also coincides with our upcoming mid-term cum end of first year review, undertaken jointly by the government and the donors. This is a critical moment because we may well be shut down and our contract cancelled; frankly I would not blame the donors either.

The meeting gets underway and I am surprised by the director's opening remarks. While he clearly states that our company has managed to field two very different team leaders, both with serious character and technical issues, he praises the company for their technical and backstopping inputs. The donors, even more surprisingly, weigh in with similar comments. The meeting is not such a complete catastrophe as I had feared it would be; but it is hard going nonetheless, especially when both government and donors express a lack of satisfaction with the other member of our international team.

As lunchtime approaches, the donors sum up the review findings. First, the project has come within a hairsbreadth of closure. Second, during the next, final year of activities, they will be monitoring progress far more closely. Third, the second international team member must leave and a suitable replacement found. Fourth, and non-negotiable, I must be named as team leader while continuing in my technical director role.

Now this leaves me in an impossible situation. While I will try my hardest not to let the company and the project down, I cannot simply up-sticks from the UK and move fulltime to Botswana. I have family responsibilities, and they will always come first, as well as obligations to other clients because, yes, I still have a few. What to do?

The problem is taken out of my hands because as options are passing rapidly through my mind, our donor says "while I insist that you assume the role of team leader, I do not mean that you must move to Botswana. We have spoken internally, and are prepared to accept that you spend approximately a month in and a month out of the country. Of course you will continue to use as many days as needed from the UK to support the project from a distance."

Oooph! That is a great relief. A quick call back to UK to provide detailed feedback and our company is on board and breathing the same sigh of relief as me. They rapidly find a replacement for the second international position who is able to mobilise rapidly, and proves a success.

Getting the donor nod for the second year of the project takes some of the personal financial pressure off my shoulders. During the first year, I was obliged to go so often to Botswana to firefight that I have burnt through all my allocated days for the entire two years, and of course have already been paid for them. By taking on the team leader role, my budget line is replenished as is my income for at least the next twelve months.

Back in Northampton, we have been toying with the idea of building an extension on that piece of land to the side of the house that had attracted me to make the purchase in the first place. We imagine that we can afford a single storey extension that will allow us to expand the kitchen and give me a more private office.

Actually, we are not just toying with the idea but have gone a step further by calling in a young architect for suggestions. He tells us immediately that the work is very doable and goes on to give us a sound piece of advice via a question.

"What do you think are the two most expensive parts of building an extension?" he asks us.

I look at Véro for inspiration and then reply for both of us "I would imagine they must be the digging of the foundations and the building of the roof."

"Precisely. Basically, what lies in between are a few bricks and the occasional window or door; not very expensive items. You are thinking about a single storey extension but I recommend that you find a few thousand pounds more and build a two-storey extension. By doing that I calculate that you will enlarge your living space by about forty percent. Upstairs, your small third bedroom could become a double room with *en suite*, and we can fit in a fourth room as your office at the front. Downstairs, you can have a toilet and then a laundry room. The kitchen will be doubled in size so you will be able to dedicate half to a breakfast room and we could put in French windows to the garden thus providing an enormous amount of light. I think you will be pleased with the result!"

My wife is looking happy with that news, so we give approval for the architectural plans to be drawn up. Next we get a couple of small, local building companies, recommended by friends, to give us quotes. The cheapest is not much over twenty-five thousand pounds all in, including some basic decorating.

Our next stop is the building society to see if they will up our mortgage to cover the cost of the extension. As always, they need to send out a surveyor to value the house now and estimate its value after the work (as if they do not already know the result!). No matter, for an eighty-pound fee, the surveyor comes to the house and, after only ten minutes poking around, tells me that I would be a fool not to do the extension. He explains that in Northampton, a town based on the shoe trade from the end of the nineteenth century, two- and three-bedroom terraced houses are plentiful because they were built by the shoe companies for their workers and managers but four bedrooms are rare. They were constructed predominantly for the factory owners and top-top managers. In recent years, of course, Barratt, Persimmon and the other builders of new houses have come in to built estates of larger houses on land around the town but close to the town centre there is a real shortage of four bedroom properties. The surveyor estimates that by building the extension, we will quadruple our investment ... and so the building society is delighted to lend the extra money.

At the start of the work, we are told by the boss of the company we select to build the extension that it should take around eight weeks. In reality that stretches to eight months – with many silly instances attached to their work. Like for example when a friend of Véro's who is staying with us comes back to the house unexpectedly in the late afternoon and finds the workers sunbathing on deckchairs in our back garden drinking my beer. Like the day I arrive back from Botswana, suitcase in hand, to find a worker plastering the wall of the new hallway. He is doing a pretty poor job as he has left bumps all over the place. When I tell him that the walls should be flat, he challenges me to do a better job than him. I take the proffered trowel and show him the skills I learnt while plastering walls in Cordon! On another occasion, I find an electrician busy at work fitting plugs and switches; and discover that he is forgetting to put the green and yellow collars over the bare earth wire. But no matter, before the end of the Botswana work our extension will be finished.

My first action in the team leader role is to go through the remaining budget; the first time I have been able to look at it in so much detail. I see immediately a big red flag that our accounts had missed: there remain oodles of cash on the budget lines for short-term technical assistance. While the second of the team leaders tried to learn on-the-job such complicated technical procedures as satellite image analysis as part of the rangeland map development, he had missed the obvious solution: that of bringing in specialist help. Within a week, we locate a young and rather brilliant South African to come over to Gaborone to handle the analysis of the satellite imagery while, at the same time, I sign a contract with my old project in Dakar to send over their best field botanist to run the ground-truthing side of the work. Within two weeks we have the core activity of our project up and running hard.

My old forestry friend flies in from Dakar and is soon organising the fieldwork with the relevant Batswana technicians. They delimit twenty-five field sites, just as we had done across Senegal back in the late-80s and, as the rainy season comes to an end, they measure annual vegetation production at those sites. Our young South African then enters the field data into an algorithm and 'hey-presto' the data from our satellite imagery transforms on his computer screen into vegetation production data; the outline of our first rangeland map is produced. I then ask the young fellow to divide the vegetation production data (that is expressed in tons per hectare) by the annual feed requirement of a 'standard tropical unit' (in Botswana one unit is about equal to a large cow!) and (again) hey-presto, a second map appears on the screen; this time for the rangeland carrying capacity. This is the number of head of cattle or other herbivores that a square kilometre of pasture could support throughout a year. We quickly arrange a short presentation of the work, inviting in our donors and senior government representatives. The whistles of surprise that greet the first map is all the praise we need. The project is getting back on the road.

While several of my national teammates are out in the field with my former colleague from Dakar, they take the opportunity to ask him about the Senegalese ecology centre. This leads to an official Botswana government request that our project should organise a trip from Gaborone to Dakar to learn more about the centre's experiences, the challenges they faced and the solutions found to overcome problems; a real South-South experience-sharing mission.

No sooner requested than we are booking air tickets and our hotel in Dakar. The ecology centre in Senegal is pleased to have added Botswana to its list of international clients and is equally happy to cement the relationship by hosting our visit. It will be nice for me to go 'home' to Dakar where I have not been for about a year and meet up with my old teammates.

While I have no doubt that the trip to the centre will be highly beneficial for my Botswana team, I am a little concerned about the peripheries of the trip. Botswana is a very modern society, well organised, with little corruption or cheating and possessing a highly stable political system thanks to the foresight and intelligence of Sir Seretse Khama, the father and first president of modern Botswana. Contrast this with several of the West African nations in which I have worked ... I say no more!

Among the Botswana team, I have one special buddy, a very large, strong but gentle technician and leader of the field botany team. As we all arrive at the little Gaborone airport in the morning, he gives me one of his trademark bear hugs and says teasingly "Don't worry my little friend, I will be your bodyguard in Dakar!"

"Anticipate a reversal of that role," I counter.

We have rather an odd trip ahead of us. The easy part is the Gaborone to J'burg flight. We have all done that many times before. But from J'burg we are to catch a flight with the now defunked Air Afrique to Abidjan in the Ivory Coast, wait there for four hours and then take another flight to Dakar; arrival in Senegal is anticipated at 3 am tomorrow morning.

Our flight to Abidjan is called and we walk on to the tarmac to board an old, very old, Boeing 747. The team of eight who I am accompanying on the trip rush up the stairs like a group of schoolchildren, excited to be making their first trip to West Africa. I follow rather less enthusiastically behind, noting a long crack in the fuselage that runs down the side of the plane and past the starboard wing attachment. This does not fill me with too much confidence but I tell myself that the J'burg airport authority would not allow a dangerous plane to fly.

We take off on what I can only describe as the flight from hell. As soon as we are in the air, we (there must be less than fifty people onboard) are served a very basic lunch, more of a leftover breakfast. One of my team asks for a glass of water, and is told that there is practically no drinking water on board. A beer then? There is no alcohol either and little else in the soft drink line. Three of the four economy class toilets are out of use, and the one still functioning is beginning to smell very badly.

Finally, at around 6.30 pm, we land in Abidjan. Our stopover should be until around 11 pm. And at least we will be given a different plane. But, as I shepherd my (by now) bemused colleagues through the transit corridors, a young Ivorian, wearing his airport identity card on a chain around his neck, comes up to me and asks if I speak French. He tells me that we must follow him and hurry because a curfew has been installed in Abidjan – their civil war is about to begin – and the curfew starts at 7.30 pm. We must go quickly, he tells me. I translate the message to my colleagues and we all trot after the member of ground staff, soon finding ourselves back on the tarmac and boarding the same old, very old, Boeing 747.

As we take-off, the captain comes on line and tells us that our flight pattern is being slightly modified; instead of travelling directly to Dakar, we have to detour to the Cameroons via Nigeria. We stop off in Lagos and a few passengers get off and even fewer come on board.

One very fit looking young man hobbles to the seat next to me. He tells me that he is an international football player from the Cameroons and is travelling on this flight all the way to the US for a knee operation. He has just flown into Lagos from Yaoundé and now learns that he will fly straight back there before the plane turns around and heads for Dakar and finally, for him, the trans-Atlantic leg to New York.

We do finally arrive in Dakar, exactly at 3 am as our tickets had originally predicted. However, we have managed more than double the flight kilometres in getting there!

Despite having taken the same Boeing 747 the whole way, none of our luggage comes out on the carousel; indeed, not a single bag does. The last thing we all need at 3 am is to queue up and provide a sleepy airline staffer with the details of our missing bags. At least yours truly had the foresight to put a change of clothes in his carry on.

Two of my old project drivers are waiting patiently to collect us and take us to our hotel. My old personal driver, Malick, who started his career driving my family around town, tells everyone that will listen to him *"tu sais, c'est mon patron – lui, c'est mon patron"* And of course, apart from me, no one else can understand a word of what he is trying to tell them about me having been his previous employer!

Luckily, at the ecology centre, lack of English is not an issue for the majority of the Senegalese staff. The field botanist has been assigned to look after us during the trip and makes a big scene of welcoming the technicians that he had recently trained in field botany during the map-making exercise.

Senegal is the land of *Teranga*, often translated by the less knowledgeable to mean simply 'hospitality'. In reality, teranga is not a simple word but rather a summation of all those acts of kindness, respect and culture that embody a feeling of belonging to a community. My Botswana colleagues are shown true Senegalese teranga throughout their stay at the centre.

To get the study tour underway, we start by splitting the team into two more manageable groups and each receives a guided tour of all the different activities of the centre before meeting up in the conference room to discuss their observations. As we talk through our impressions of the technical aspects, our director asks about the institutional process that led up to the creation of the business that the centre has become.

One of my ex-colleagues looks across at me and asks in French "would it be helpful to speak to the minister who helped guide the centre through the institutional phase?"

I translate to my Batswana colleagues and they agree it would be a brilliant idea, but query how can you fix a meeting with a person as important as the Minister of the Environment?

My Senegalese colleague, understanding the gist of the exchange in English, takes out his cell phone and speed-dials a number. I can hear him chatting with the person at the other end of the line and they fix a time, just prior to lunch, the next day.

When the connection is cut, I receive a nod and am able to tell my team "we can go to see the Minister tomorrow just before lunch." I then turn to my old friend and thank him for fixing the appointment.

Our director turns to me with a surprised look on his face and asks the question "how was that possible? In Botswana we would need to book an appointment at least a month in advance to see a minister."

"Because my friend is the secretary of the minister's political party, as simple as that," I reply.

The following morning, we are received with great pomp in the ministry. They are delighted to receive a visit from the Botswana delegation of the Ministry of Agriculture, apparently a first for the country. We are soon passing into the office of the minister himself. The next surprise for them is that he welcomes them in perfect

English. The second surprise is that he comes over to me and shakes my hand hard and asks "how are you doing, Malcolm?"

Now the Batswana are really confused! How come the Senegalese Minister speaks such fluent English and how did I get to know him personally? One of my colleagues plucks up the courage to ask the questions and the minister replies with a laugh saying that he did his doctorate and then became a lecturer in the UK and, once upon-a-time, had a teaching colleague; he nods towards me. A small world.

After the pleasantries that help my team to relax, the minister gets down to business and explains that laying the egg that was to become the centre was extremely painful but watching it hatch was a pleasure and seeing it grow into the beautiful creature that it has now become has made all the effort worthwhile. He goes on to say that problems will always crop up, but deal with them calmly and keep an eye on the results you wish to achieve and all will sort itself out.

The team leaves for home after a week in Dakar and the knowledge and experience gained with the friends at the centre provides them with a new impetus to succeed.

I take the opportunity of being in Senegal to travel straight back home to Northampton; I do have a family I miss and a freelance consulting business to run, after all. But I am due back in Botswana soon for a final push before the end-of-project review that is to signal the official end of our project.

That final meeting comes around a few weeks later. We all make a big effort to get our rangeland and carrying capacity maps printed within the ministry – and they do look really good – and are a first for the country. We decorate the walls of the conference room with A0 sized maps and it is nice to see that all the senior members of the ministry have copies proudly displayed on their office walls too.

I work hard to get everything written up and ready for the meeting. Not only is the end-of-project report finished but so is the business plan for the (we hope) future ecological monitoring centre of Botswana.

The meeting starts with proceedings led by the senior representative of DFID and by the government director. All goes well with the review of the past year's progress. Indeed, the review team is very happy with what has been achieved. The meeting seems to progress quickly, so quickly that we soon get down to the closing statements. My whole team hold their breaths as the DFID representative stands up.

"We have overseen a project that is definitely of two halves, of two years. The first half was, quite frankly, atrocious and almost led us to pull the plug on the financing. But we do not need to go back over that; all that needed to be said was said in the review of a year ago. What we do need to do ..." and he looks around the team, both national and international, "... is to summarise the past year, the second year, and I can only think of a single word to sum it up and that word is 'exceptional'. What a change a year brings! Congratulations to you, Mr Director, to Malcolm and to the whole team. I have looked over the accounts of the project and, thanks to that first year when little was spent, there remain considerable funds in the budget. Given the progress made in the second year, I am recommending that the project be allowed a no-cost extension of a third year. You have my support but we will require special approval from the UK government in London."

Sadly, the UK government does not approve the extension, despite taking due note of the progress made in the second year and the quantity of funds that remain in the accounts. The logic (that my Batswana colleagues consider 'illogic') is that the Botswana economy has made such great strides over the past few years that it is now considered a middle-income country and therefore no longer qualifies to receive UK development funds.

As one of my Botswana colleagues says with considerable irony at our closing down meeting "prizes are usually given for excellence but here our country is punished for doing well."

During the two years plus, and the twelve missions I make to Botswana, I find the country, the people and the social inclusion attractive and calming. Botswana really is a country I could (in another life) settle down in. Gaborone itself is a little boring; rather like a Milton Keynes in Africa but with real cows, not concrete ones. However, the countryside is beautiful and fascinating with a high likelihood of coming across an enormous bull elephant standing in the middle of a country road (as indeed we did). The Okavango Delta is a region to be visited and marvelled at. How can a delta exist more than a thousand kilometres from any ocean?

The Kalahari Desert, in the west of the country with a good part shared with the neighbouring Namibia, is on the doorstep of Gaborone. However, having wandered around the Sahara Desert in Mauritania, Chad and Niger, the Kalahari is not really a desert, it is more akin to the Sahel of northern Senegal and southern Niger. Within the Kalahari live the incredible 'San People', often called the Bushmen, who lead a hunter-gatherer existence with their incredible knowledge of nature and an even more incredible language, based on tongue clicks. They are perhaps the oldest living race of humans on the African continent and, in modern times, have either withdrawn into the Kalahari or been integrated into the wider society.

Such are a few of the wonders of nature that Botswana offers. AIDS took a good shot at destroying the country and its economy, leaving innumerable children to be raised by aging grandparents, but the country is resilient and is now taking AIDS in its stride.

Corruption, a plague across many countries of the world, is heavily condemned in Botswana and the economic result is that average incomes are high and rising. A beautiful and interesting country and a lovely and welcoming population.

During those two years of magic and while I am enjoying my four hundred plus days working in and for Botswana, my work on other fronts is not at a complete standstill either. Granted, Botswana represents the majority of my work efforts during the period 2000-2002 but I am still managing to keep other important clients served and, I hope, satisfied with my support. The most important of them sees me continuing to work in Guinea-Conakry for my friend Chris Kopp's company as well as going back to Senegal for a couple of months for the company that runs LDI in Madagascar. These three years are busy, very busy but highly satisfying intellectually.

However, with so much time being dedicated to Botswana, and not forgetting Guinea and Senegal, I am starting to be obliged to refuse the overtures of new clients while juggling with my time to keep other regular clients satisfied. On a single occasion, I am pushed to go through a 'never again' episode lasting an entire fortnight. What happens is that I am contracted by one company to do an input that involves an overseas visit followed by two weeks of intensive UK-based input, mostly to analyse M&E data and write up the report. At the start of the intense UK section, I receive a call from another important client who begs me to take on a major French to English translation for them. Despite saying that I am already fully booked, they will not be put off because, in their words, this is an emergency. We know each other well enough that I am simply told 'come on, you can find a way', And of course there always is a way.

My way is to set my alarm clock on vibration at 4.20 am (not to wake Véro) and to get to my office in a dressing gown by 4.30 am.

I get served breakfast at the keyboard and continue working until 12.30 midday with frequent mugs of coffee arriving full and leaving empty. Midday marks the end of the day for the first company. A thirty-minute break for lunch, a brisk walk around the garden in lieu of digestion and I am back at my computer for the start of the day for the second company with work for them continuing until 9.00 pm. I last at that pace for the entire fortnight but cannot believe that I would have lasted much longer. On the positive side, I have two happy clients and a very happy bank manager.

This intense period in my work life also marks an important time in our daughter's life. As she enters the home straight of her A levels, she starts receiving invitations from different UK universities to come to visit. We are not sure how our daughter comes up with her choice of universities because none of them could be much further from our home in Northampton. She reels off the list that she has applied to: Kent in Southeast England, Swansea in South Wales, St Andrews in the east of Scotland and Aberdeen in the far north of Scotland, that last one practically within the Arctic Circle! The teasing begins that she wants to be as far away from her annoying little brother as possible and, in that case, why did she not go for Northern Ireland or indeed the University of the Falklands?

I end up taking her to visit Swansea on one trip. She declines that one. We then take a plane from Luton to Edinburgh, rent a car there and overnight in the beautiful capital of Scotland. I receive some very strange looks as we check into our hotel where I have reserved a room with two single beds. Luckily we have both brought our passports and the suspicious receptionist can see that we really are closely related! In the evening, we wander the streets of Edinburgh close to our hotel and spot a French restaurant with bright lights shining inside. On entering, we discover that we are the only clients, probably too early for anyone else, and are seated by a young French man.

We chat with him in French and discover that he is the owner, chef and, tonight, providing the service too. He takes our order and walks off, towards the kitchen.

Once out of sight, Mélanie asks "dad, explain something to me, why did you order the house red with the meal, why didn't you choose a bottle from the list?"

"Well," I reply, "there is of course always the price to check but more than that, you can often judge the quality of a restaurant by the house wine they serve. If they serve a *piquette* (plonk) you know that the restaurant is likely not up to much either but if the house wine is good, you know the restaurant takes pride in its business."

Twenty minutes or so later the chef cum waiter comes back with our first courses and then brings a large carafe of wine to the table. He fills my glass with a couple of centimetres and, surprisingly stands back to await my commentary on the wine ... that is not usual with a house wine. My instincts prick a little.

I go through the protocol of tasting a new wine: noting colour, sniffing the *bouquet,* and then tasting and holding the wine in my mouth to allow it to penetrate the different taste bud zones on my tongue before finally swallowing and seeing what sort of taste re-mains in my mouth. Monsieur is watching me closely, Mélanie too.

Finally, I declare "this is excellent and is most certainly not your house wine. I believe that you have just served me a Burgundy and likely a very good one, possibly from Gevrey-Chambertin but I really am not sufficiently expert to say more."

"From an Englishman, I am really impressed," he replies with a laugh and goes back to the bar and returns with an empty bottle to show me that I was quite close. "I overheard your daughter's question and your reply and wanted to test you out so I served you one of my best bottles rather than the house red. Well done."

The following morning, we drive from Edinburgh, crossing the beautiful Forth Road Bridge and follow the signs to the ancient university town of St. Andrews. This university is Scotland's answer to Oxford and Cambridge and possesses an impressive academic reputation made even more appealing by a certain Prince William who decides to do his studies there and, by a pretty young lady, who came with a fishing rod and managed to hook the prince.

But the university does not attract my French Miss, too snobby she tells me after her interview with a lecturer followed by a guided tour with fellow students. Despite getting the required grades, the university did not get my lady. That honour went to Aberdeen, the university of the Silver City.

And not to forget our chirpy boy. He is now almost fifteen and full of character. One afternoon while I am working in my office he returns from school with an equally chirpy friend.

The friend asks "Mr Marks, what do you really do for a living? David tells me that you travel to different countries and work as a biologist. But what specifically do you do?"

"Well, that's a bit complicated to answer quickly. I do lots of different things, usually working with the US or UK governments to help other countries. Let me show you these," and I extract a roll of maps from my Botswana work, "they are maps that I have just helped to make in Botswana."

He takes one look at the maps and scoots out my office saying to David "you see, you see, I told you he must be a spy!" And the kids leave the house to get up to some gentle mischief and certainly spread the rumour.

8

New Travels, Old Countries

I feel sad to have come to the end of the Botswana work. Also to be leaving such a wonderful country and people, at least for the time being. I feel justly proud of the two consultants from South Africa and Senegal who came in so rapidly and effectively, making my job that much easier in the process. I am thankful to the local team who stepped up to the mark and of the donors at DFID who kept faith in our ability to turn things around after that dreadful first year.

But leaving lovely places, indeed leaving not so lovely ones too, is the destiny of all consultants. Finishing the Botswana work simply means that I am moving on to the next chapter in my career. Overlapping with the Botswana work, I also manage three visits to Guinea-Conakry, starting off the first assignment in the capital with the initial team leader. He departs the project when he is asked and refuses to move from Conakry to the northern town of Labé. His replacement is a gentle young man whom I had gotten to know very well in Senegal, several years back.

On my second trip to the project where I am now reporting to the new team leader, all my time and work is based in in the country-side around Labé. I arrive in the town at the moment when the new team leader and his family have just moved into their rental house in this northern town. We are sitting at the dinner table enjoying a marvellous Thai meal when his wife tells me that she had a new washing machine delivered this very afternoon, and do I, by any chance, know anything about washing machines?

"I'm not sure how to answer you," I reply. "If the machine is not working, I will not be able to do anything more than check that the electricity is getting to the motor. What seems to be the problem?"

"No, it works OK but everytime I switch it on, it runs fine for a few minutes and then starts bouncing and jumping across the room, until finally it manages to pull the plug out of the wall socket" she replies.

Her husband laughs at this description but admits that it is true and he is baffled.

"I bet I know exactly the problem," I state, "did you remember to remove the immobilisation bolts out of the back of the washing machine? Those are put in by the manufacturers to hold the rotating drum stable during transport otherwise you would risk the drive shaft getting damaged."

We go to the laundry room, I pull the machine away from the wall and turn it around to check the back, and there they are: four bronze bolts still proudly in place! A few turns with an adjustable spanner and the bolts are removed and the washing machine ready to go. Madam loads in a basketful of washing and then the soap powder, and offers me the honour of the first push of the 'start' button. The machine hums, water enters, turns bubbly, the drum turns and the machine stays firmly in place.

I really enjoy my work in Labé. It is interesting, the local and international teams are friendly and committed while the countryside of the Fouta Djallon is some of the most beautiful I have ever seen. My opinion of Guinea changes too from the negative one I had following my first trip there in 1995 to a very positive one after my recent missions in the country.

I also go back to Senegal, for a full two months. I am part of a team of three that is working with the US mission to develop two major pieces of work. The first is to undertake a review of assistance activities in the fields of agriculture and natural resources management undertaken with US funding in Senegal over the past forty years; indeed, since independence in 1960. This is a massive and varied piece of work and we are well supported by several of the Senegalese specialists at USAID who constitute their institutional memory. The second, and (perhaps) more important piece of work, is to extract the major lessons learnt from that first piece of what worked and what did not, and use them to develop a prospective proposal for activities that might be used in future projects.

Being back in Senegal also gives me a fresh opportunity to catch up with close friends both at my old project and in general, people like 'old Alan' (Mr Cockroach) who recently celebrated his eighty-third birthday and still seems to be going strong.

Part of our work analysis requires a period of extensive travel around the Kaolack and Sine Saloum areas, following which we are to travel on to Tambacounda for an additional piece of work that has been latterly added into our ToR.

The first part of the trip is to re-visit the sites of some old, small-scale agriculture projects and check the level of sustainability of activities that were introduced by the US a couple of decades pre-viously. During this trip, one of our team, an American, mentions that he had been a Peace Corp volunteer more than thirty years previously and had lived in a village not far from our work site. We agree to make a small detour so that he can go back to visit his old village for nostalgia's sake.

Our large 4-wheel drive vehicle enters the small village composed of individual compounds enclosed by protective barriers of rough stakes interwoven with prickly '*Balanites*' branches. Immediately we are noticed by a crowd of small and noisy children, then by a group of smiling-faced girls and ladies who shyly cover and then uncover their faces with bright cotton scarves, and finally by several elderly men who maintain a calm dignity, typical of their age group.

The children and the women respectfully let the elderly gentlemen through to be the first to greet us. They shake our hands and say 'a *salam malikum*' and '*nan-ga-def*' as is typical in their society.

One elderly gentleman who sports a single tooth at the front of his gummy mouth moves across to my American teammate and enquires "*Malik? C'est toi?*" (is that you?)

They fall into each other's arms, hug and chat in Wolof for a long moment. Finally, 'Malik' (the name my colleague was given by the villagers three decades ago), comes over to me and presents his 'brother' that he has not seen for more than thirty years. He explains that the American Peace Corp believes in total immersion and integration (at least it did when he started his two-year assignment back in the late 1960s) whereby, after a short intensive language training, the young volunteers enter, often remote, village communities and are 'adopted' into a family with whom they remain for the entire two years. During this immersion, most of the American youngsters become totally fluent in the local languages and adopt many of the characteristics and habits of their adoptive families.

Regretfully we soon have to say goodbye to the villagers and head off to our next site. As we drive along, I can see that my American colleague has large tears in his eyes as he sits quietly in the rear seat.

"Heh, buddy, what's happened? Why so sad?" I ask concerned for him.

"Did you see how old my 'brother' looks? What would you think his age is, at least 70 or so, no? Actually he's the same age as me but looks more than twenty years older. I cannot get that image out of my mind. I remember him as a handsome young man of twenty, now look at him. That is the result of the harsh life those villagers live."

The recently added part of our ToR is to carry out an evaluation of a current project and, for that aspect, we travel to the south-eastern town of Tambacounda. Evaluations, the second part of M&E work, are always nervy events for the project team. There is always self-doubt and the leaders of the team inevitably ask themselves is our project doing its work correctly and adequately? Will the evaluators find any of our hidden failures (there are always a few tucked away!)? Will our approach to working with the participants be appreciated? And many more questions of uncertainty.

The project we are looking at is trying to promote different means of ensuring that the use of local natural resource is becoming more sustainable. It is also supposed to target help to the *very poorest families* (note that target population) to begin income-generating activities. Their *modus operandi* is to use local technical staff to visit villages and explain the project's ambitions and activities. Villagers are then provided with a list of potential cash-generating activities, with the most popular being cattle fattening or fruit tree planting. Villagers are then asked to select one or more of the activities, if interested of course. The project assists in two main ways, the first is by capacity building to help the villagers with their new activities, the second is by providing cash incentives to start such activities. The cash assistance ranges from fifty percent of the total budget for something like cattle fattening up to ninety percent for activities like tree planting; and there lies the problem we quickly uncover.

On our first morning in Tamba, two vehicles roll up to our hotel. One contains two members of the international technical team and the other has a couple of field technicians and their driver. We quickly deny the assistance of the internationals, as we want local staff to feel they can speak freely with us. We leave in convoy with the local technicians and visit a village nearby that the project itself has selected. The three of us in our team are sufficiently savvy to know that we are about to be taken to a village that the project will consider to be 'successful'. This is fine for us because we decide logically that if they are taking us to one of their best villages, should we happen to find issues, this will reflect badly on the rest of the project sites. And within thirty minutes we find just that.

Our first stop, selected by the project technicians, is at a farmer's compound who is fattening two cows in his stable that adjoins his home. My American colleague asks him in Wolof why he decided to join into this specific project activity.

His response is unsettling, for he replies to us, also in Wolof, "it was a no-brainer. The project told me that they would fund me 50/50 for a cattle fattening project and since I intended to buy a cow anyway, I decided to join and so instead of buying a single cow, I got two for the same level of investment!"

I ask the next, and deliberately leading, question "has everyone in the village done the same thing as you?"

"Well no, of course not. A cow is expensive and so most villagers cannot afford even the fifty percent to buy one."

Eh bam. There lies the fault in the project's model. In reality it is not helping the very poorest villagers who are supposed to be its target population because the very poorest cannot afford the fifty percent required to buy a cow or whatever activity the project might be proposing to them. Instead, the project is helping only the wealthier families who have the money available to invest.

We confirm this conclusion by going to speak with families that we are told by the same farmer are among the poorest in the village. They confirm our suspicions by telling us immediately that they believe the project is avoiding them because they are too poor to be helped.

Sometimes projects get it wrong, despite having the very best of intentions. We return to Dakar and make our report to the donor hierarchy, are thanked and told that they agree that the model is seriously flawed. The project soon closes.

We finish our two main reports. The first one is of broad interest since it points out a historical sequence of what has been done in the past, what has worked and what has not; facts that are today more of an academic interest but might help to prevent the same errors being repeated in the future. However, the second report, that proposes activities that could be included in future projects based on successes drawn out in the first, is the one that the mission is really waiting for. Our reports form the basis of one or two project that should start in the not too distant future.

In mid-2002, as my work in Botswana begins to draw to a close, I start receiving phone calls and emails asking my interest in being considered as a long term team member of 'an upcoming project in Senegal'. Our prospective report has indeed been used to help design a new project and that project will soon be put out to tender. Some who approach me by phone are companies with whom I have worked in the recent past while others who contact me by email are often unknown to me.

One American company, for whom I have never worked, went as far as to ask my availability and then recommend that I read the two reports that they had thoughtfully attached to their email. They considered that I might find them of interest in reaching a decision about joining their team. I open the attachments and find that they are sending me the two reports that I developed and lead-authored for Senegal!

I reply, thanking them for their interest, and pointing out (very much tongue in cheek) that the Malcolm Marks to whom they are writing is the same person who had written the two reports they had kindly thought to send me! And indeed this carelessness on their behalf did convince me *not* to join their team!

Meanwhile the Washington company I worked for in The Gambia tells me that they would like to include me in their team but I will only be allocated a long term position if there is a suitable opening available (I guess that is fair enough), but they say that I would still be obliged to sign an exclusivity agreement based on that half-offer (which I consider not so fair).

In contrast, my friend Chris Kopp in Arkansas calls and says that if I am willing to join his company's team, they will ensure that there is a long-term position for me no matter what. Logically, I sign an exclusive with his company.

By one of those twists of fate, my former company soon learns, a little too late, that one of the long-term positions really does need my skills because it is all about environmental policy and M&E but, because of my exclusivity with Chris' company, they must now take that company as a partner on the bid in order to get me into their proposed team!

Nothing is ever sure in the consultancy world so, while I believe we are in a very good position to win the contract, one just never knows and I so continue to look for and accept other work assignments. Two are upcoming, the first in Morocco with a new company based in Italy and the second back in Benin for Jorgen's German company.

First off, I am employed by the Italian company to undertake the work in Morocco as their specialist in environmental monitoring. The work is on a new protected areas project funded by the Global Environment Facility of the World Bank. There are potentially several missions to be undertaken over the course of the project and this does guarantee me a good level of future work in Morocco just in case our team does not win the Senegal bid.

My first mission in Morocco starts in late November 2002 and is to occupy me until close to Christmas. The project itself looks really interesting and is getting me right back to my original ecology roots. I am to undertake considerable travel both along the Mediterranean and Atlantic coasts as well as into the Atlas Mountains to help set up plant and animal monitoring systems in three national parks and ten Sites of Scientific Interest (SSI); potentially fascinating work for me. I arrive for my first day in the ministry in the capital Rabat and am invited to attend an opening meeting chaired by the director of the project.

He starts the meeting by reading out aloud in French my CV, sneering as he tells the entire audience that I have little relevant M&E and ecological experience in Africa. I find that odd because I started working on the continent as a lecturer in ecology in Nigeria in 1979 and, apart a few years as a teacher in the mid-80s, have worked exclusively in and with the continent ever since. My credentials in M&E are now well known in the development world.

I counter by saying "I agree that I have little experience if one does not count the last twenty years that are clearly described in my CV."

He responds in a very nasty and racial manner about the inhabitants of the countries to the south of the Sahara in which I have worked. I rapidly grasp the fact that this mission is not going to be easy with him in charge.

After trying to establish his credentials as the alpha male (I was going to write 'alpha dog'!), he leaves the room and I can get on to plan the work for the next month or so with my new colleagues. Several of them tell me openly that the director is difficult and that I must try not to get annoyed with him. However, since this trip has started with a racial attack on friends and colleagues from the many African nations I have had the pleasure to work with, I confess to feeling very prickly at this moment and I will not be so polite if this guy tries to attack in the same way again.

During this initial trip to Morocco, I have two main activities to undertake. The first one is to visit all three national parks and several of the SSIs while the second is to write up the details of how I propose to the project that the environmental as well as general project monitoring should be carried out. Once my proposals are accepted, I will lead on the future environmental monitoring work itself.

I am to spend a bit more than two weeks on the road visiting some of the sites with relevant colleagues. We set off only a couple of days after my arrival in Rabat with the first part of the trip taking us to the northern coast of Morocco in order to visit the Al Hoceima and Boujibar National parks. Not only do these parks offer fantastic birdwatching opportunities, they also have unbelievable geological formations that are really eye-catching even to a non-geologist like me. While we are taking a guided walk around the coastline of the Al Hoceima National Park, I notice barbed wire fences surrounding a small rocky peninsular jutting into the sea. I ask the reason for the wire and am told that the peninsular is a part of the coastline claimed as Spanish sovereign territory.

"But a part of Spain on the African coast belonging to Morocco?" I query.

"Yes, disgraceful isn't it," one of my colleagues replies. "The Spanish occupy several small enclaves along the coast that we consider is Moroccan territory. However, we would need a passport and a visa to enter. You, of course, could enter with just your European passport."

That got me thinking about the hypocrisy of nations. While Spain is always making bellicose noises about the legality of Gibraltar being a British Overseas Territory, it quietly occupies several tracts of Moroccan coastline.

The saying 'don't do as I do, do as I say!' springs to mind

The next part of our trip takes us to the National Park of the High Atlas Mountains. On the drive south we stop in the little town of Meknes and I am surprised to see cafes openly serving local wine to all-comers. In the capital Rabat, even to drink a small can of beer, one is obliged to go into a four- or five-star hotel while here in Meknes, the cheap and pretty rough wine of the region is available to all.

From Meknes we travel into the lower Atlas and pass the night in a small hotel before heading up into the mountains and well above the snowline. Despite this being only early December, I have to confess that I have never, in my entire life, felt as cold as I do today. At convenient moments I pull my suitcase out of the back of the car and sequentially keep loading up with layer after layer of extra t-shirts and jumpers until I resemble quite closely the Michelin Man!

Our park trip is fascinating and I get to appreciate and like the three civil servants who travel with me and act as my guides to the parks and to Morocco generally but eventually we have to return to Rabat and I must get down to report writing and the development of the monitoring system.

My work is progressing well and so I give a presentation of ideas and results to the team in order to obtain any relevant feedback that I can add into the report. The director is, thankfully, out of town but his boss, the *Directeur de Cabinet* to the Minster attends and ask some relevant questions. At the end of the presentation, he invites me to his office and pours us both a cup of strong coffee.

"I enjoyed your presentation, it was clear and concise and the staff have told me that you know your subject and have struck up empathy with them. I also heard that you had some early problems with the director. Has that settled down now?"

"The staff are all great, helpful, knowledgeable and friendly. As for relations with the director, well I hope so but I haven't seen him for the last few weeks while we were in the field and now he is out of the office but I hear he is back tomorrow. Anyway, I only have three days left and then I am home to UK, just in time for Christmas."

"Will your work be finished?" he asks.

"I will certainly have a very advanced draft for you, but my contract allows a few extra days of work from home and this will give me a little extra time to ensure that I complete the final report and carefully proof read it. Also I am due back in Rabat in a couple of weeks so that any remaining issues can be cleared up then."

"That all sounds good. Thanks for all your efforts and, by the way, congratulations on your excellent French!" He shakes my hand and I go back to my office. What a pleasant man.

With only a couple of days remaining until I am scheduled to fly home, I get my head down and my report is coming along nicely. On my final afternoon I stay late in the office to get some final tables drawn up and looking 'pretty'. All I really need to do now in order to complete my report is to check through it one last time to iron out any typos and then add a couple of small paragraphs at the front by way of a summary.

I start to pack my computer and papers away. I have to get back to the guesthouse within thirty minutes or so or I will miss dinner. After eating, I still have to pack my suitcase and then I want to get to bed early, my taxi for the airport is arriving at 6 am tomorrow morning.

"Give me your final report now," comes a familiar aggressive voice from behind me."

"Good evening Director. I still have a few bits to complete but I will email it to you in the next two days as is written in my contract."

"If you have not finished then you should not go home but stay here to complete" he says in a voice that steadily rises throughout the sentence and ends in a shout.

Very calmly I reply, "I am going home because it is Christmas in a couple of days and I will not miss being with my family for such an important occasion."

"That is not an important occasion, it is a Pagan ceremony," he continues shouting, going quite red in the face.

By now, I am beginning to get a bit annoyed with the foolish and very rude fellow and say back as calmly as I can "It is most certainly not a pagan ceremony but the celebration of the birth of Jesus Christ."

"Your Christ is nothing special, just another prophet, not even on par with Moses," he informs me.

I look over my shoulder and say back to him, as calmly as I can, "Director, you may believe exactly what you wish because frankly I do not give a damn."

At this point, he loses it. He screams, rants and becomes hysterical, throwing insults at me and clenching his fists. Until now, I had thought of him as just a silly bigot but I can now see that he has some serious issues and has completely lost control of his temper. And I am not prepared to be aggressed by this fool and so I stand up to face him; I am several inches taller, many years younger and a fair few kilograms heavier. But my posture does not shut him up, he continues screaming, insulting and threatening until the door to the room bursts opens and in walks the *Directeur de Cabinet.*

"I have heard too much of your screaming *M. le Directeur*, that is quite enough from you. Malcolm, thank you for your work and all your efforts. I think it best that you leave the office now. Have a safe trip home."

I arrive back in UK the following day, finish my report quickly and send it off to Morocco and to the Italian company that has hired me. My payment for the mission is transferred rapidly into my bank account, arriving a few days after Christmas. My resignation goes in equally rapidly. While I am prepared to put up with difficult conditions during my work, I am not prepared to accept harassment, racism and bigotry during the execution of that work. The director stepped too far over the line for me to accept such behaviour.

New Year 2003 comes around and my present for the year arrives on the second of January when I hear that our team has indeed won the Senegalese contract. The work on my component is for a total of three years and a couple of months. We are to mobilise as a team in early February. The rapidity of our mobilisation creates a problem for me due to a follow-up assignment I had agreed to do for the German company at their project in Benin, now entering its second phase. I am a little sad about this because I like the staff at the company head office, the team leader in Cotonou has become a close friend, the national director is very supportive of our activities, and indeed I enjoy visiting Benin with its thousands of little Hondas that create roadblocks at unpredictable times of day. But I feel that if I am to let them down, I need to be totally honest and tell them quickly so they can make alternative arrangements.

I make the call to the company office in Germany and tell them that I have accepted a new long-term post in Senegal, starting in

February, and so am not available to undertake my next mission for them. Their response is to say that if I am no longer available in February, why not go now in early January; and so I do.

The first part of my mission is based at the project office in the Ministry of Forestry in the capital Cotonou. Because the dates of my mission have been brought forward by a few weeks, I arrive at a time when only the team leader and the national director are in their offices. The rest of the team involved in the monitoring activities, who will be working with me, are out of office for a few days at a civil service training programme.

The German company has also sent out to Benin a young member of their staff to shadow me during my work as a means of gaining some experience and insight into consulting work. She is sharing my ministry office. During the first few days, and in the absence of my national counterparts, I concentrate hard on developing a new training programme that I must soon present to a different group in the ministry on 'How to carry out environmental audits'. The young lady gets on with some company work that she has brought from Germany.

Three days into my mission, the team leader puts his head around the door to invite me to his house for dinner that evening. His Nigerian wife, hearing that I am in town, is going to cook for me one of my favourite Nigerian dishes: goat meat pepper soup; the pepper is made from the hottest chilies, not peppercorns!

My friend then asks the young German lady how her work is going. She says OK but asks to speak to him outside. Some confidential company business, I assume.

Fifteen minutes later, the team leader comes back to my office, minus the young lady, and sits down.

"Heh buddy, do you want to know what she said, that young girl?" he asks.

"Only If it's not confidential," I reply.

"She said she wanted to report you to me because in all the time you have been here, not once have you interacted with any staff apart from the national director and me."

"What did you say?" I ask chuckling slightly.

"I didn't say much. I told her to follow me and I went to knock at every door where the staff usually work. She discovered that there are no other staff in the building. I then gave her a good ticking off and told her that she is lucky that I do not report *her* to head office for insulting you. I also said that she is fortunate to be able to work and learn from someone as experienced as you. She is waiting in my office and I am going to tell her to come up here and apologise to you."

"Let it go, I don't need an apology. She is young and learning and I don't want to embarrass her further."

A few days later, as we travel to different project sites, she asks me what important lessons she should learn to become a successful consultant like me. My response includes: Be a sponge; soak up as much information as you can. Be humble; never assume that you have all the answers or that you are more expert than the people you are helping. Try to learn; what you learn today will serve you tomorrow. Keep calm; you will always come across someone who wants to trip you up. Finally, respect and provide capacity building help to all the local staff you work with.

On that last point she asks a question that I have been asked many many times in the past. "But if you train your local counterparts too well, surely that puts you out of a job?"

I nod an agreement but go on to add "In principle, I can see why that might seem the case but try to imagine a young technician who is helped by me, shown my respect and learns sufficiently well to get promotion or to move to a higher post in a different project. When that person encounters a problem or needs help or is asked to recommend a consultant for other work, who do you think they will tell their boss to contact?"

Once the staff training at the ministry in Cotonou is finished, we go off into the field where the project's main activities are underway based in three massive forest blocks near to the centre of the country. The nearest major town is Parakou, one of the towns in which we are staying. The project is trying to build up small commercial enterprises based on renewable forest resources. One enterprise we visit is breeding 'bush rats' or agouti to be sold into the Cotonou market while another has whole villages working within a honey producing cooperative. I am told that we really must investigate this project more closely because it is being helped by a French couple who have given up France to live and work in Benin.

We drive into the forest taking small, tracks that only a four-wheel drive can negotiate and, after an hour or so bumping along, come into a clearing in which stands a most magnificent house built totally of local materials. It has two floors and must contain several bedrooms, given its size, and a massive terrace out-front with an unhindered view into the forest.

Two fit looking middle-aged French come out to greet us and take us for a visit around their home. No words are sufficient to explain the simple splendour of what they have created in this very remote spot.

But we are here to work not remain captivated by this incredible sight in the forest. We leave on a hike through the forest that is to last all afternoon and the walk gives me the opportunity to chat with our host. He is working on beekeeping not because he particularly likes bees – although he proves to be a specialist – but rather as a way to help protect the forests from bushfires. Noting my surprised look, he explains that the traditional way to collect honey, a product that has real value in the major towns of Benin, is to find wild bee swarms (mostly in holes in trees) and to smoke them out with fire. Then the hole is hacked to make it sufficiently large for the comb to be pulled out. Not only does this behaviour kill the hive, the queen and all the young nymphs who might eventually become queens, it almost invariably starts bushfires that destroy the vegetation and any animals that cannot get away.

He researched beehives and found that some traditional one could be made by weaving tightly packed grass into a sphere with an entrance at the front. These are placed several metres up in forest trees and they invariably attract wild swarms.

He is teaching around fifty families how to weave their own hives, select the trees where they can be affixed and, importantly, how to use simple smoke generators, locally produced from recycled materials, to calm the bees at honey harvesting times. He has also persuaded the families to create and join a beekeeping cooperative. It is this group of villagers that has attracted project funds and the aid money has been used to purchase some quite modern material such as a centrifuge, hygienic washing facilities as well as sealable jars and labels. Their commercial enterprise has been able to negotiate much higher prices for the honey from companies based in the capital who are attracted by the volume of honey on offer and its far superior quality and hygiene. A winning combination.

The win-win of his beekeeping activities is that the beekeepers can only generate a solid income if their hives are left in peace. Woe betide any hunter who decides to set a fire to drive game animals towards his nets or guns!

Of course everyone in my group is curious to know how he and his wife ended up living in the middle of a forest in Benin. The story he tells us is incredible and leaves us all incredulous. He explains that they came across the village, located a short distance from his present home, by chance during a trekking vacation. He and his wife arrived in the village and immediately were swept up into a big festivity of celebrations for the White Saviour that their folklore said would, one day, arrive to help them.

As anyone would do, he tried to explain to the villagers that he was a simple holidaymaker and perhaps they should wait a little longer for the long anticipated saviour to arrive. But they would have none of his excuses. They made him a chief, they gave him hectares of forest and they helped him to build his first, rather rustic home. Basically he had two options: disappear back to France and never return, or move to Benin and spend his time helping the villagers. He decided the latter and is now dedicating his life to the area. And, by his actions, he has, of course, proven the veracity of the village folklore!

My project is using him for considerable consultancy work that seeks to build the capacity of the villagers with the twin objectives of vastly improving their incomes while helping the forests to regenerate. One important sign that the forest is improving dramatically now that bushfires are being curtailed is the arrival and growing size of a small herd of buffalo while, just prior to our arrival at his home, there were sightings of a pair of West African wild dogs – very rare animals indeed – that probably crossed into Benin from the neighbouring Togo.

9

Back to Senegal

Mélanie is well into her third year at the University of Aberdeen, reading anthropology. The *wee lass* is proving herself a Chamaeleon yet again by picking up a Scottish accent; but, to us, that is preferable to the strong American one she obtained in Dakar while at the American School! We now get calls as she rides on the bus to the university campus to tell us that she is looking at '*wee bonny seals*' that are swimming in the North Sea or that '*last night, you ken, I had a wee dram too much*'! She loves university life, the freedom being away from us but knowing that we are always there, just in case. Her studies are going well and the finals of her degree are only a few months away, then on to the fourth Scottish year and the hope of getting a Masters at the end.

David is now seventeen, less confident than his big sister and with considerably less application to his work. He is also the cleverest of the family. The French have a saying for people like him '*intelligence au service de la paresse*' and his response is that it has been proven that more intelligent people always appear to be lazier simply because they take the time to reflect. In a roundabout way that may prove our point!

His A-level exams are in June next year and, because of his apparent lack of application, we are secretly a little worried about them. We recently spoke to his economics teacher, a lady who favours leopard-print clothes. She tells us that she is fond of David but that he can best be compared with an onion: as you peel away one layer and feel you know the beast a bit better, you find a different layer revealed underneath. She tells us that getting to know and motivate our son has been quite an adventure, and continuing the onion analogy, but often makes you want to cry!

For a short while his family nickname becomes 'onions' but that is rapidly changed to 'skunky' when he arrives home one evening at the weekend with a white band dyed into his hair at the crown of his head!

School work aside, I am also worried about my son because my work in Senegal is about to start and so I have soon to leave Northampton. On the positive side, good friends in Northampton and the parents of his best friend, say there is plenty of room in their home for him to stay with them during the times that Véro is in Senegal with me. But we cannot take advantage of their kindness and I insist that we put in place a financial arrangement that means we pay them for the weeks that David stays in their home. Thankfully, educational costs like these are covered by the project. All the same, it is a difficult decision to make and results in Véro splitting her time during the first year or so between being with me in Senegal and with David in Northampton. When he gets his A levels and goes off to university we can reassess the situation.

For the start of the project in early February 2003, Véro and I go off together to Dakar and meet up with the rest of the senior team. The team leader is my old friend from Niger days, we have another expat in the shape of a likeable young man from the US. The fourth member of the senior team is an ex-member of the Forestry department in Senegal who is known affectionately by everyone as the '*Colonel*', his last rank in the paramilitary forestry cadre.

We are all together in Dakar for a week or so of team-building, initial work planning, meetings with donors and with the government; all the usual project start-up activities. We are also together to recruit more junior staff such as drivers and secretaries. Our young American colleague and his wife are both recent members of the Peace Corp and both perfectly fluent in Wolof. His wife is hired as a short-term consultant to help with such tasks as getting grouped estimates for air conditioners, refrigerators, computers, stoves and ovens, even furniture. The team leader hopes to make savings by buying for everyone in bulk. She is also charged with getting adverts into the local newspapers for drivers using a PMB (private mailbag) address at the central post office.

As the main activities of the project are to be based initially in the south-eastern town of Tambacounda, my senior colleagues and just about all of the technical team are soon going off to the town to look for personal and office accommodation. I, alone of the four seniors, get to reside in Dakar since half of my work activities, that of influencing environmental policy, can only be achieved by working with senior government officials in Dakar. The other part of my work, monitoring and information management, will require me to travel to the project sites and I expect either to rent a very cheap house in Tamba or stay in one of the few small hotels that have recently established there.

Véro finds us a lovely home in an area that touches on to the sea called Yoff Virage. Yoff is the part of Dakar where the airport is situated, about two kilometres by road from our new house, while *virage* indicates a bend in the road which indeed exists at the point where one leaves the tarmac road to the airport and enters into the group of houses where ours is situated close to the shore. In our little village, there is a small supermarket and a bar cum restaurant.

Our new house has three bedrooms, perfect for when the kids come to stay, a very large sitting room that sits on two levels allowing us to have a dining area on the raised part and a cosy sitting room on the lower one. A spacious kitchen sits just to the rear of the dining room. There is a front garden, down to grass and a few shrubs, with a garage at the side while at the back of the house is the servant's quarters where a maid will live; once hired. The real beauty of the house is, however, the roof terrace. We get to the terrace via a spiral stairway that starts in a small internal garden and finishes at a glass door that lets on to the roof. From the roof, we look straight over to a rocky cove and beyond that the Atlantic Ocean. At least that is the manner that we were persuaded by the owner to rent the house. Within a couple of years, other (illegal) properties begin to spring up in front of us, pretty much blocking our once perfect view. I also find a car, a second hand Renault Laguna purchased from a garage that imports cars from France. I get one of my old drivers and project mechanic from the ecology centre to check over a few cars on offer at the import company and drive out with the Renault.

He teases me by saying that for a big boss, I really should be going for a Merc or a Beemer; but such luxury has never been my style – and you should see the state of some of the roads I have to drive on!

Véro is now very experienced in finding good quality maids. Experience has shown that if one is prepared to pay above the local rate, then a well-trained lady, fairly fluent in French, can be found and retained. She has found that the best place to look for a maid is to make a visit to the catholic nuns who run maid training schools. A bag of groceries and a bottle of wine gains her access to the sisters and our new maid is presented, interviewed and comes to work for us. I also hire a guard, called Diallo who originally hails from Guinea (just like 80% of the Diallos in Senegal). He lives in a small house with his wife and umpteen children, very near to our new home, but spends most of the days and nights camping out in our garage.

In Senegal, as in much of Africa, a house guard is rather like an insurance policy. If you do not have one, you are sure to be burgled while if you do, the chances are much lower. Our Diallo is a polite, rather frail and elderly gentleman, who would be incapable of stopping any burglar worth his salt. But Diallo works in an unofficial brotherhood with all the other guards in the neighbour-hood. His tools of trade are a machete, rarely used and only then for opening coconuts not for chopping up burglars, and a whistle that occasionally is. Whistles are used by guards to signal if a burglary is in progress or to follow the path of a fleeing burglar should he try to run away. My only experience of an attempted burglary in Senegal was when we lived in the area called *Sacré Cœur 3,* several years previously. Then the unfortunate person was caught, a painful local punishment meted out and he would have been thrown over the Dakar cliffs if I had not intervened. Burglars learn quickly that some houses are best left alone.

My colleagues in Tamba find themselves suitable homes in the town and also rent a sizeable building to be our office. My main office is in Dakar, in the Forestry Department building where I have a large room. My secretary has a smaller one just down the corridor. Our project director, a nice young man and a serving officer of the department, has an office resembling a presidential suite next to mine. All is ready for us to get on with our proper work.

The post office calls the wife of my young colleague, now our re-cruitment lady, to tell her that there is mail to collect. She goes with a project vehicle and comes back with the back of the pick-up full of mailbags. We have received thousands of applications for the four driver positions. Everyone has to help in sorting the mail or we will never get any drivers hired. We soon start to see that most applicants have applied on 'a wing and a prayer'. Usually there is nothing in the envelope except a photocopy of a driver's licence. Those all go into the rejected pile since we do not even know if they can speak any French or know how to drive in the bush. But, even with the best will in the world, we soon discover that we can never get to the bottom of the mail bags of applicant letters because the post office rings an hour later to tell us that they have more bags for us to collect.

Finally, I ask the team leader "why do you want to go through this lengthy process and then hire unknown people? Why don't we hire drivers that are known to us or recommended by the donors or the ministry?"

My other colleagues agree (with a certain amount of relief when they see all the mailbags that are now piled up in an office). The Colonel rings the ministry, the team leader rings the donor office while I ring former colleagues at my old project. Within twenty minutes we have four recommended drivers, all experienced in bush driving ready for employment. My assigned driver is officially called *Pape* but he tells everyone that his name is Moctar Niang, in homage to a past and well respected director of the forestry department with whom he had once worked. Another of the chauffeurs is my old driver Malick from my ecology centre days who will go to Tamba with the rest of the team.

In order to get the project up and running quickly, we need to develop our five-year workplan. This is to be a whole team effort and so I travel down to Tamba to join the others. The road, after the town of Kaolack, is terrible with innumerable stretches of road, each several kilometres long, that are almost impossible to drive along due to the profusion of deep potholes in the tarmac. Luckily our 4-wheel drive vehicle is robust; I doubt a saloon car would make the journey undamaged. Although we leave Dakar at 7 am, we do not arrive to the outskirts of Tamba, a distance of only around four hundred and sixty kilometres, until almost twelve hours later. Just in time for dinner at the little hotel that has newly opened at the entrance to the town.

The following day we meet up in our conference room and each team leader: the Colonel, myself and the young American make presentations of the broad lines of each of our activities. Most of these were developed in our contract proposal but very few of the seniors and none of the more junior team members will have had access to that document so this is also a good information sharing exercise and the first opportunity for the team to ensure that we develop synergy between the four sets of activities (remembering I have both environmental policy and M&E to cover).

My own activities are rather easy to describe for I exist in a team of two; and the second person is still to be recruited. I have two broad and separate activities to undertake. The first is my usual work in M&E, and it is relatively easy to lay out the different activities to be undertaken and their timing over the periods of a single year and for the entire five years. The second set of activities is more difficult to predict; many experienced development workers would say impossible. This is where I am to try to influence changes in environmental policy; areas where there are stiff economic interests at play. For example, the recently voted Law on Decentralisation theoretically transfers management decisions for community lands and forests to the local communities themselves. However, the Hunting Code has recently been rewritten and is in line to pass through the National Assembly and be voted into law by the deputies. Sadly, some of the Hunting Code rides roughshod over the Decentralisation Law since central government provides, and will continue to provide, licences to the rich hunting lobby with little reference to the local communities; despite a law (of Decentralisation) taking legal precedent over a code (of Hunting).

Similarly, community forests cannot be cut for timber or charcoal production without the community sign off but, and nonetheless, the relevant government bodies still hand out forest exploitation licences, mostly to Dakar-based businessmen with the right political connections. Lots of difficult work on the horizon and likely a veritable struggle in sight to obtain cooperation from the powers that be. I have no illusions about the difficulty of this side of my work.

The Colonel is responsible for working with the local communities to develop forestry management plans that theoretically, once approved, hand forest management officially to the local communities. But again, if the forestry department refuses to sign off on these plans (for example if the government is about to hand out charcoal exploitation licences in the very forest to be covered by a plan) then all his team's work will come to nothing and the pillaging of local forests will continue unabated, despite the law in place that is theoretically meant to protect them.

Finally, our young American colleague is responsible for selecting and supporting the development of market chains of selected non-woody forestry products in the community forests as well as some non-traditional agricultural products.

The overall idea of the project is excellent, if a little foolhardy given the obstacles we face. Our young American supports the sustainable use of selected forestry products, the colonel ensures that local communities receive legal protection of their local resources, and I work to ensure that the national laws available to protect the community forests operate and are unambiguous. I am also to monitor the results of all our activities and the progress made towards achieving the project's overall ambitions. Is all that possible? We like to think it is but the whole team has doubts; there are just too many vested financial interests at play.

A few of the potential market chains for community forest products look very promising indeed. One is the use of baobab fruit, the so-called 'monkey bread' because the hard pulp inside the fruit looks like pieces of dried white bread. Another is the fruit of the jujube tree, and a third is a forest vine called *Saba senegalensis* with its fruit locally known as *madd*.

But even assisting market chains and their development is not without difficulties and deliberate hindrances. For example, and like all fruit, *madd* must be gotten rapidly from forest to market and on to the consumer or it will spoil. A favourite trick on the long road from the forests in the south of Senegal to the major markets around Dakar is for government agents to halt lorries on the bumpy road from Tamba to the capital and query the number of sacks loaded on the lorry. If the bill of lading says, for example, 80 sacks of fifty kilograms, the transporter may well find an agent will query this number of sacks and insists that the lorry be unloaded by hand so the sacks may be counted. After unloading – with, of course, required breaks so that the agent may have lunch, coffee breaks or a smoke – the lorry is then reloaded while the number of sacks are recounted. Inevitably, certain agents will insist that there are one or two extra sacks. That results in either a 'fine' or, if contested, unload and recount. As the transporter sees that the fruit will soon become damaged and overripe and he risks losing his entire cargo, guess what he eventually does in order to be allowed to continue on his way? There are several such checkpoints along the road from forest to market and so transporters are sometimes obliged to pay several "tolls" to government agents in order to get their produce to market in time. Clearly, the price of tolls has to be borne somewhere along the market chain. While consumers can exercise price control by simply refusing to purchase forest products should they become too expensive, individual collectors of the fruit in the forests of the south have little control over the ultimate sale price. They are, therefore, invariably the ones who lose out financially. They also happen to be the poorest and most vulnerable. Our project is seeking ways to strengthen the market chains so that all links are improved and each receives its fair share of the value that passes along the chain.

Among non-traditional agricultural products, we have come across fonio, a traditional cereal, and bissap, the basis for Vimto that I used to drink in the pub gardens as a child! Interestingly, bissap belongs to the same family as the red-flowered Hibiscus that many people grow in their Dakar gardens.

Before officially adopting these different forest and agricultural products, we carry out in depth market research studies to understand better the potential levels of production, the demand for each product and the interest of the local population to be involved with us in developing or strengthening these market chains.

For the baobab fruit, there is already considerable in-country demand for the white bread-like pith. Also baobab leaves are used as a vegetable in stews while the bark is peeled and used for cord. However, little of these products, and several other potential ones from the baobab, are exported, and here lies the real value of the species. Our young American colleague manages to tap into an Italian family-run firm called the Baobab Fruit Company. Several members of the family pay us a visit and we are to learn the full panoply of products that the incredible baobab offers. They tell us that the large outer husk of the fruit which is relatively hard is perfect for polishing and turning into jewellery and other household products. I have a carved box on my desk made from the two matching halves of the fruit. Open up the husk and one finds not only the 'monkey-bread' but also numerous baobab seeds as well as a pinkish filament that attaches the seeds to the pith and the inside of the husk. Some of the seeds are retained locally for germination and the growing-on of small plants in local nurseries but the majority are pressed and an oil extracted that has a wide range of cosmetic uses. The filaments are the one part that no-one thought anything of. That is until the Italian company tells us that it contains more antioxidant per gram than anything else known to man. Suddenly, we have uncovered another hidden treasure from the baobab tree!

Turning to the agricultural side, our young colleague begins to explore a semi-cultivated member of the grass family called *fonio* which goes by the scientific name of *Digitaria exilis*. I have to confess that when he mentions this crop during our planning meeting as a potential candidate for inclusion as a non-traditional agricultural product, I am rather surprised. During my days as a lecturer in Nigeria, one of the common and pernicious weeds of local agriculture that I studied and wrote about in the French scientific journal, *Acta œcologica*, was a close cousin of fonio called *Digitaria ciliaris*.

Our Senegalese colleagues tell us that in southeastern Senegal, fonio is considered to be a famine crop that is usually grown on very poor or stony soils where other crops struggle to survive. However, once we start to investigate the scientific side of fonio, we find that it was once a common crop from Egypt of the Pharaohs right across to West Africa. But today, the majority of fonio is grown in Guinea followed by Senegal and then The Gambia. Further research tells us that the medical world is rather in awe of fonio because, although a cereal, it has no gluten, is rich in vegetable proteins and is considered an ideal carbohydrate food for diabetics. On the negative side, local ladies tell us that husking the grain is a long and tricky process and, for this reason alone, they are not interested in producing larger amounts to feed into our nascent value chain. That is until we come across the 1996 invention of Mr Diakité of a fonio husking machine.

A few strategically placed machines speed up the grain processing for the ladies while in France we come across a company called Gaia that proves an initial outlet for much of our production.

The final piece in the local jigsaw is how to ensure that the collectors of forest products like *madd* and Baobab fruits and agricultural products like bissap and fonio are paid the true value of their work. Traditionally, so-called 'Collectors' go through small, isolated villages with old pick-up trucks or, where the forest trails allow, with small lorries. They offer ridiculously small amounts for these products with a take it or leave it attitude; forcing the forest dwellers to accept the offer or receive nothing for their work.

Our project makes an early check of the forest and farm gate prices and compares them to sale prices in the larger, regional markets of Tamba, Kolda and Kédougou. The difference is staggering, often at least a tenfold increase and sometimes even a twentyfold difference. Clearly, there is a very wide margin that can be tapped to ensure that the local producers receive a much fairer return on their efforts.

The first thing to do is to investigate how the producers we are seeking to help, traditionally set their sale prices. We quickly discover that decisions on prices are left to individual families; hence the take it or leave it attitude of the collectors. Our research also shows that these individual families almost never know the amount that their goods are then sold on for in the local, regional and national markets. What to do to force through higher prices?

The team decides on a two-pronged process, the first is based upon the telephone link that exists between staff based in regional towns, and other staff living in or close to villages that we are seeking to help and who work with the local families. Market prices for the relevant produce are relayed on a weekly basis and provide our agents with the information needed to help the producers understand the value of their products and thus to determine more suitable selling prices. The second step is to try to bring together the individual producer families into tightly knit producer-groups; the easiest way is to consider these as village cooperatives. Part of my monitoring work is to see what impact the project is having on the incomes of the several hundred families that have signed up to work with us.

The baseline for the project was developed during our start-up phase but now that our two-pronged approach is up and running, I return to a sample of villages to obtain comparable data. When we collect income data, we always work in private with individual household heads rather than collect such data in open groups. The added privacy of such moments allows us to have more confidence in the accuracy of what we are being told, and it also allows us to dig more deeply if we hear something that sound strange, unusual or irrational.

I sit down with the first household head using one of our *peul*-speaking village agents to help with translation. I start by asking how many sacks of baobab fruit the household sold at the last collector's visit. I am told eight sacks of fifty kilograms. I then ask at what price? At this point the villager roars with laughter and goes into a long explanation, interspersed with many guffaws.

When our villager finally stops chuckling, my agent turns to me, also trying not to laugh, and explains "when the lorry came to the village, our participant here was offered the usual, ridiculously low price for his sacks. But, since he last sold baobab fruit, the village has set up its cooperative and fixed the minimum price it would sell to the collectors. The collector in the lorry, of course, did not know this and refused his requested price and drove on to the next house; receiving the same price response from his neighbour and then the next and the next. When he arrived at the end of the village, no one had accepted his low price offer. This left the collector a simple choice: leave the village with nothing and lose his day's work or pay the higher price. He paid."

While our successes at this level are starting to become evident, the colonel is having trouble in getting the initial community forest management plans through the forestry department and sadly there is no common model on which we can base our new plans. The simplest way, therefore, is to hire a couple of senior forestry agents to develop the first plans and then use those as the basis for future ones. Although this does sound rather like a form of abuse of power, it does help get us over another hurdle.

While the M&E side of my work is going well and I have recently hired a very bright young assistant from the ecology centre, the other side of my work on influencing environmental policy is proving very slow going. Changing policy or even ensuring that an existing policy is applied is not like clicking fingers. Rather, it is first about convincing and then finding a well-placed champion to help push changes through. At the beginning of my work I tried to be rather less subtle by threatening to put journalists in random lorries to try to catch government agents from illegally 'taxing' forest products on their way to market. But was told in a very friendly manner by a senior civil servant that this would result in '*mon ami*' receiving a one-way ticket home!

On the project side, we have just heard that our team leader is to leave, why I am never to find out.

I am asked by the lead company to assume the leadership role until a new person can be appointed; two or three months at max., I am told. Having recently celebrated my fiftieth birthday in Dakar, this was certainly not the belated present I wished to receive. It is hard to see a friend, and someone I respect, have to pack up and leave. I certainly do not wish to be the replacement in this situation but there is little alternative until the lead company appoints someone else. The task of temporarily taking over at the head of the project is made that much harder because I do not work for the lead company (my contract is with one of the subcontractors). I am now obliged to jump through administrative hoops to undertake even simple tasks like signing cheques for local salaries. Furthermore, while I have assumed this new role, I am still expected to continue to do my environmental policy and M&E jobs with no additional assistance provided. I now try to spend half my time in Tamba with the team and half in Dakar to continue policy work as well as representing the project at frequent donor or government meetings. Roll on the arrival of the replacement.

Another enormous worry for me is my health. On the morning of my fiftieth birthday, when Véro and I are supposed to be getting a small party together for that evening, as I shave I notice a lump, a bulge, just below the jawline on the left side of my throat. What on earth? My usual attitude to health is to leave well alone, let my immune system do its job and cross fingers that the problem goes away; a typical male attitude, I know. But Véro is more sensible and insists that I go there and then to see a doctor that we hear has a very good reputation. Luckily, I can get to see him within the hour.

He starts off with the usual questions, then an intense examination with much prodding around my throat and neck. As the examination continues, I get steadily more concerned because of what he is not saying.

Finally, I say "doctor, I would prefer that you tell me outright what you consider is the issue, why the lump has suddenly appeared."

"Are you sure you want to know my thoughts," he asks, and in response to my nod he continues, "I believe you have cancer. Perhaps Hodgkinson's or a form of leukaemia, I'm not sure. We will have a better idea after we do a lot of tests. For the moment, I want you to go for blood tests, an ultrasound on your throat and chest x-rays."

He sits at his desk and scribbles out various prescriptions, handing them over with firm instructions to go for the tests this morning. He promises to call the laboratory to get me seen straight away.

Long story, a little shorter; I go first for the blood tests, then for the x-rays and finally the ultrasound; the results of all to be picked up the following day. I then go home and try to make the best of my birthday party, pretending cheerfulness although some of the guests do twig that something is wrong.

First thing on Monday morning, I put a call through to my old GP surgery on the Billing Road in Northampton and (bless you Dr R.) get put through immediately. I explain what is happening on the health front and the good doctor asks me to fax all the results through, then to come back to UK as soon as possible for more checks.

A week later, I am home in Lime Avenue and put an early call through to my Doctor. He tells me that he has his first patient at 9 am and so I should come to the surgery at 8.30 and he will see me then.

I confess to being very nervous as I enter the surgery. After all this could be the moment that we all dread happening to us.

As I walk across the room, the doctor's first words put my mind a little more at ease "It's OK Malcolm, you have none of those dreaded diseases. I thought that when I saw your very healthy set of blood results and now the shape of that impressive lump tells me that it is not cancerous. Sit down, relax. I want to examine your throat."

After a good prod and a fruitless check for swollen ganglia under my armpits and in my groin, the doctor confesses that he has not the faintest idea of what is causing the lump and better that I go to see a specialist at the local hospital.

No sooner said than done. Initially, the specialist is baffled too.

"I need to take a biopsy to see what's in there", he says extracting a syringe and attaching a very, very long needle to it. This is rapidly pushed into my neck and he draws out a yellowish fluid.

"It looks like glue," I say to him.

"More like saliva to me," he responds. "I believe what you have is called a 'Plunging Ranula'. We'll first confirm with an ultrasound and then a scan but it certainly will need to be excised. Before we do that operation, I know that you will have read all about plunging ranula on the internet and end up knowing more about them than me! For the operation, you have two options: either I do it under the National Health Service here in Northampton or I can do it in a private clinic in Milton Keynes."

Chatting over the two options with Véro, we decide to go the private avenue for one simple reason: if I go via the NHS, the date of the operation is unsure and liable to last minute postponement while at the clinic, I can be operated in a week. Since I am taking unpaid leave, the longer I wait for the NHS, the more salary I am losing. It would be a false economy to try to get the operation for free at the local hospital.

I spend a couple of days in the clinic and the plunging ranula is, with a certain amount of difficulty the surgeon tells me, dissected out.

Why the name? Well, 'ranula' comes from the Latin word '*rana*' which means 'frog' (the lump in the throat like a frog, get it now?). The plunging part refers to the crazy bunch of salivary glands that somehow managed to pass down through the muscular floor of my mouth and then fill up with liquid. How many other people do you know who can claim to have had or even know someone who had a Plunging Ranula? Not many, I bet!

I come home with a big bandage around my neck covering over the dozen or so external stitches; my tongue tells me that there are loads more stitches inside my mouth.

David has just received invitations from a couple of universities – Plymouth and Gloucester – to go for an interview cum look around. Four years after ferrying the Miss to all the most distant universities in the country, I have fewer miles to go with my son.

We drive into Cheltenham, where one of the University of Gloucester campuses are located, and this beautiful town appeals to my son aesthetic appreciation of architecture far more than Plymouth and so will be his home for the next few years. And he really did say that about the architecture, totally surprising me!

Back in Senegal, after the operation, we get an unexpected phone call from the youngest of Véro's three brothers. He is in the air force and is being posted to Dakar for a three-month period in case the French population of Ivory Coast needs evacuating from the ever more bloody civil war that had started up as I had led my Botswana team over to Senegal, and is still going on in the country. He is a military aircraft mechanic and co-pilot of a Transall, a slow and enormous cargo carrier. He has asked for permission to stay with us rather than in barracks near to the Dakar main port and his application has been approved. We are both very fond of the young guy. I have known him since he was six years old while when he was born, Véro invariably demanded, as the big sister, to give the new baby his bottle. They are fifteen years apart in age.

One morning as we are both getting ready for work (Véro is now a relief teacher at the International School of Dakar), she suggests to her brother that he should bring his crew back for dinner that evening.

"Great thanks but I will bring the dessert," he says jumping into the jeep that has just arrived to pick him up.

That evening as I walk through the door of the house, I spot a large jute sack standing at the entrance to the kitchen. It is full of pineapples, and I hear Véro's brother explain to her that he got the pineapples today while in Abidjan. What an international life we lead!

In reality, the crew is obliged to make frequent training flights, not only to ensure that the plane is in perfect working order but also to practice rapid landing and take-offs from small runways. On one occasion when, by coincidence, I am in Tamba, he phones through to tell me that the plane is on its way to the tiny airport in Tambacounda. Would any members of my team like to visit the plane? Of course, everyone wants to be there and have their photos taken while sitting in the cockpit. The Colonel even suggests that he is the senior officer on board, much to everyone's amusement and gentle ribbing.

Almost a year after my friend was obliged to leave Senegal, the company finally recruits a new chief of party; an American gentleman with impressive numbers after his name. He has a sterling reputation in Sahelian forest management and we all agree that this is just what we need to help the Colonel push through forest management plans and me to better influence policy in central government. The only fly in the ointment is during my annual leave in France, the new boss has the nerve to move me out of my assigned office in the ministry and install me in another, smaller one on the other side of the building and away from the forestry colleagues with whom I work.

On returning from leave and walking into my office, I find the new gentleman sitting behind my desk and using my computer. He simply says "I prefer this office so I have moved your papers out and moved in here myself!"

Not the best beginning to a working relationship, especially since he is meant to be based in Tamba, and a firm slap in the face for me holding the fort so long during the interregnum.

On the home front, Mélanie has been awarded her Masters in Anthropology while David has passed his A-levels and so is off to the Cheltenham campus of the University of Gloucester.

Our daughter has decided that she would like to try out international development work and is looking for an internship with a reputable international organisation. By an enormous coincidence, a few days later, I am in the little Tamba hotel where I stay during my trips there and am having a drink with the head of the Senegal office of 'Care', a large and very reputable international NGO. I mention that Mélanie has just got her Masters in anthropology and is looking for an internship. He responds by telling me to get her to apply to Care, but goes on to warn me that she should expect no recruitment favours; fair enough.

She goes through their strict selection process and, on her own merits, lands one of their coveted internships – based in Dakar! My girl will come to live with us for six months.

The three of us are on our roof terrace overlooking the ocean, chatting one evening, when Véro and I start to discuss, totally out of the blue, what we should do with our Northampton home. Now that Mélanie is working, David is in Cheltenham and we are living in Senegal, why are we keeping an empty house and still paying the mortgage and all the bills? Additionally, everyone's preferred home is in Cordon and Véro and I will certainly move there when this contract finishes.

"Let's sell it," Véro suggests and, in late 2005, we do.

Out of Africa

My contract finishes in mid-2006 and we pack our container, sell our car and leave Senegal for the very last time. While the work was satisfying, Senegal has changed in many ways, not all for the better. We certainly did not enjoy this stay as much as we did the first time round. I feel happy to leave and not stressed at all about finding the next contract.

Our UK home is, of course, sold but Cordon still waits patiently for our return. We have even added to our little kingdom there. During our first time in Senegal we had bought a small rundown house in the courtyard, which the children nicknamed *'La Petite Maison'* or the Little House while, during the current trip, we had the opportunity to buy the ruined remains of a large old barn that sits on the opposite side of our courtyard.

When we first bought our house in Cordon in 1981, the sellers of our house had also offered us the chance to buy their barn; for the grand sum of £3,000. The floor area of the barn was approaching one hundred square metres and it stood higher than the neighbouring houses and had three upper floors in addition to the ground floor. That was the optimistic view, anyway.

Our decision to say 'no thanks' was an easy one since we simply did not have the extra cash in 1981 but, even if we had, I doubt we would have made a different decision. The roof was lacking literally thousands of tiles and had leaked for many, many years. So much so that several of the major beams were rotting and the leaks had severely damaged the upper walls, made of *pisé* (compacted mud).

Pisé was once a building material much favoured by our neighbours across the Rhône in Isère where they did not have easy access to the quantity of building stones that are common on our side of the river. While *Pisé* is a very good insulator, it does not do well when wet, actually it dissolves, and that is exactly what was happening to the upper walls of the poor barn. So much so that the roof periodically lost a batch of its tiles that came crashing down to the ground. One such tile – they each weigh one kilogram and so can do a lot of damage from such a height – decided to fall from the top of the roof and down to the village road just as *M. le Maire* happened by in his car (the tile missed by the way!).

One registered letter later and the poor owner of the barn is given a stark choice: either repair the roof (we are talking at a cost in the region of £20,000 at this time) or demolish the building. The latter is the only real option for the owner since the cost of demolition is quoted at about a third of the price of the repairs. In desperation, and some debt, the owner asks me and a friend who lives on the other side of the barn (now demolished) if we would like to buy the plot. We make a joint offer of a few thousand euros, go off to see our respective *notaires* (solicitors) and we are now owners of the vacant land; actually there is a bit of the lower walls, constructed of local stone, still standing to delimit the plot. Once we have received building approval, in come our friendly builders, *les Frères Franco*, and up go two 'garages' (they are really barns). My side has fifty square metres of floor space and I ask the Franco brothers to add a second level meaning that we can park our car inside during winter and still have an incredible amount of storage space on the ground and first floors. Our container arrives and the contents are quickly stored in our new barn.

What to do about work now? We decide to take a couple of months of sabbatical and use the time to start advancing the work in the 'Little House' with a view to renting it out in a year or so. I also, rather tentatively, send out a few CVs.

The sabbatical proves to be more wishful thinking than anything else because only a few weeks after leaving Senegal, I take a phone call in English from a Polish-based company.

"Dr Marks, we have your details in our database and would like to bid you on an EU livestock project in Botswana to develop their M&E system. Would you be interested?"

"Yes, in principle" I reply with little hesitation remembering how much I enjoyed my time in that lovely country just a few years back.

"Great. What daily rate would you anticipate?" the voice asks.

I mention the daily salary rate that I received while working long-term in Senegal, converted to Euros, and receive, frankly, a rather rude response with an offer of half that amount per day.

"Good luck in finding even a very junior consultant at that rate," is all I can think to say to the Polish company. Nonetheless, I politely say goodbye and wish them luck with their bid before hanging up. As I cut the call, I think that is the last I will hear about the project. No matter.

But it is not, for half-an-hour later the phone rings again in my office and, this time, the caller speaks to me in French. "M. Marks, we are a French consulting company and would like to bid you on a livestock project in Botswana. If you are interested could you give us an idea of your daily salary rate?"

I do and he accepts my fee rate with absolutely no haggling. I agree to join their team.

But the sketch is not yet finished. As I put the receiver back in its cradle, the phone rings immediately and I am once more talking to the Polish company. The young man says rather sheepishly, "my managing director wishes me to tell you that we are prepared to accept your rather steep consulting fees. May we now bid you on the project as we have a great chance of winning?"

"I'm afraid that you should have spoken with your MD before calling me the first time because another company has come in and accepted my rate without argument. I am sorry for you but it is not very clever to haggle overmuch with experienced consultants. Goodbye."

The French company wins the consulting contract and I am off to Botswana next week for a month of technical input. The contract is rather nice since it provides two missions per year, each of one-month duration. My little consulting company, Development Ecology, is resurrected!

It feels really good to be back in Gaborone. During my previous trips, a few years back, I had discovered a small hotel-apartment, close to the African Mall in the centre of town, with prices that compare very favourably with the Cresta Lodge Hotel. The real advantage of the apartment is that I have good cooking facilities and so am not always obliged to eat in restaurants.

In contrast, the SADC building where I am now working is in Kololi and so rather far from the centre of town but I soon get a minicab driver to pick me up in the morning and bring me back in the evening. But I do miss the ease and sheer numbers of West Africa's yellow taxis!

My work for the livestock project revolves around developing and running their M&E system and, using the results obtained, to write the project's progress reports for delivery to SADC and the EU paymasters. My first couple of missions, now and then again in early November, are to be based in Gaborone. Subsequent ones will see me travel to regional SADC offices, including to Mauritius no less!

The first mission is basically to set up the M&E system, select indicators, and show the technical team where to enter data for their assigned indicators into a series of spreadsheets. I am setting up the spreadsheets in such a way that immediately a new value is entered into a data table, it is automatically sent to a self-generating graph. These graphs can then be copied and pasted straight into the progress reports and the explanatory text added. I have tried to design the system to be as automatic and user-friendly as possible.

My current work has progressed well and the team have bought into the system design. I will provide the individual, on-the-job training to the team during my follow-up visit later this year.

Mission over, I arrive in J'burg International to take the long-haul flight to Europe and from there to Lyon. As I arrive at the flight information board, I see that my flight is showing 'cancelled'. That is likely to cause me considerable trouble because the next flight with that airline is not until tomorrow. I walk towards the company's information desk meaning to ask if they have booked me on another flight but find that it is tightly locked. What to do now?

I notice that a BA flight to Heathrow is to leave in a couple of hours and so I go to their desk – which is thankfully open – and explain my situation and flash my frequent flyers card. I am told politely that their flight is full but I could try to get a last minute seat at the check-in. I join the queue and eventually arrive at the head of the check-in queue. I explain my situation and am told sorry, we cannot give you a seat at this moment because it looks like we are completely full. Please check back closer to take-off time.

I decide to play the gentle nuisance and move to the side of the queue but remain standing just off the desk. Several times I am told that I might be more comfortable sitting down in the hall but I stay stubbornly fixed in place. Half an hour later I am joined by a young lady who is in the same predicament as me. She decides to be stubborn too. Time passes and finally there remains no one in the queue, just the lady and I standing just off to the side with the BA ladies doing their final paperwork. Twenty minutes before anticipated take-off, a BA hostess calls our names and hands us our tickets, oooph.

We walk quickly to the plane, chatting us we go.

On taking our seats she says "I heard the hostess call you Dr Marks. Do you happen to be Malcolm Marks?"

"Actually, yes I am but how do you know me?" I ask, feeling that I may have met the lady in the past and forgotten her face.

"I work for the WWF and we spoke several years ago when I tried to recruit you for a job in the Oban Hills in Nigeria. Do you remember?"

And indeed I do. My first job on leaving London University was as a plant ecology lecturer at the University of Calabar in southern Nigeria. Soon after arriving in Calabar, I had also been appointed director of the botanical gardens and the university's enormous nature reserve. A few years after leaving Calabar, I ended up teaching biology in Northampton and, one afternoon, had received an unexpected call from the WWF. This superb international organisation had approached me to become the first director of a new Gorilla nature reserve being set up in the Oban Hills, north of Calabar. Family constraints had forced me to refuse the offer.

"I certainly do remember the offer for the Oban Hills work and I was really sad to have to decline but my second child had just been born and there was no way that I could take a new infant to a place like the Oban Hills. Who did you manage to get as the director?" I asked.

"Your old colleague and friend Dr Reid" she replies.

I remember back to this lovely character who taught animal ecology with me and lived in the house that backed on to ours. He adored the forest far more than the classroom and had a penchant for capturing wild animals and keeping them around his house, including a pair of crocodiles. They escaped from their enclosure during a rainstorm and one found its way into our back garden, surprising Véro as she hung out the washing. The other took refuge in a drainage ditch where it remained undiscovered for over a year until I heard stories from two young French children about the eyes of a giant frog poking through the duckweed that floated on the water surface.

"Wow, now that's a name from the past. I haven't seen him since 1983 and we last spoke on the phone in 1985. Do you know how he is doing?" I ask.

"I'm so sorry, obviously you do not know? He passed away a few years ago. He had returned to live in South London with his partner and I heard that he was killed in a burglary gone wrong."

I stand there shattered trying to digest what I am hearing. This lovely guy who recovered from a rattlesnake bite as a student and then for years toyed with death by catching unknown species of African snakes, jumped in ponds to grab crocodiles and had a collection of insects and spiders that provided many new species to science was killed by a burglar in Brixton. What is wrong with our world?

Time passes far too quickly, Mélanie has now been working in London for Christian Aid for well over a year. She started as a temp one afternoon in 2005 and never left. Now, in late 2006, she is still there in a permanent fulltime role. David has just started his final year at Cheltenham while we are living permanently in Cordon although starting to look around for a larger house and garden.

The time arrives for me to make my second trip to Botswana. My work will keep me in Gaborone until early December. On my first morning back in the country, I arrive at the project office in the SADC building but find only the secretary present. She hands me a letter from the project administrator and it reads:

'Malcolm, so sorry that the team is not around. We have to be away from Gabs for the first two weeks of your visit on a training programme in a couple of other SADC countries. I am sure that you have sufficient work to occupy you until we get back for the training you are going to provide to the team. Kindest'.

Not a very efficient use of my time. And, to be strictly honest, I have very little work for the project to occupy me; certainly not for two weeks. I do what needs to be done, basically to develop the latest quarterly report, but that only takes a few days, leaving me with around another eight working days to amuse myself in the office.

I have decided to stay once more in one of the serviced apartments that I now prefer that is near to the African Mall. Close to the mall and not far from the Cresta President hotel is a bar cum restaurant that I like to go to occasionally for my evening meal, always accompanied by a few glasses of strong and excellent South African red wine. With advancing age (I am now going on 54), I have drifted away from beer drinking and invariably stick to red wine. I find this far less demanding on my nocturnal bladder as my prostate begins to age too!

This evening, being only a few short weeks before Christmas, there is a company Christmas party going on at the far end of the restaurant. The party seems to be more oriented around glasses and bottles than the few plates of snacks on their tables. While the youngsters and not so youngsters appear to be having a fun time, they are neither loud nor rude; just a group of people laughing and having fun together sharing the spirit in the lead-up to Christmas.

I have just finished my meal of steak, tomatoes and noodles and the waiter has already taken my plate away and is now behind the bar refilling my glass with a rather tasty Cape red; I feel good, relaxed and am thinking of home and the Christmas we will soon be spending together.

Two of the youngsters stop at my table and say *"Dimella rra* (hello sir), we have all seen that you are sitting here on your own while we are having a great time with our company party. *Rra*, it is not right that you are alone with Christmas coming so soon. Please come and join us."

"Dimella rra, dimella mma," I say replying to the greeting from the young man and his wife, "that is kind of you but you are all having such a lovely time together that I would not dream of disturbing your fun."

"No *rra*, we insist. If you stay here alone, none of us will be able to enjoy our evening. Please come." And the young man leads me back to his friends and I spend a pleasant hour or so with his group.

I am citing this occasion because, for me, it typifies the kindness and openness of the Botswana people that I encounter on a daily basis. And, I have to ask the question, would we Europeans show such kindness if we saw an obvious foreigner sitting on his or her own in a restaurant? I very much doubt it.

Back in the office the following day, I decide that since I still have at least six or seven 'free' days until the team comes back for the training I have prepared for them, the best use of my time is to do an intense internet search for more consulting work. I start with a Google search based on 'vacancy' + 'M&E' + 'consultant' and, by chance, come up with several possibilities, all based in Africa. While I have always enjoyed the work I have done in around fifteen different countries on this continent, I do despair about ever obtaining an assignment on a different one. M&E is a skill that travels so why have I never been offered an assignment in South America (OK, I do not speak Spanish or Portuguese) but why never in Asia?

The following day, I do more Google searches using a variety of different terms. One possibility outside of Africa pops up on my screen. This is short-term work for an enormous UK-funded programme that needs a specialist in M&E and information management for a ten-day assignment. Perfect. However, the advert goes on to say that the person selected must have fifteen years of experience in the technical area of M&E (tick that criterion) but also ten years of experience of working in the country. I have never been there. The advert was posted by a UK-based consulting group that I have never previously come across.

What should I do? Should I just give up? But no, given my excess of free time, I decide, notwithstanding the lack of country experience, to make a tentative approach by email to the company. Basically, I am honest upfront and say that while I have the fifteen years of M&E experience required, indeed that I have written several of the manuals on the subject, I have never set foot in the country. I go on to argue that M&E skills travel well and I foresee no valid reason that would prevent me from carry out the work in this new country. And, I ask myself, 'why do they need so much experience for a ten-day mission?'

The following day I receive an email back from the company and get a big surprise. The message starts with "Hi mate, what are you up to now? I haven't heard from you for quite a while."

I read on and find the message is sent by the first chief of party that I had worked for in Guinea-Conakry and it seems that he is now a senior member of this London-based consulting group. He knows me and my work well, especially in the field of M&E, and goes on to agree that the required length of country experience is excessive. He tells me that it was only inserted in the advert to cut down on the number of unqualified applicants they would otherwise have received. After he makes a quick check with a couple of my referees, I am offered the job, to leave as soon as possible after finishing up in Botswana.

I make my way home to France and sit down with Véro to share our news. I tease her by saying that I am soon to go off on a trip outside of Africa to a country that has rather a lot of water. She laughs and replies that during my absence in Botswana, she had been persuaded by a rather esoteric friend to go with her to visit a fortune teller. The first thing that the French version of Mystic Meg had announced is that Véro is destined to go to a country with lots of water.

Now where an earth can that be?